Celebrating 150 years

The Pictorial History of Fort Worth, Texas

1849 — 1999

Landmark Publishing, Inc.
4410 W. Vickery Blvd., Suite 101
Fort Worth, Texas 76107

Library of Congress Data:
Oates, Paula J., Editor,
Celebrating 150 Years, The Pictorial History
of Fort Worth, Texas, 1849-1999
Landmark Publishing, Inc.

Includes Index and Bibliographical references
ISBN 1-928582-02-8

First Edition

Landmark Publishing, Inc. books are available at special discounts for bulk purchase for sales promotions, premiums, fund-raising, or educational use. For details contact:

PRESERVING HISTORY
4410 West Vickery, Suite 101 · Fort Worth, Texas 76107
1-800-886-0689
1-817-377-3399

Printed in the United States of America

Acknowledgments:

At the conception of this book, the sesquicentennial celebration seemed a long time away. I foresaw no problems; simply gather the photographs and devise an interesting layout in which to present them and their captions.

The first photographs, with the assistance of Ken Hopkins at the Fort Worth Public Library, came with little trouble. Where, I thought shall we get others? Then the strangest thing began to unfold with my first visit to a potential contributor. Eager to help, Ruth Karbach, Curator of Thistle Hill, suggested several others to contact. They, in turn, had a few names to add. The list grew and the layout changed as did the concept. It became a brushfire, one I had no desire to extinguish. In retrospect, I believe nowhere but Fort Worth would people have embraced the idea so wholly, making my task a pleasure as well as the most fascinating of learning experiences.

What started as a pictorial history has evolved into a compendium of treasured photographs, some familiar images, some never before in print; and of short essays and straightforward facts, written by experts in each field, submitted by those who know their stuff. This work is not meant to be a definitive history of a city, but perhaps instead a spark. I hope you will strive to learn more about this twice-selected All American City - visit the libraries and museums, enjoy the vast and varied forms of entertainment from the Stock Show to Bass Hall, from the Omni to Shakespeare in the Park, shop Sundance Square and admire the city's architecture, experience Fort Worth. We have more than enough to please any palate and it is ours to appreciate and enjoy!

Please take a moment to read the appendix. Here you will find the particulars for location, admission information, hours of operation, etc. for our contributors. Visit and learn more than would fit in any book about your city.

No work of this type happens without the help of those people eager to help. I want to thank especially the gracious Ruth Karbach, Curator of Thistle Hill. From the moment she opened the door of the grand mansion, she opened also a world of historical treasurers. To Quentin McGown of Texas Wesleyan University, not only for allowing access to his postcard collection but for his priceless expertise. To Jim Noah, Retired Battalion Chief, Fort Worth Fire Department, for having the foresight to write it all down, and his willingness to share it. To Dr. Richard Selcer and Dr. Ben Proctor of Texas Christian University; to Speaker Jim Wright, former Speaker of the House of Representatives. To Major Clay Church of the 301st Fighter Wing at Naval Air Station - Joint Reserve Base Carswell Field, Jo Linda Jara Martinez; to Dalton Hoffman, Jr. To Officer Curtis Chesser & Captain Bryan Sudan of the Fort Worth Police Department, to Judy Alter, of Texas Christian University Press, and everyone who had anything to do with the Sesquicentennial History Symposium, the "hotbed of historians" gathering.

To Donita Maligi, of the University of Texas at Arlington Library, Special Collections; Paul Davidson of Tarrant County College, Northeast Campus; and Mr. Billy W. Sills of Fort Worth Independent School District Archives; to Ken Hopkins of Fort Worth Public Library; Sarah Biles of North Fort Worth Historical Society, Michael Pullin of Southwestern Baptist Seminary, Dr. Cheri Wolfe of Cattle Raisers Museum, Louis Sherwood and Sherry Parker of Texas Wesleyan University, and Bobby Bragan of the Fort Worth Cats. To Britt Stokes of Acme Brick, Hollace Ava Weiner of the Fort Worth Jewish Archives, and C. Jane Dees of the Museum of the Science and History.

To Douglas Harman, of the Fort Worth Convention and Visitors Bureau, whose very appearance, not to mention office, speaks of his dedication to Fort Worth's heritage, and Jeanette Hodges of the Lancaster Street Post Office. To Grimes and Rachel Fortenberry of Travis Avenue Baptist Church and Joy M. Thomas of Mt. Gilead Baptist Church. To Joy Webster of the W. T. Waggoner building; Fernando Costa, Planning Director, City of Fort Worth; Joyce Williams, Dick Ramsey, Bill Morgan, and countless others whose forgiveness I ask as I know I have forgotten a few.

And to the people of Fort Worth -- those who endured the once-desolate plains to farm a plot of land they could call their own; the veterans of the Civil War who came determined to make a new life, and to those who pushed the cattle; the men and women who toiled at the packinghouses and the railroad yards; the people who worked a line at the bomber plant or processed a part order for an oil-rig in west Texas; those who drove a truck, served a meal, or opened a shop day after day to provide a service; the people who fought a fire, walked a beat, worked the 11 to 7 shift at the hospital, delivered the mail or taught school. These are the people who have made our city prosper.

Finally, to the expert staff of Landmark Publishing, Inc., especially Ernie Hammond, Operations Manager; Jason Petty, Director of Marketing; Lisa Blake, Administrative Assistant; Lynda Fralish, Production and Operations; and Julie Guess, Production. Most of all, to Robert Akin, Jr., - thanks, Bob, for the foresight and the faith.

Paula Oates, Editor

(Photo Courtesy of the Quentin McGown Postcard Collection)

The front endsheet photograph is from the Dalton Hoffman, Jr. Collection. "Fort Worth From the Air" (photo by Ennis C. Helm), *The Progress of Fort Worth, an Annual Report by the City of Fort Worth, Texas, 1926-27,* Stafford-Lowdon Co., Fort Worth, Texas, 1927.

Please note back endsheet photograph, which was taken from approximately the same southwest angle, seventy-two years later.

The mark of greatness is often viewed as a total package. Fort Worth is truly a great city. Having twice been named an All-American City, Fort Worth is the benchmark for many Texas cities. The one aspect that lends itself to being our strongest attribute is the people of this city. Fort Worthians' pride runs deep, as well it should, from our western heritage to our love of world-class culture. Here you see boots at Bass Hall, and we make them look good.

Early influential visionaries took the time to see to it that our city would be looked upon to set the standard. Amon Carter, Sr. would not allow a certain city to the east of Fort Worth to lay claim to the Centennial celebration; Kay Kimbell amassed an internationally-renowned art collection; W. R. Watt expanded the Southwestern Exposition and Rodeo, a family tradition that continues today. Ed Bass created Bass Performance Hall to elevate the level of our entertainment experience.

Do you ever wonder why we study history? Some feel that it is so we learn from the past to avoid making the same mistakes twice. To the historians, we do so to honor those who have had a hand in shaping our world. The events and people that have made life better need to be recognized. I hope that this book will inspire the reader to learn more about this unique city. Take the time to discover a few things ... the museums and the libraries that are at our disposal, the Fort Worth historians who have the answers, and the appendix of this volume. . . where your journey begins.

The reason Fort Worth is a great city . . . . . you never meet a stranger!

Bob Akin, Jr.
Publisher

Fort Worth, Texas
Ca 1852
(Courtesy of the Quentin McGown Postcard Collection)

Fort Worth, Texas
Ca 1876
(Courtesy Fort Worth Star Telegram Photograph Collection, Special Collections Division, The University of Texas at Arlington Libraries)

Celebrating 150 Years - The Pictorial History of Fort Worth, Texas

Introduction by Richard Selcer

Some wag once said, "If you think a picture is worth a thousand words, try taking a picture of 'The Gettysburg Address'." Pictures are a wonderful record, but by themselves they can never tell the full story; they need the interpretation that only a well-written text can provide. But having said that, there is no denying the impact that pictures have on the imagination. They "dress up" a story as no verbal or written explanation can, no matter how eloquent. A picture of "The Gettysburg Address" is impossible, but an accompanying picture of the scene that day, of Lincoln giving the historic speech, would be a wonderful adjunct to the story, not to mention a priceless artifact.

Pictorial histories of Fort Worth are nothing new. Up to early 1999 there have been eight, not a bad record for a city only a hundred and fifty years old, and part of that time predating photography as a mass medium. Even so, most of those volumes suffer from one (or both) of two problems: 1) sameness of visual images because they have tended to go to the same sources for their pictures; or 2) limited vision by their compilers in terms of what they wanted to accomplish. The earliest attempt to chronicle Fort Worth by camera was C.L. Swartz's *Views of Fort Worth, Texas*, privately printed in 1901. The cover of the 5x6¾ inch book boasted "50 views for 50 cents." It was produced on a shoe string— literally. Instead of being bound with glue and stitching, it was held together with string passed through two holes and tied in a knot. Charlie Swartz (sometimes spelled "Schwartz") came from a family of what were quaintly known as "camera artists," who moved to Fort Worth in the mid-1880s. Brothers Charles, John, and David all went into the photography business as partners and occasionally as friendly rivals, while brother William was their "advertising agent." Working out of his studio at 700½ Houston, Charles published the first views of significant Fort Worth buildings, providing a priceless legacy for later citizens. But it was brother John who took one of the most famous pictures in the history of the West when he snapped the portrait of the Wild Bunch gang in December, 1900 and put it on display in his window. It led directly to their downfall by providing pictures for wanted bulletins. That photograph has since been reproduced countless times showing the five impeccably dressed outlaws coolly looking into the camera. Even Hollywood could not improve on it, though they tried by adapting it for a movie poster for 1969's *Butch Cassidy and the Sundance Kid.*

But Charles Swartz, not John, did the greater service for the cause of local history by publishing his photo album of fifty Fort Worth buildings, public and private. Ironically, he was killed "in the line of duty," although photography is not usually considered a dangerous occupation. It was a few years after the book came out that he was hit by a train while setting up his camera in the vicinity of the Our Lady of Victory Academy on South Hemphill. He was preparing to photograph a railroad switching track when a train struck him. Today the Swartz volume is counted among the rarest of Fort Worth memorabilia; I only know of two copies in existence, one in Yale University Library's special collections, and the other in private hands in Washington state.

The Swartz brothers and other old-time photographers got their start when shooting any kind of picture was still an ordeal, requiring them to make up their own plates, their own paper, and, for outdoor shoots, stand in the hot sun for hours to turn out a single 11x14 print. Indoor pictures required the use of choking flash powder and with that came the ever-present danger of fire. Some of those early cameras were 16x20 inches around with a 14 foot bellows stretched out in front of them. The advent of wet-plate technology and smokeless flash powder made the process easier, but still no picnic for the cameraman. Wet plates involved pouring a chemical solution on a glass plate and exposing it while still sensitive, a time period of up to four hours duration when a picture could be made on it. The first wet-plate pictures known to have been taken in Fort Worth were of the Texas Spring Palace in 1890 by O.C. Greer, the "Dean of Fort Worth Photographers." By the time Swartz produced his *Views of Fort Worth, Texas,* photographers were using the dry-plate method which relied on coated paper rather than glass plates and revolutionized commercial photography as a new mass medium.

We do not have any sales figures, but Swartz's production must have been successful because six years later A. Owen Jennings published another volume of pictures titled *Greater Fort Worth in 1907; Gateway to the Great State of Texas*. The production values were of a slightly higher quality although still a far cry from the coffee table standards of later years. And it accomplished something else the Swartz volume did not; it was reprinted by the Fort Worth Lion's Club in 1961 as a service project, so it still occasionally turns up in flea markets and garage sales.

Sixty-six years passed before the next pictorial history of Fort Worth, the awkwardly titled *How Fort Worth Became the Texasmost City*. Put together hurriedly in 1972 by the expert team of Ron Tyler, a local museum curator, and Leonard Sanders, a hometown author, for the Amon Carter Museum of Western Art, the public first saw the results of their efforts as an exhibition in 1973 celebrating the one hundredth anniversary of the city's incorporation. Unlike Swartz's and Jennings' modest efforts, this book provided text to accompany the pictures and thereby could take its place on the history shelf as a genuine chronicle of Fort Worth. The Amon Carter's director described it as "the first documented pictorial account of early Fort Worth."

Just as important, it was intended as a major contribution to the preservation of local history, which traditionally was taken for granted or else left to the occasional newspaper stringer doing a special report. What Tyler and Sanders discovered right off was that the pictorial record for early Fort Worth was mighty sparse. Sheer expense and intimidating technology might have discouraged the efforts of most would-be Matthew Bradys, but cannot be blamed entirely for the paucity of early images of the city. Unlike, say, Dodge City, Kansas or Denver, Colorado, Fort Worth, it seems, did not possess any dedicated shutterbugs running around snapping candid pictures with their bulky box cameras of anything willing to stand still for three minutes -- not in the nineteenth century anyway.

Several unpublicized disasters help explain the paucity of old Fort Worth photos: flood and fire have wiped out more than the ravages of time. Two disastrous fires in the studios of professional photographers are recalled by long-time residents, but only one of those fires can be chronicled. On the evening of July 24, 1925, a conflagration engulfed the studio of George M. Bryant at 705½ Main Street. As the *Fort Worth Record* described it the next day, "[A] heavy volume of smoke... rolled from the storerooms over the studio where countless negatives depicting the history of Fort Worth for many years were victims of the flames." There is no way of telling what images were lost or even how many, but there is a hint that the number was probably substantial because Bryant had purchased the studio thirteen years earlier from John Swartz, which suggests that he may also have purchased at the same time Swartz's personal library of images, going back to at least the 1880s. In 1949 when the Great Trinity Flood struck the city, another long-time professional photographer's studio near the river bottom was wiped out, along with all of its collection. The details of that tragedy have since been forgotten. It is fair to say that the city's photographic history has suffered losses in almost Biblical proportions, being spared only plagues and locust infestations.

The photographic record of Fort Worth, such as it is, also shows a definite lack of imagination. Before 1900, surviving photographic images show a few views up and down Main Street and some group portraits of various solid citizens posed in front of equally solid buildings. A decade or more earlier, Matthew Brady and Alexander Gardner were able to capture more vivid images during the Civil War while dodging bullets than local photographers were coming up with at their leisure with Fort Worth as the subject. Tyler and Sanders had to deal with the fact that not only were the numbers of pictures at their disposal frustratingly few, but the subject matter of even those few was extremely limited: not a single view of Hell's Half Acre, the section of town that first put Fort Worth on the map, nor of the city's Black or Hispanic or Oriental population. (Yes, there were a few Chinese and even an opium den or two in operation before the end of the city's second decade!) The only Black residents to appear in the entire book are the servant of Dr. and Mrs. Julian Feild, shown holding the bridles of their carriage horses (p.111), a couple of janitors in the First National Bank (p. 157), and a track repair crew on the streetcar line (p.176).

This was not by design of either the authors or the museum but out of necessity. Equally depressing, *How Fort Worth Became the Texasmost City* contains no interior views of the clubrooms, dance houses, theaters, hotels, or of the city's pride and joy, the natatorium and the opera house. If anybody was taking inside photographs before 1900, they were seemingly not saving the results for posterity! (Recently, some interior views of Fort Worth saloons have been turned up by a local researcher; these were unknown at the time Tyler and Sanders were gathering their pictures.) The variety of outdoor shots to choose from in 1972 was not much better. No railroad station, farm houses, cribs (of the sort occupied by "soiled doves"), soldiers, buffalo hunters or even buffalo contributed to the story of *How Fort Worth Became the Texasmost City*. There are also more horses to be seen than women in these early views of Fort Worth.

The roster of contributors to the *Texasmost* volume numbered more than twenty private individuals plus various official collections including the Fort Worth Public Library, the *Fort Worth Star-Telegram*, the Museum of Science and History, and Amon Carter's own collections. Yet Tyler and Sanders were able to assemble only 131 usable images covering the period from 1849 through about 1920. Logic suggested that there were more pictures out there, but they ran out of time before they could chase down all the possible leads among long-time residents of Fort Worth.

Tyler and Sander's book was very well received, and had the unexpected effect of opening the floodgates for pictorial histories, although none of the volumes that followed in the next twenty-six years measured up to their standards of scholarship. The main reason for that is the next four pictorial histories that followed were all contract books aimed at an audience of corporate sponsors rather than true history buffs. One positive effect the Tyler-Sanders volume had was that henceforward, no one would attempt to produce a pictorial volume without providing at least a rudimentary narrative to go with the illustrations. In 1980 the Fort Worth Chamber of Commerce sponsored a new pictorial volume, *Fort Worth: The Civilized West*, with text by Caleb Pirtle III, an award-winning newspaperman and Western writer. Ron Tyler returned as photography editor. This time both men worked on contract. Like many similar city histories, the concept for the book was first sold to Fort Worth by a commercial publishing house hoping to cash in on a ready-made market. In this case, the Continental Heritage Press called their roster of municipal histories "The American Portrait Series." Fort Worth joined Houston and San Antonio as the Texas representatives in the series. Unlike *Texasmost*, *The Civilized West* contained no endnotes, but it did include a standard bibliography and extensive picture credits. Reflecting the marketing strategy of the publishers, nearly a quarter of the text was designated for corporate histories of those fifty leading businesses in the city who underwrote the cost of the book. In this sense, *The Civilized West* was not so very different from *Views of Fort Worth, Texas* or *Greater Fort Worth* in 1907. Both Charlie Swartz and A. O. Jennings were on the same page as the Continental Heritage people, conceiving their projects as money-making ventures to cash in on people's natural curiosity about their hometowns.

The third pictorial history of Fort Worth followed this same tradition. *Where the West Begins: Fort Worth and Tarrant County* was put out in 1985 by Windsor Publications. The Northridge, California company was on the same mission as the Continental Heritage Press, namely to sell a ready-made history to the city under contract. This time the Historic Preservation Council for Tarrant County sponsored the project. Tarleton State University history professor Janet L. Schmelzer was hired to write the text, with Amon Carter Museum assistant curator of photographs Carol Roark taking over the Ron Tyler role of "picture researcher." To her credit, Roark came up with several usable pictures of Native Americans to illustrate our earliest history, although none in a Fort Worth or Tarrant County setting. However, as in *The Civilized West*, it was the corporate capsule histories that drove the wagon. Handling the "Business Biographies" section was Weatherford College instructor Darleen Garrett. The twenty-two businesses profiled in that section underwrote the costs of publishing. The book contained, besides 203 delightful pictures, a "selected bibliography" to satisfy the more scholarly readers, but no separate listing of picture credits. Hitting the stores in 1985, *Where the West Begins* made Fort Worth the seventh city in Texas to get the Windsor treatment. To its credit, the book contained some remarkable photographs, dug up by Roark, which had never been published before, and many color pictures, another first in pictorial histories of Fort Worth.

After *Where the West Begins*, the pictorial histories began to look depressingly the same: expensive coffee table books with less and less attention to scholarship. In fact, there seemed to be an inverse correlation between retail cost and level of scholarship. To raise production values, however, and therefore justify raising the price for buyers, they turned increasingly to modern, full-color pictures which provided dazzling eye candy but had little connection to historic Fort Worth. The period photos used by Swartz, Jennings, Tyler and Sanders, were old hat and ho-hum. Modern "readers" required fancy pictures produced in professional dark rooms.

In 1990 Windsor Publications returned with *Fort Worth: New Frontiers in Excellence* with Mike Patterson credited as the "author" of the skimpy text. In 1995, the Fort Worth Chamber of Commerce published *Fort Worth: Catching the World's Attention*, with Mike Pelecchia as author. This volume gave up all pretense at assembling genuine historic photos of "Cowtown," preferring to use only modern, color photos in the layout. Then in 1999, the Chamber of Commerce, apparently deciding they should contribute something lasting for the city's 150th anniversary, published *Fort Worth: A Sesquicentennial Celebration* turning once again to Mike Pelecchia to write the text that accompanied the pictures. The most notable thing about this volume is that it was the first to tap the substantial post card resources of city residents, reproducing an even dozen of such images from decades earlier, thus bringing the pictorial story of Fort Worth full circle to the turn of the century.

Now comes the present volume to take its place alongside the other pictorial histories of Fort Worth. It benefits from many "new" views of Fort Worth and its residents that have surfaced in the last fourteen years. The city's sesquicentennial (1849-1999) has provided the spark to produce this book as well as the inspiration for many long-time citizens to dig through their trunks and bureau drawers searching for old family pictures. A significant addition to this work is the large number of post cards made available to the compilers. Picture post cards were part of America's love affair with photography in the latter decades of the nineteenth century. The post card craze was a direct descendant of the practice of handing out *cartes de viste* (or CDVs) as calling cards in the mid-nineteenth century. This craze did not hit Fort Worth until after the turn of the century, long after some of Fort Worth's most famous and potentially picturesque moments had already occurred, such as the founding of the fort, the annual "long drives" through town, the completion of the first railroad into the city in 1876, or the Texas Spring Palace of 1889-90.

The earliest postcards were made and sold by the U.S. Post Office beginning in the 1870s for a nation which even then was already in a hurry. Around 1880 the first picture post cards made their appearance in America, bearing primitive images of buildings, landscapes, and simple lithographs. Businesses quickly jumped on the bandwagon, recognizing a ready-made form of advertising that could be mailed to potential customers, or just handed out by the wagon-load to a highly literate citizenry. But something odd happened on the way to the mail box. People who sent and received them were not so much interested in using this cheap and easy form of correspondence to let the folks back home know where they were in their travels, as they were in acquiring as many of the things as possible and storing them away in shoe boxes to swap with other collectors and eventually pass on to their descendants. Picture post cards became a collectible item in the same way that stamps or Indian arrowheads or bottle caps were. On May 19, 1898, a Congressional law allowed "private mailing cards" to be printed up by private companies and sold by the millions, though the later practice of writing a personal message on the back was prohibited. A warning printed on the reverse side from the picture stated, "This side is exclusively for the address." Only years later was the reverse side divided in half with a place for both the address and a short message. Even before that time, the collecting craze was already in full swing thanks to two developments during the 1890s: first, improvements in the manufacturing process made colored images possible; and second, the Columbian Exposition in 1893 gave the hundreds of thousands of tourists who came to see it something extraordinary to show the folks back home.

The oldest existing Fort Worth postcards cannot be dated any earlier than the turn-of-the-century, but soon after that they began being produced in profusion. The earliest were on pale blue card stock and required only a 1 cent stamp to mail anywhere in the United States. Everything that did not move, in the form of commercial buildings, homes, gardens, etc., served as suitable subject matter for the photographers and artists who furnished the visual images to the printers. The favorite views of old Fort Worth seemed to be street scenes, especially of Main Street, prominent public buildings (especially the County Court House), churches, bird's eye views, and, oddly, people posing behind cardboard cutouts in studio shots. (One of the most popular cutouts depicted one of those new-fangled automobiles with the subject appearing to be either the driver or a passenger. It was as close as many people would ever come to the actual experience of driving.) Artists sometimes touched up the photographs, for instance adding a sun shining above the courthouse.

The gap in the Fort Worth historical record between proper versus improper subject matter shows up in local post cards, too - or rather

The dignified "Alaska" building at Tenth and Main had become the moderately-priced Delmar Hotel by 1930. Notice the "White Way" lights leading down to the Majestic Theater on Commerce Street; both were razed to build the Convention Center. *(Courtesy of the Dalton Hoffman, Jr. Collection)*

does not show up, because no risqué cards have ever surfaced. As far as we can tell, there were no "underground" picture post cards produced using local subjects or local settings. Shady ladies and shady places were off limits, possibly because the Comstock Law could be tough on anyone sending such things through the mail.

Unlike one-of-a-kind photographs, the sheer numbers of postcards produced of the same subject insured that many favorite Fort Worth scenes were preserved for posterity, and some of the best appear in this book. It is likely that at some point in the future, an entire book of historic Fort Worth post card views will be published, drawing from the enormous collections of several dedicated local "deltiologists" (postcard collectors) who call Fort Worth home. At present, their collections represent an untapped gold mine of Fort Worth history.

The twentieth century brought a veritable flood of visual images of Fort Worth. The reason had as much to do with cultural developments as with technology. Once the modern newspaper age arrived with the *Fort Worth Press* (1921) and *Fort Worth Star-Telegram* (1925) competing for readership with both morning and evening editions, photographers were routinely dispatched to every newsworthy event in tandem with reporters. Journalism, as they say, is "the first draft of history," so it is no accident that Fort Worth's history has traditionally been chronicled by newspapermen — and women — from Buckley B. Paddock through Mary Daggett Lake, Boyce House, Oliver Knight and Mack and Madeleine Williams. The two newspapers were soon building enormous photo libraries (known as "morgues" in newspaper lingo) for the use of their staff writers. The problem was, newspapers are not in the archives business, so when the collections grew too large, and when the *Fort Worth Press* eventually shut its doors, thousands of photos were tossed out for garbage collectors, as opposed to historical collectors. A priceless record was thus lost.

In the meantime, Great Events tend to attract hordes of shutterbugs snapping away trying to capture the moment. Among the best examples of Great Events in modern Fort Worth history that brought out the photographers, both amateur and professional, Camp Bowie (1917-1919) and Casa Mañana (1936-39) loom the largest. But a pictorial history of only Great Events tends to give the impression that the city's history was nothing *but* great events, in between which people stood about like actors between scenes, waiting for their next stage entrance. Pictorial images of ordinary folks going about their daily lives are the greatest of all historical rarities. After all, why would anyone want to take pictures of the mundane?

Shutterbugs eventually discovered that Fort Worth has a particularly rich visual history with its heritage of cowboys, longhorn cattle, outlaws and lawmen, soldiers and showgirls, steam engines and giant bombers, visiting Presidents and flamboyant preachers. Fort Worth is a city rife with legends, both established and in the making. The city known at different times as "Cowtown," "the Paris of the Plains," and other colorful names, has always been bigger than life, either producing or attracting the likes of Cullen Davis, Butch Cassidy and the Sundance Kid, the Texas Spring Palace, and the Kimbell Museum. And that magic shows no sign of abating any time soon.

This is a wonderful time for a new pictorial history of Fort Worth to appear, and not just because of the Sesquicentennial. As we approach the end of the twentieth century, the city is rapidly changing, beginning with the booming, high tech economy. The city's expanding population also makes it one of the fastest growing urban areas in the nation, creating a remarkably diverse population. So far, newcomers and old-timers alike are showing a wonderful appreciation for Cowtown history, as demonstrated by the broad support for local historic preservation and the strong sales of local history books. While Fort Worth is a city galloping toward the twenty-first century, it remains a city with one foot squarely planted in the past. Nostalgia sells by the bushel basket locally, which is why the multimillion dollar Sundance Square re-development incorporates the brick streets, old buildings and historic themes that it does. They are pleasing to the eye and good for business!

Today Fort Worth has much to be proud of; so it is fitting that at the end of the twentieth century - as the city celebrates its sesquicentennial - we pause to look back. Has it really been only 150 years since Major Ripley Arnold first planted the flag on the bluff overlooking the Trinity? We have come so far. But not so far that we are in danger of forgetting our roots. Fort Worth has Historic Fort Worth, Inc., the Tarrant County Historic Commission, several historical societies, strong neighborhood associations, deep-pocketed benefactors, and a collective pride in its rich culture that shines through in the Northside Stockyards area, Sundance Square, and the world-class museums, art galleries, and performing halls.

In another fifty years, when our Bicentennial rolls around, what images of the present-day city will Fort Worthers cherish? Alliance Airport perhaps? The Bass Performance Hall? The Texas Motor Speedway? What old landmarks will no longer be with us except as postcards or "Kodak moments"? Will the Flatiron Building, the Northside Coliseum, "Trader's Oak," the Main Street Bridge, and the T&P Station be nothing but memories in another half century? Will there still be a herd of longhorns on Exchange Avenue in 2049? Whatever Fort Worthers are looking at then, hopefully the pictures in this book will help remind them where they came from, and new generations will go to whatever kind of libraries they have then, whether electronic or hands-on, and learn about their city. It's a great one.

Dr. Richard Selcer is a historian of Military and American Civil War. He holds a Ph.D. from Texas Christian University and has taught at both the International University of Vienna, Austria and the Kiev, Ukraine University. He has also taught for the Tarrant County College, and the Dallas County College systems as well as Texas Christian University. He is author of numerous books including: The Fort that Became a City: an Illustrated Reconstruction of Fort Worth, Texas 1849-1853 / drawings by William B. Potter: text by Richard F. Selcer, Texas Christian University Press, 1995; Hell's Half Acre: The Life and Legend of a Red Light District, (Chisholm Trail Series No. 9), Texas Christian University Press, 1991; Almanac of American Life: The Middle Period, 1850-1875, Facts on File, 2000. Legendary Texas Watering Holes: The Great Saloons of the Lone Star State, Texas A&M University Press, forthcoming.

Fort Worth - From a Rich Heritage to a Promising Future

Douglas Harman

Combine a cowtown's wildness with modern civilization and a great big slice of American culture, and you come up with a town called Fort Worth, Texas. It is a city of "Cowboys and Culture".

Fort Worth is fortunate because key community leaders developed D/FW Airport, museums, gardens, convention and equestrian facilities and historic preservation in a manner that has positioned Fort Worth to be a strong destination. The community leaders who preserved the Stockyards to become a major historic entertainment district deserve our praise. They took an obsolete livestock business area, saved it from obliteration and turned it into a unique entertainment area where Fort Worth can exhibit its important Texas heritage. It includes many historic landmarks, Billy Bob's, The White Elephant Saloon and now the Fort Worth Herd of Longhorns.

Fort Worth has had great success in the revitalization of the north part of downtown, an area known as Sundance Square. And as the dust settles on the successful 1998 bond program, the city government has the great opportunity to begin the process of convention center renovation and expansion. The studies called for exhibit space expansion, new meeting rooms, and a ballroom. The timing could not be better for these improvements. Now the city has the chance to use the Convention Center as a major stimulus for the revitalization of the south end of downtown. In addition to the Convention Center, there are already major highway and transportation improvements being implemented in the south part downtown to the east and the south of the Center.

Towns like Fort Worth were a critical part of the Western frontier. However, most cities shed their buildings along with their heritage from the early frontier period. Fort Worth is an exception. Through the years, Fort Worth, known with cowboy directness simply as "Cowtown", has by luck and planning preserved its extraordinary Western Legacy. From the cattle culture of the stockyards to the fine art in the museums, Fort Worth holds a storehouse of Western Americana. Visitors expect to experience "the West" when they come to Texas, and Fort Worth gives them that authentically

Fort Worth is unique as one of the few large American cities to maintain a thoroughly Western flavor. Horse trailers, cowboy hats and spurs are a common sight in town. Fort Worth has not only preserved its historic buildings, but has kept its traditions alive — it is truly still a city "where the West begins."

Douglas Harman is president and C.E.O. of the Fort Worth Convention and Visitors Bureau. He is a former city manager of Fort Worth, and professor who is also a writer, political cartoonist, history buff and collector of Fort Worth memorabilia and spurs. He has been president and C.E.O. of the Fort Worth Convention and Visitors Bureau since 1989.

(Courtesy of the Fort Worth Convention and Visitors Bureau)

Foreword

by Dr. Ben Procter

On June 6, 1849, Major Ripley A. Arnold positioned forty-two men of Company F of the Second Dragoons on the Clear Fork of the Trinity River, his mission that of guarding East Texas settlers against Indian incursions. Within two months he relocated his men to a more advantageous spot, a high bluff overlooking the river, and designated this site as Camp Worth in honor of Brigadier General William Jenkins Worth, who had distinguished himself in the recent U.S.-Mexican War. Three months later, November 14, 1849, the United States War Department officially named this area as Fort Worth, thereby establishing a permanent outpost on the North-central Texas frontier.

In 1999, the sesquicentennial year of its existence, Fort Worth is celebrating its heritage and history, proud of the progress of the fifth largest city in Texas. And what an impressive record its citizens have fashioned over the past one hundred and fifty years! After suffering the hardships of frontier living in the 1850s, the initial settlers endured the loss of men leaving to fight for the Confederacy in 1861 and withstood the ravages of Reconstruction by unfriendly government officials, both civilian and military, until the population in 1866 dropped to a low of 175 people. As a result, Fort Worth soon assumed the title, with an accompanying logo, of "Panther City," suggesting that its environs were so placid and its ambiance so dull that citizens discovered a panther sleeping in a street.

But by 1873 this image began to change. Because of the efforts of such merchants as Jacob Samuels, William Jesse Boaz, and William Henry Davis, educators Addison and Randolph Clark, and newspapermen K. M. Van Zandt and Buckley B. Paddock, Fort Worth was incorporated, and with a mayor-council form of government the city began to grow. By 1876 the Texas and Pacific Railway designated Fort Worth as its eastern terminus, especially since cowboys considered the city as a "jumping off" point for respite before continuing to drive cattle northward along the Chisholm Trail to the railheads in Kansas. As a consequence, meat packing became the principal local business, along with accompanying enterprises. And by 1900, with eight more railroads linking Fort Worth to areas of the nation, the city attracted a populace that made it the fifth largest in the state.

In the first half of the twentieth century Fort Worth continued to grow and expand. For instance, it became a military and defense center. During World War I the U.S. Army established Camp Bowie in west Fort Worth, where 100,000 soldiers received instruction and training; the U.S. Army Air Force also converted three airfields into aviation training establishments. In 1942, after the outbreak of World War II, Consolidated Vultee Aircraft Corporation (later bought out by General Dynamics and still later by Lockheed) became the largest aircraft manufacturer in the area; and, together with a bomber base, that in 1948 became Carswell Air Force Base, where the U.S. Strategic Air Command stationed its B-36 bombers, Fort Worth thrived because of military contracts and accompanying personnel.

Other ingredients also affected continued growth. With the discovery of oil in West Texas prior to and after World War I, such oil refining corporations as Sinclair, Texaco, and Humble (later Exxon) selected Fort Worth as a home base as well as a center for oil exchanges and field equipment. Equally important during the first half of the twentieth century was the leadership of Amon G. Carter who directed the economic and political fortunes of the city. Besides building the Fort Worth Star Telegram into one of the state's foremost newspapers, he directed the construction of Casa Mañana (theater-in-the-round) and Texas Frontier Centennial in 1936 to rival the State Fair in Dallas. As a result of his forceful guidance, the city became the recipient of much needed federal funds during the depression years of the 1930s. Carter was therefore largely responsible for such projects and edifices, most of which are still in existence--Will Rogers Memorial Center (and auditorium), Botanic Garden, John Peter Smith Hospital, a public library, forty-eight public schools and playgrounds, low-cost public housing, a high school gymnasium, and the largest high school football stadium in the state (Farrington Field).

The Pictorial History of Fort Worth Texas: Celebrating 150 Years, scripted by Landmark Publishing, Inc., with an introduction by local historian Richard Selcer, has captured the spirit and flavor of this sesquicentennial year -- the institutions and businesses and leaders that created a vibrant civilization and distinct culture for that city "where the West begins." A number of classic pictures thus record a "cowtown" ambiance.

After all since Fort Worth was a major center for cattle drives after the Civil War, meat-packing businesses arose in the 1880s that culminated with the establishment of Swift and Armour branch packing plants on Fort Worth's "north side" in 1902. To promote these livestock-meat packing industries, city officials and merchants initiated a Fat Stock Show in 1896, which became so popular that promoters moved this annual event to the Northside Coliseum in 1908 and renamed it the Southwestern Exposition and Fat Stock Show (which has become the Southwestern Exposition and Livestock Show).

Landmark Publishing, Inc. has focused upon the major industries that dynamically affected the political and economic life of the city for most of the twentieth century The photographs remind readers of the vital importance of the railroads, the oil and gas industry, and the continued military presence as well as the effect of such visionary leaders as Amon Carter.

In depicting the growth of Fort Worth from a small village on the Clear Fork of the Trinity to a major city, Landmark Publishing, Inc. has lifted out of the annals of local history a number of endearing pictures, which reflect not only the endeavors and activities of citizens over the years but also the building of a unique culture and way of life. Where else will readers be able to find a better tome that captures the ambiance and spirit of Fort Worthians during this sesquicentennial year? Photographs depict agencies of a growing metropolis--unique pictures of the city police and fire departments, churches that have become notable landmarks, nationally recognized museums located in the Arts/Cultural district, institutions of higher learning such as Southwestern Baptist Theological Seminary and Texas Christian University, historic structures such as the Texas and Worth hotels as well as the restored Thistle Hill mansion, and recreational and athletic facilities, ranging from the Lake Worth Casino and Bath House (1920s) to Bobby Bragan's Fort Worth Cats Texas League baseball team in 1931. Hence, Celebrating 150 Years: The Pictorial History of Fort Worth, Texas is, according to an old refrain, "a wonderful trip down memory lane."

"The Texas" hotel was built in 1921, Sanguinet & Staats, architects. Known later as Hotel Texas and now Radisson Plaza Hotel. Best remembered as the last ovenight stop for President John F. Kennedy. *(Courtesy of Acme Brick)*

Dr. Ben Procter, professor of history at Texas Christian University, received his doctorate at Harvard University in 1961 after receiving B.A. and M. A. degrees at the University of Texas, Austin. He is the author of numerous books and textbooks on Texas history as well as Not Without Honor: The Life of John Reagan, for which he received the Sommerfield G. Roberts Award in 1962. He has been cited as professor of the year at TCU, is a Fellow of the Texas State Historical Association, and received the Texas Writers Roundup Award in 1972. Dr. Procter is also author of Just One Riot, Episodes of the Texas Rangers in the 20th Century, Eakin Press, 1991 and William Randolph Hearst, The Early Years, 1863-1910, Oxford University Press, 1998. He is currently working on the follow-up to this title.

KAY GRANGER
12TH DISTRICT, TEXAS

WASHINGTON OFFICE:
435 CANNON BUILDING
WASHINGTON, D.C. 20515
(202) 225-5071

DISTRICT OFFICE:
SUITE 740
1600 WEST 7TH STREET
FT. WORTH, TX 76102
(817) 338-0909

Congress of the United States
House of Representatives

ASSISTANT MAJORITY WHIP

COMMITTEE:
APPROPRIATIONS

SUBCOMMITTEES:
TRANSPORTATION
MILITARY CONSTRUCTION
LEGISLATIVE BRANCH

Congresswoman Kay Granger's Statement on Fort Worth

"The magic of Fort Worth lies in its diversity – diversity of population, opinion, and experience – and the fact that diversity works to our advantage. This diversity shows in our reverence for our old west history, preserved so effectively in the historic Stockyards area. Then a five-minute drive to West Fort Worth and you're in the arts Mecca of Texas, the Cultural District with its world-renowned museums and a rejuvenated zoo. These attractions draw scores of visitors interested in exciting arts and exotic animals. A trip north on I-35 takes you straight into the 21st Century and Fort Worth's future when you enter the Alliance Corridor, home to some of the world's leaders in technology and industry. And our thriving downtown brings all of this together in a way other cities envy. Of course, none of this ignores the beauty and strength of our neighborhoods and the activism which enables us to coordinate our efforts and cooperate in a way that brings everyone to the table. After all, in Fort Worth, everyone has something to offer."

Kay Granger was Fort Worth's first woman mayor, first Republican woman to serve in the U. S. House of Representatives from Texas, and first woman to represent district 12 in the House in almost a decade. She was elected to Congress in 1996 and re-elected in 1998.

CELEBRATING 150 YEARS

THE PICTORIAL HISTORY OF FORT WORTH, TEXAS

1849 — 1999

Paula Oates, Editor
with an Introduction by
Dr. Richard Selcer
Landmark Publishing, Inc.
Fort Worth, Texas, 1999

Main Street, Ca 1879

(Courtesy Fort Worth Star Telegram Photograph Collection, Special Collections Division, The University of Texas at Arlington Libraries)

Main Street, looking north from Front Street (now Lancaster) Ca 1878

(Fort Worth Public Library)

Early Views of Fort Worth

Main Street, looking north to courthouse, Ca 1885

(Courtesy Fort Worth Star Telegram Photographic Collection, Special Collections Division, The University of Texas at Arlington Libraries)

Tarrant County Jail and Labor Day Parade on Belknap Street. Ca 1895.
(Courtesy Fort Worth Public Library)

Main Street looking north from between 9th and 10th, Ca 1895

(Courtesy Fort Worth Star Telegram Photographic Collection, Special Collections Division, The University of Texas at Arlington Libraries)

Houston Street, Ca 1900

(Courtesy Fort Worth Public Library)

1856	***1856***
First United States Post Office established - Main Street - by Julian Field, first postmaster. July, first licensed stage coach arrives in Fort Worth	***Fort Worth wins vote to be county seat***

Looking south on North Main to the recently built courthouse Ca 1900
(Courtesy Fort Worth Star Telegram Photographic Collection,Special Collections Division, The University of Texas at Arlington Libraries)

Old North Main Viaduct over the Trinity River, Ca 1905
(Courtesy Fort Worth Star Telegram Photographic Collection, Special Collections Division, The University of Texas at Arlington Libraries)

The Anheuser-Busch Brewing Association Building and yards, Fort Worth, about 1905.
(The Quentin McGown Postcard Collection)

Bluff Street view of courthouse with jail at the left Ca 1905
(Courtesy Fort Worth Star Telegram Photographic Collection, Special Collections Division, The University of Texas at Arlington Libraries)

Looking north from Jennings Avenue Viaduct with Carnegie Library in the distance. Ca 1905
(Courtesy Fort Worth Star Telegram Photographic Collection, Special Collections Division, The University of Texas at Arlington Libraries)

Iron bridge over the Trinity River with the courthouse and jail in the background. Ca 1905
(Courtesy Fort Worth Star Telegram Photographic Collection, Special Collections Division, The University of Texas at Arlington Libraries)

The Railroad Arrives, July 19, 1876

Twenty-six car train of horses and mules from W. O. Rominger Horse and Mule Company of Fort Worth, Texas, 1917.
(North Fort Worth Historical Society)

In March of 1923 # 601, the first of seventy Class 600 locomotives that would eventually arrive from Ohio was delivered to the T&P Railroad.
(Tarrant County College NE Campus)

April 12, Confederate States of America fire on Fort Sumpter; Texas secedes from the Union. Tarrant County votes in favor of secession by a 28 vote majority of 800 votes cast

Galveston taken by Federal forces

Santa Fe Depot, 1971. Built in 1899 as the Fort Worth and Denver City Railroad Union Depot.
(Courtesy Fort Worth Star-Telegram Photograph Collection, Special Collections Division, The University of Texas at Arlington Libraries.)

T&P locomotive #900 (Tarrant County College, NE Campus)

Texas & Pacific Passenger Terminal, 1931
(Tarrant County College, NE Campus)

Texas and Pacific Passenger Terminal.
(Courtesy Fort Worth Star-Telegram Photograph Collection, Special Collections Division, The University of Texas at Arlington Libraries.)

This is believed to be the interior of an early T&P Office
(Fort Worth Public Library

Texas and Pacific Diesel #2000 alongside older 900 series locomotive.
(Courtesy Fort Worth Star-Telegram Photograph Collection, Special Collections Division, The University of Texas at Arlington Libraries.)

The Original Tarantula Map was created in 1872 by B. B. Paddock and used on the masthead of his newspaper. It depicted the city as a hub for railroad and stage lines

(Tarantula Corporation)

1902 -- Fort Worth begins a six decade alliance with the meat packing industry

Swift and Company won a coin toss and selected the site south of Exchange Avenue. Armour and Company located on the north side of the street. Both plants opened in late 1902 but launched a Grand Opening in March of 1903 to coincide with the annual Live Stock Show. Armour closed in 1962, and Swift in 1971

(Courtesy of North Fort Worth Historical Society.)

Armour & Co. Show Team — Ca 1914
(Courtesy of North Fort Worth Historical Society.)

Swift and Company, with view of box cars waiting on the tracks, Ca 1918
(Courtesy of North Fort Worth Historical Society.)

1867

Chisholm Trail opens with the beginning of the cattle drives northward.
Ford the Trinity at Daggett's Crossing

(Courtesy Tarrant County College, North east Campus.)

The Chisholm Trail

The first successful cattle drive along the Chisholm Trail that ran from south Texas through Fort Worth to Kansas was in 1866. The cowboys drove the herds in from south of town and went north toward the river, following what was first a nameless street, later Rusk and now Commerce Street. From early spring to late fall, for eighteen years, the cattle came. By 1884, more than three million cattle later, travel up the trail had virtually ceased. This bronze sculpture, known as Texas Gold, is located on North Side Drive and stands as a monument to the longhorn, and the cowboy; both one of a kind.

(Courtesy Fort Worth Star-Telegram Photograph Collection, Special Collections Division, The University of Texas at Arlington)

North Fort Worth Historical Society Presents The Stockyard Museum and Collection

The Bad Luck Wedding Dress

A dress that has brought personal misery or disaster to everyone who has worn it or planned to wear it? Yes.

David VanHorne left Marie in 1889 to seek gold in Oregon. Although he declared his love for her until his death many years later, they were never reunited. The dress was passed on to their daughter, Evelyn Henrietta VanHorne to wear for her wedding. Her fiancee, who was in France during World War I, was killed in a mine field just a few days before the wedding. The War was already over, and he was on his way home to her. She never married and died at the age of 79, an "old maid".

David and Marie's granddaughter, Alta Marguerite VanHorne, wore the dress at her wedding, but six months after the wedding, her husband, Daniel Patrick, took multiple sclerosis and died with the year.

The dress was put away and not worn for many years. In 1949, Alta VanHorne Patrick Buker, wore the dress for a historical tour she was giving through her home. The next day she became ill and was bedridden for more than a month, a total mystery to the doctors as to her illness. She did recover, but the dress has never been worn again ..

This dress is now on display at the Stockyards Museum, located in the historic Livestock Exchange Building. The Museum grants visitors an insight into an era when a man's word was his bond, and a handshake was his contract. Focusing on the living history of the Fort Worth Stockyards and the community that surrounds it, exhibits take you into the world of cattlemen, cowboys, and commission companies. Photographs tell the story of men and women who made a decent living in hard times working for two giant meat-packing plants.

Relive the days of riding a streetcar, putting the card out for the iceman, crowning the Stock Show Queen, and seeing a movie in a plush theater -- with just one screen. The museum is the home of the electric light bulb that once lit the backstage door at the Palace Theater in downtown Fort Worth. It has been burning since 1908.

Native American artifacts from many tribes speak of the days before the coming of Major Ripley Arnold's dragoons and the building of the fort on the banks of the Trinity.

Trace the route of the 1986 Texas Sesquicentennial Wagon Train as it wound its way around the state. Gifts presented to the wagon train from communities along that route are on display.

Members of the North Fort Worth Historical Society worked many long hours restoring the museum's interior for its opening in 1989. Now they volunteer as hosts to visitors who come from around the world to discover the Fort Worth Stockyards..

Come enjoy the Stockyards Museum, a labor of love, which honors a rich heritage.

North Fort Worth Historical Society

The Birth of The Stock Show and Rodeo

The National Feeders and Breeders Show, shortly after the construction of the Coliseum in 1908.

(Courtesy Fort Worth Museum of Science and History/Fort Worth Stock Show Collection)

1870 - 1872

Texas readmitted to the Union in 1870; Following year, K. M. Van Zandt purchases the Quitman Herald; B. B. Paddock arrives and becomes the editor of The Democrat; 500,00 cattle driven through the city

1873

Hyde Park, Fort Worth's first park, established at present day 9th Street; Paddock creates Tarantula Map; Standard newspaper published by J. K. Millican

Hereford herd in north central Texas, 1975
(Courtesy W. T. Waggoner Memorial Library Historic Photograph Collection)

(Courtesy Fort Worth Museum of Science and History/Fort Worth Stock Show Collection.)

Texas and Southwestern Cattle Raisers Association

Texas and Southwestern Cattle Raisers Association was founded by 40 cattlemen in 1877 in Graham, Texas, under the name of the Stock Raisers Association of Northwestern Texas. These cattlemen created the association to fight cattle theft in the region.

In 1893, cattlemen dropped the regional name for the more appropriate title—Cattle Raisers Association of Texas. In so doing, it brought in cattlemen from other small, regional associations to strengthen the original Northwestern group.

In 1921, the cattlemen adopted the name of TSCRA at the request of the Panhandle and Southwestern Live Stock Association, the group formed by Charles Goodnight to protect the Panhandle during the days of the big trail fights. The bigger, stronger association boasted members from throughout the Southwestern United States as well as from Mexico, Haiti, New York, Michigan and other outlying states. Today, TSCRA has over 14,000 members ranching in Texas, Oklahoma and surrounding states.

TSCRA Field Inspector, Slim Hulen
(W. T. Waggoner Memorial Library Historical Photograph

TSCRA has gained worldwide respect through the vigilance of its inspectors, who became Special Texas Rangers in 1893. With more than a century of law enforcement behind them, the inspectors remain the backbone of TSCRA.

At present, TSCRA maintains a staff of 32 field inspectors stationed strategically in multiple-county districts throughout Texas and Oklahoma. The number of cattle, number of members and the square miles of area involved determine the size of each district.

TSCRA field inspectors, whom the late cowman-author J. Frank Dobie compared favorably with the Texas Rangers, Scotland Yard and the Royal Canadian Mounted Police, remain in the forefront of beating back the ever-present threat of cattle theft. The Texas Department of Public Safety and/or the Oklahoma Crime Bureau commission the inspectors, all certified peace officers, as Special Rangers. They are charged with the primary responsibility of investigating livestock thefts and other ranch-related property losses. They also serve as agents of the association's members in claiming and determining ownership of stray cattle or any cattle held in question. These inspectors may also inspect some cattle shipments from individual ranches, when requested, before movement to other ranchers or feedlots in or out-of state. Investigations and inspection of shipments are performed without regard to an individual being a member or not.

Texas field inspectors also supervise TSCRA brand inspectors conducting inspections of cattle at Texas' 140 auction markets and terminals. TSCRA has 72 brand inspectors who inspect over 5 million head of cattle yearly. These inspectors record a complete physical and color description of each animal including sex, age, class and horn information in addition to earmarks and brands. This information, including the name of the consignor, is compiled on a computerized form which, in turn, is sent to the Fort Worth headquarters where it is microfilmed and entered into the association's computers.

Many cattle thefts are solved and thieves apprehended through the use of TSCRA's brand inspection program and its computers.

Since September 1997, the Association has been responsible for similar inspection of all horses processed at commercial slaughter plants in Texas. The Texas Legislature conferred this authority in order to meet a recognized need to identify stolen horses.

TSCRA also publishes monthly a Missing-Stolen Livestock Bulletin. This bulletin, which may include information on stolen or strayed cattle and horses, stolen saddles, tractors, trailers and other miscellaneous ranch property, is distributed nationally to approximately 1,000 other law enforcement agencies.

TSCRA also maintains a complete card index file of over 138,000 recorded brands in Texas.

As the association has grown, so have the challenges to cattlemen beyond cattle theft. TSCRA is recognized as a spokesman for the Texas cattle industry statewide and nationally on legislation, animal care, regulatory matters and other things which might affect the best interests of cattlemen. TSCRA works closely with the National Cattlemen's Beef Association, the Cattlemen's Beef Promotion and Research Board, the US Meat Export Federation and the Texas Beef Council, all of which it helped found, as well as other livestock groups on issues of mutual interest.

TSCRA has expanded its services to include health and life insurance for members, their families and employees, assistance in getting workers' compensation insurance through the TSCRA group purchase program and credit card services. The association also publishes an award-winning twice-monthly membership newsletter and, for 85 years, has published *The Cattleman Magazine*, one of the nation's most respected and quoted livestock trade journals.

1999 TSCRA Annual Convention Trade Show
(Courtesy The Cattleman Magazine)

Fort Worth's north side was the home of the TSCRA from 1923 to 1950
(Courtesy W. T. Waggoner Memorial Library Historic Photograph Collection)

This bronze, "The Brand Inspector", greets visitors to the Cattle Raisers Association and Museum at the Seventh Street location

(Courtesy Cattle Raisers Association)

Intended to involve youngsters in educational programs aimed at furthering the livestock industry, Baby Beef Clubs sprang up across the country. The first annual meeting was held in Fort Worth in 1913.

(Courtesy Fort Worth Museum of Science and History/Fort Worth Stock Show Collection.)

Fort Worth's National Feeders and Breeders Show 1916.

(Courtesy Fort Worth Star-Telegram Photograph Collection, Special Collections Division, The University of Texas at Arlington Libraries.)

FROM CATTLE TO CULTURE: FORT WORTH'S WEST SIDE ADVENTURE

Delbert Bailey, Publicity Manager
Southwestern Exposition and Livestock Show

From cattle to cannons, then a Texas Centennial, a flavor of culture, and now a Sesquicentennial for Fort Worth, the area known as Will Rogers Memorial Center has seen it all while manifesting positive horizons.

Pioneer Khleber Miller VanZandt was a major in the Confederate Army. After the Civil War, he settled in Fort Worth and built quite a reputation as a cattle rancher in Tarrant County, operating in what is now Fort Worth's West Side. As the United States anticipated involvement in World War I, the Army utilized a number of acres belonging to the pioneer family to establish a military reservation—Camp Bowie—to be used as an artillery training range and a mounted cavalry base. The government released the land to the VanZandt family after the war.

As plans were established in the early 1930's for Fort Worth to become involved with the State of Texas Centennial in 1936, the City obtained title to 100 acres of land that lay south of Camp Bowie Boulevard and west of University Drive. This effort was due in large part to the political and civic influence of Amon G. Carter, publisher of the Fort Worth Star-Telegram.

Carter pressed the City to make a bid to the State of Texas to host the official Centennial reflection. Utilizing political clout in Washington, Carter promoted a plan to construct on the tract a massive civic center that would serve as a focal point for the state celebration. Through Carter's influence with President Franklin Roosevelt, plans were laid for the edifice that would include an auditorium and coliseum, plus a landmark facility that became the Pioneer Tower. The federal government's Works Progress Administration provided funds and workers for construction.

As work began in 1934 on the Tower and Auditorium, Carter suffered a tremendous personal loss. His close friend, Will Rogers, met death in a plane crash in Alaska. The publisher, at his expense, arranged for the air transport of Rogers' body back to Oklahoma for burial. In a mode of his expression of friendship to Rogers, Carter petitioned the City of Fort Worth to name the new municipal structure for the entertainer/humorist. The entire 100-acre tract was titled Will Rogers Memorial Center.

Carter wanted the facility to open as the center piece of the Texas Centennial. However, a competitive bid by the City of Dallas found favor with the Texas Legislature and that city was named as official Centennial host. This infuriated Carter, a setback from which he never recovered. He insisted that Fort Worth city fathers proceed with completion of the civic facility, and promised to join in funding an extravaganza in Fort Worth to honor the State's Centennial.

In the interim, dissension among planners, architects and builders on a structural engineering plan for the coliseum brought delays. It was a general consensus that a "remarkable edifice" be constructed, one that would benchmark construction of such facilities, that had size to house thousands of patrons, and that had minimal viewer obstructions. But how was such a building to be constructed?

The answer came from a young construction engineer named Herbert M. Hinckley (1897-1938). His innovative, somewhat radical, views on a free-span domed building brought further delays, but was granted permission to proceed. Hinckley had staked his reputation on the design (which uses a unique way of connecting radial arches at a peak) despite doubt by many "experts" of his time. As the Texas Centennial arrived in 1936, the Pioneer Tower (another of Hinckley's designs) and Auditorium had been completed, but the Coliseum was still under construction. The Coliseum, dubbed the world's first such free-span domed building, did not become usable until 1937. Hinckley fell by the wayside in receiving praise for his engineering feat but went on to build another such building at Louisiana State University. He died of heart failure before his 41st birthday.

Accompanying the major construction project was the inclusion of a massive outdoor amphitheater, complete with dining hall, that became known as Casa Mañana (the house of tomorrow). The theater stage was circular and rotated to present two staging areas in the shape of one-third of the circle. The remaining third was "backstage," which housed dressing areas and prop storage. As the scenes changed, the stage was rotated 120 degrees to present another view or entertainment venue. Again, such a configuration was unheard of in the entertainment industry.

Casa featured table seating in a semi-circle off the stage apron and seating in the back area. The stage was at the base of a natural rise in the terrain, situated near University Drive and what is now Harley Avenue. As the terrain climbed westward it gave a natural setting for the patron seating. A lengthy façade stretched across the west entrance, giving the appearance of a medieval castle. Today's Casa Mañana is a stationary "theatre-in-the-round."

Carter's intervention to insure a better Centennial "show than Dallas" included the fact that he personally paid Broadway Producer Billy Rose a daily salary of $1,000 to present a premiere event at Casa. To support the showcase, a "Frontier Village" was created on the site, along with a facility known as Pioneer Palace, complete with façade to complement Casa and equipped with a massive bar from which liquid spirits flowed.

Due to material shortages during World War II a bronze statue of Will Rogers, commissioned by Carter to Artist/Sculpture Electra Waggoner Biggs was delayed in its dedication to Fort Worth citizens. The bronze was to be placed on a grassy area north of the Pioneer Tower. Carter imposed upon another close friend, then Army General Dwight D. Eisenhower, to speak at the official dedication of the bronze in 1947. The artwork features Will Rogers astride his favorite horse, Soapsuds, "Riding into the Sunset."

The Southwestern Exposition and Livestock Show moved its "official home" from North Fort Worth to the Will Rogers Memorial Center in 1944. To the political dismay of residents of the North Side, the Stock Show had outgrown its space there. The West Side's

First jail constructed at 2nd and Commerce
Fort Worth's first sworn police officers

City incorporates March 1; first city elections; first Mayor W. P. Burts, serves until 1874

(Courtesy Tarrant County College, NE)

34th annual convention of the Cattle Raisers Association of Texas held in Fort Worth in March of 1910
(Courtesy W. T. Waggoner Memorial Library Historic Photograph Collection)

extensive land area was more conducive to the growing livestock exhibition and entertainment enterprise. Remnants of the Texas Centennial structures—the Auditorium, Coliseum, a horse barn and the Pioneer Palace Building—were ideal for use by the Stock Show. For the debut event in 1944, the Stock Show set up a large number of tents for show arenas and covered stalling for horses.

The Stock Show has grown to become Fort Worth's most attended annual event, causing a yearly economic impact in excess of $110 million during its three-week stand. Working in close harmony with City government, the Stock Show has partnered almost $20 million of its profits into a spacious, world-class show facilities which are second to none in the show place industry.

Progressing with a planned land use for the Will Rogers complex, Fort Worth has become home to world-renown museums with a variety of themes and displays for public education and enjoyment.

A treasure to Fort Worth and art lovers throughout the world, the Amon Carter Museum houses an extraordinary collection to support the study and appreciation of American art. The family of Fort Worth publisher and philanthropist Amon Carter (1879-1955) founded the museum to house his collection of paintings and sculptures by Frederic Remington and Charles M. Russell.

The Carter boasts one of the country's most active art museum publishing programs. Since 1962, over 100 books have been published independently and in conjunction with major publishers. The Museum closed in the summer of 1999 for a building expansion program that will triple the size of its display galleries. Carter Downtown at 500 Commerce Street will be a temporary service gallery until the reopening in the fall of 2001 of the (new) Amon Carter Museum, located on West Lancaster Street at the northwest corner of the Will Rogers complex.

The Kimbell Art Museum, located on West Lancaster Avenue north of the Pioneer Tower, was opened in 1972 by the Kimbell Art Foundation which was established by Kay Kimbell in the 1930's when he and his wife purchased their first paintings. The Kimbells continued to collect artworks. When the successful local entrepreneur died in 1964, he bequeathed his art collection and entire personal fortune to the Foundation to establish and maintain a public art museum of the first rank in Fort Worth. Shortly thereafter Mrs. Kimbell contributed her share of their property to facilitate the full implementation of her husband's wishes.

By 1966, the Foundation board adopted the policy to "form collections of the highest aesthetic quality, derived from any and all periods in man's history, and in any medium or style." The museum offers a full schedule of public programs to promote appreciation of the collection and special exhibitions, including symposia featuring guest speakers, lectures and gallery talks by the professional staff.

Chartered in 1892 as the Fort Worth Public Library and Art Gallery, the Modern Art Museum of Fort Worth is the oldest art museum in Texas. With a focus on modern and contemporary art, including paintings, sculpture, works on paper and international contemporary photography, the Modern exhibits works from its extensive 3,000-piece collection.

Educational programs such as lectures, adult and children's classes and workshops, summer art camp and occasional family activity days are regular features of the Modern, which also operates The Modern at Sundance Square in the historic Sanger Building (ca. 1929) at Houston and Fourth Streets in downtown. By 2002 the museum will move to a new home with greater exhibit space, a restaurant and state-of-the-art auditorium with classrooms and studios. The new facility will be just east of the Kimbell.

In 1939, the Fort Worth Council of Administrative Women in Education advanced a proposal to establish the Fort Worth Children's Museum which was opened in 1945 in two vacant classrooms at De Zavala Elementary School. Having operated in a former private residence for over a decade, the Museum opened its current location at 1501 Montgomery Street in 1954.

Changed in 1968 to Fort Worth Museum of Science and History to better reflect the types of exhibits and special educational opportunities available, it prides itself on additions such as the Noble Planetarium, Amon Carter Science-Education Wing, Bruce Shulkey Hall of Texas History, science, medical and health offerings. In 1983 the grand Omni Theater, which embodies a revolutionary concept that gives viewers a sense of active participation in the film, was opened. The Museum offers fascinating, educational and entertaining experiences to well over a million annual visitors.

Plans are nearing completion to construct two additional museums in the Western Heritage Center, planned for construction in an area just south of the Museum of Science and History. The initial tenant of the Western Heritage Center with an opening in fall of 2001 is the National Cowgirl Museum and Hall of Fame. The Cowgirl Museum will house displays, art, photographs and historical memorabilia with regard to ladies who have impacted the Western Heritage of America.

Wearing grit and determination like a badge of honor, the cattle raiser has traveled an arduous yet rewarding journey through time, and personifies all the best qualities of the American character. What better time than now to create a vital, new museum that will preserve the memory of the old ways, while celebrating the future of the new. The forthcoming new Cattle Raisers Museum is destined to become that museum and also will be housed in the Western Heritage Center. A small facility is presently located at 1301 West Seventh Street.

To summarize the influence of the area, a media visitor a number of years ago offered a truism: "There's more cowboys and culture within a square-mile area than in any other within the United States." If you asked, all of Fort Worth and hundreds of thousands of annual visitors will agree.

1873

Fort Worth Presbyterian Church organized; The city's first Volunteer Fire Company organized as the Hook & Ladder Co. # 1

1874

G. H. Day elected Mayor, serves until 1878

North side Coliseum and Livestock Exchange Buildings, Fort Worth. (Ca 1915)
(Courtesy of the Quentin McGown Post Card Collection)

Overview of the midway of the Will Rogers Memorial Center in 1952 looking East from the Coliseum. Carnival, produced in conjunction with the Stock Show, was run by Gene Ledel. Train in lower right is now used on the Rusk to Palestine excursion. Building shown as "cafeteria bar" is the old Pioneer Palace from the 1936 Centennial Celebration; original bar is now in the Round-Up Inn. Can also see Farrington Field and downtown Fort Worth skyline.
(Courtesy Fort Worth Museum of Science and History/Fort Worth Stock Show Collection)

The Spring Palace

Texas Spring Palace *(Courtesy The Fort Worth Public Library)*
Upper right corner shows the VIP invitation to the opening of The Texas Spring Palace, 1889. *(Courtesy Quentin McGown)*

The Spring Palace was Fort Worth's "exposition of the resources and progress of the lone star state". Inspired by St. Paul, Minnesota's Ice Palace and Sioux City, Iowa's Corn Palace, the city decided to build a tribute to Texas products. B.B. Paddock was named president of a company charged with fund-raising for the project.

Designed by Armstrong and Messer, the St. Andrews Cross-shaped building was constructed in thirty-one days at a cost of $ 35,000. The second season, it was enlarged at a cost of an additional $10,000.

The main dome measured 150 feet in diameter, with numerous smaller domes and towers. Only Texas materials were used. The foundation stone was from Texas quarries and east Texas pine was used throughout. Decorated with horn and hides, palmettos, shell, and minerals, the goods were used to form geometrical figures. The interior walls and beams were inlaid with ores; polished woods were used as well as the agricultural products of the state. Wheat, corn stalks, rye, moss, cactus, cotton, even Johnson grass decorated roofs and curtained the windows.

Above the portico a coat of arms, made of cotton, corn, moss and grain, stood 15 feet high and measured 20 feet across. An eagle, wings spread, made of colored corn cobs sat atop and the shield upon which the eagle stood was made of cotton and corn. The words TEXAS SPRING PALACE were inscribed on the coat of arms. A large indoor fountain and a raised band platform along with the spacious auditorium was on the first floor. The music room was draped cheesecloth, pleated and held taut. Strung popcorn, peas and straws on threads were used to decorate each panel. The ceiling was entirely covered in popcorn. Many counties were represented with special exhibits.

Opening on May 10, 1889, the ceremony was a nation-wide story. It was called a "fairy-castle", and the "pride and glory of Texas". Luke Short had paid $5 for a gaming concession, and visitors came from as far away as Boston and Chicago.

The first season ended, however, in the red. Not to be deterred, the second season Fort Worth added one hundred feet on each wing and tried again. The second season was a success - that ended in tragedy.

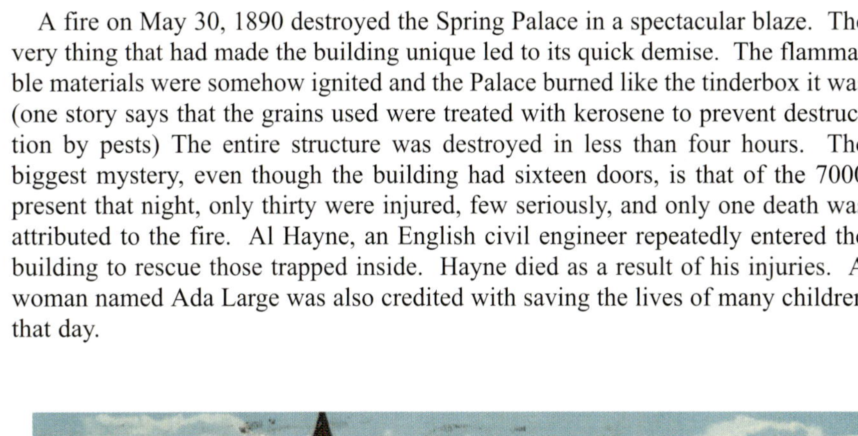
A fire on May 30, 1890 destroyed the Spring Palace in a spectacular blaze. The very thing that had made the building unique led to its quick demise. The flammable materials were somehow ignited and the Palace burned like the tinderbox it was (one story says that the grains used were treated with kerosene to prevent destruction by pests) The entire structure was destroyed in less than four hours. The biggest mystery, even though the building had sixteen doors, is that of the 7000 present that night, only thirty were injured, few seriously, and only one death was attributed to the fire. Al Hayne, an English civil engineer repeatedly entered the building to rescue those trapped inside. Hayne died as a result of his injuries. A woman named Ada Large was also credited with saving the lives of many children that day.

Spring Palace Photographs Courtesy The Fort Worth Public Library

The Al Hayne Memorial, pictured here near the old T&P building, stands northeast of the former site of the Spring Palace .

(Courtesy The Quentin McGown Postcard Collection)

World War I brings Camp Bowie to Fort Worth

Camp Bowie Recruits, 1917 *(Courtesy The Paris Coffee Shop Collection)*

Camp Bowie, 36th Division
(Courtesy Fort Worth Star-Telegram Photograph Collection, Special Collections Division, The University of Texas at Arlington Libraries)

Officers of the 36th Division training at Camp Bowie during World War I
(Courtesy Fort Worth Star-Telegram Photograph Collection, Special Collections Division, The University of Texas at Arlington Libraries)

Soldiers on review in Ft. Worth. April, 1918
(Courtesy of the Quentin McGown Post Card Collection)

The 61st Field Artillery Brigade trained with the 36th Division. This unit received further training in France, but the war was over before they saw battle. (Courtesy of the *Dalton Hoffman, Jr. Collection)*

The 36th Division Infantry trenches were located along Old Stove Foundry Road and ran almost to present day Benbrook.
(Courtesy of the Dalton Hoffman, Jr. Collection)

Fort Worth and Canadian Aviation

Douglas Harman

President and C.E.O., Fort Worth Convention and Visitors Bureau

On May 26, 1997 a little known page in aviation history came to life in Fort Worth, Texas at the Biennial Memorial Service for British and Canadian War Graves at Greenwood Cemetery. Fort Worth is know for its rodeos, western events and art, the Van Cliburn Piano Competition and the Kimbell Art Museum, but few people associate it with one of the most dramatic events in early aviation history which will link Fort Worth and Canada together forever.

The close relationship between Canada and the United States in the field of aviation began in 1917 when the U.S., Canadian and British governments established a joint aviation training program in Fort Worth.

The results of this unprecedented international training program were impressive. Between November 1917 and April 1918 there was a total of 67,000 flying hours and a total of 1,960 U.S. and Royal Flying Corps. pilots trained.

Unfortunately, many of the student pilots gave their lives during their training in Fort Worth. At the time there was one fatality for every 1,400 hours of flying. In total, 101 men died in training, including 38 from the R.F.C. After the war most of the remains of the deceased were returned to cemeteries near their homes. In 1924 the British Imperial War Graves Commission purchased a site at Greenwood Cemetery in Fort Worth and moved the remaining casualties to this location. Twelve Canadian and British servicemen have their final resting place at Greenwood —seven of this group were Canadians.

Although the sounds of the Canadian Jennies are long gone, Fort Worth still remembers an important early relationship between Texas and Canada. In today's era of complex defense issues and important tourism relations it is important to recognize that the Canadian-Texas relationship has deep and long-lasting roots.

Send-off parade for the 36th Division, April 11, 1918, included the troops, Miss Liberty, and a wooden float designed to resemble a tank

(Courtesy Dalton Hoffman, Jr. Collection)

Post War Parade

(Courtesy Dalton Hoffman, Jr. Collection)

Hell's Half Acre is in full swing; becomes refuge for outlaws; Reform government elected to crack down on "The Acre"; First Artesian well

Courthouse fire destroys all records; George L. Gause opens Missouri Wagon Yard; large part of his business is renting hearses

Building Boom

Board of Trade Building, built in 1889
(Courtesy of the Dalton Hoffman, Jr.)

Fort Worth Opera House
(Fort Worth Public Library)

Chamber of Commerce Auditorium, with First Christian Church at left.
(Courtesy of the Dalton Hoffman, Jr. Collection)

1876

***Daily Democrat* becomes the first daily paper; *Standard* follows soon thereafter; Two streetcars serve the city, making 160 trips per day**

1877

Fort Worth's first telephone lines installed; John Peter Smith deeds the land to the city that will eventually become JPS Hospital

Fort Worth Star-Telegram building *(Courtesy Fort Worth Star-Telegram Photograph Collection, Special Collections Division, The University of Texas at Arlington Libraries)*

Knights of Pythias Temple. The renovation of this Sundance Square anchor by the Bass Family sparked a major downtown restoration movement. *(Courtesy Jack White Photograph Collection, The University of Texas at Arlington Libraries*

Baseball Team, Panthers, established; First streetlamps, first gaslights downtown; first shipments of ice into city; first telephone

"Hog Law" passed to keep hogs from aggravating mud in city's streets; over 1000 living in "tent city"; swimming in Trinity prohibited; Mayor R. R. Beckham serves until 1880

Flatiron building, the first "sky scraper" in Fort Worth built 1907, this photo was taken Ca 1912
(Courtesy Fort Worth Public Library)

Burk Burnett Building, Ca 1920

(Courtesy of Acme Brick)

THE W. T. WAGGONER BUILDING

The W. T. Waggoner Building, constructed in 1920, is a twenty story "U" shaped building oriented toward the prevailing winds. Its numerous outside windows combined with the shape provided adequate ventilation before air conditioning.

Brick exterior walls contain extensive terra cotta ornamentation on both Houston and Eighth streets. Exterior window frames are of wood, set in type with operable lower half.

The main entrance facing Houston street is decorated with a suspended copper trimmed canopy, coach lamps on each side of the entry. Glass entry doors are at sidewalk level with brass plated handles bearing the Waggoner insignia. A secondary entrance on the west side of the building provides access to the surface parking lot adjacent to the building.

The four elevator cabs are original electrical operated, detailed with hand etched glass, the Waggoner logo, brass plated handrails and cherrywood paneling.

The main lobby is enhanced by the original Italian white marble walls which continue through the lobby in theme with the original tunnel, vaulted ceiling with molded ornate detailing.

The lobby elevator doors are also original filigreed brass. The original brass and glass mail chute is still operable on every floor of the building with the main box in the lobby being tied to the brass theme matching the brass handles and elevator doors.

Cross Timbers Oil Company's executive offices are on the ground floor, in what was formerly Landmark Bank. These offices lend an original feeling to the building with marble wainscoting on the first floor walls, marble columns extending to the mezzanine level, again bringing the tunnel vaulted ceilings back to tie into the main lobby. Much ornate work in the final finish out of the bank lends to the original decor of the era of 1920.

The original brass lettering in the street and sidewalks have been maintained to keep with the historical theme of the building.

The first three floors of the building have been restored to the original status including the hand set mosaic tile on the third floor elevator and common lobby.

The W.T. Waggoner Building has received official local, state and national historic designation.

(Photos Courtesy W.T. Waggoner Building)

Influential People

Many of the ranchers in the Fort Worth area leased reservation land for grazing from the American Indians. The story goes that Quanah Parker, a Comanche Chief, and his uncle Yellow Bear made a trip to Fort Worth in 1885 with the intention of collecting over-due rent. They took a room at the Pickwick, one of the more modern of the hotels offered by the city. Quanah met with the foreman of the Waggoner ranch, while Yellow Bear retired for the evening.

Later, when Quanah returned from his negotiating, he apparently turned down the gaslight, but did not close it completely. Overnight, Yellow Bear died, and Quanah was found unconscious near the window. A delegation of representatives returned with the Chief to deliver the body of Quanah's uncle to their people and to assure the Comanche that the death was an unfortunate accident.

Quanah Parker, son of Cynthia Ann Parker and Chief Nocona. Quanah, who has been called the last great chief of the Comanche, frequently visited Fort Worth to confer with ranchers regarding leased grazing lands.
(Courtesy Tarrant County College, Northeast Campus)

B. B. Paddock (Captain Buckley B.) was the owner and editor of the Fort Worth Democrat, an early, influential newspaper. A former scout for the Confederacy, he created the Tarantula Map depicting Fort Worth as the hub of railroads and stage lines. Through editorial influence, he pressured the city to form the first volunteer fire company. Paddock was instrumental in bringing the railroad to Fort Worth, and insuring its success as well as promoting the cattle industry. President of Spring Palace Exhibition Hall, he was its biggest proponent.

(Courtesy of The Fort Worth Club)

1882	1883
First water system completed; first streets paved with "compressing stone"; Jacob Washer opens business on Houston Street; John Peter Smith elected Mayor, serves until 1886	*Central Fire Station built;Fort Worth Opera House grand opening; 150,000 head of cattle through*

W. T. "Tom" Waggoner
(Courtesy W. T. Waggoner Building)

W. T. (Tom) Waggoner, cattle baron, oilman, was included as one of the ranchers who accompanied Teddy Roosevelt on the famous "wolf hunt". His discovery of oil on his ranch while digging for water propelled him into one of the most wealthy of the early Fort Worthians. A portion of this capital was used to build the mansion, Thistle Hill, for his daughter Electra.

Major K.M. Van Zandt

Major K. (Khleber) M. Van Zandt, came to Fort Worth after the Civil War and became President of what became the Fort Worth National Bank. A key player in the Reconstruction years of the city, his civic contributions included donating land for the railroad. Van Zandt was instrumental in bringing the post office to Fort Worth.

Burk Burnett

Samuel Burk Burnett; civic leader and rancher, another member of the famous wolf hunt with Teddy Roosevelt and liaison with Quanah Parker for lands leased for cattle grazing. First president of Southwestern Exposition and Fat Stock Show and founder of Southwestern Cattle Raisers Association. Established famous "four sixes" ranch (6666); some say he won the ranch in a poker game where he held four of a kind in sixes.

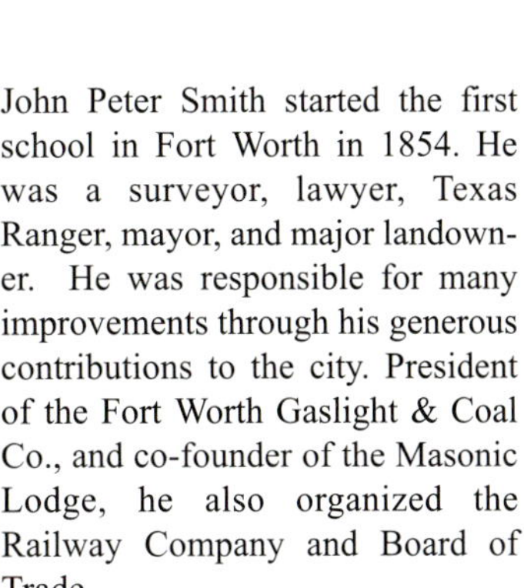

John Peter Smith

John Peter Smith started the first school in Fort Worth in 1854. He was a surveyor, lawyer, Texas Ranger, mayor, and major landowner. He was responsible for many improvements through his generous contributions to the city. President of the Fort Worth Gaslight & Coal Co., and co-founder of the Masonic Lodge, he also organized the Railway Company and Board of Trade.

Billy Rose was hired by Amon Carter at $1000 a day to produce Fort Worth's Frontier Centennial celebration which included Casa Mañana, Sally Rand's Nude Ranch, The Tiny Rosebuds, a dance hall, a musical rodeo and a nightclub with dinner, dancing and a stage show that ran twice per night.

(Photos this page, with the exception of the W. T. Waggoner photo, are courtesy of The Fort Worth Club)

1884

First free home mail delivery in Fort Worth; first full time district court; Chisholm Trail closes with the beginning of the end of the trail dirves

1884

City Directory lists 379 residents, 35 saloons; new jail built on Bluff behind the courthouse; Fort Worth National Bank opens

President Franklin D. Roosevelt with Elliot Roosevelt (driver), Mrs. Elliot Roosevelt, James Roosevelt and Mrs. James Roosevelt (in back seat) on a visit to Fort Worth)

(Courtesy of The Fort Worth Club)

Amon G. Carter, Sr. was a founder of the Fort Worth Star which bought out rival newspaper, the Telegram and became the Fort Worth Star-Telegram. He was instrumental in bringing the aviation industry to Fort Worth and was a lead player in bringing the auto industry to the area. Carter started the first radio station in the South, and followed with the first television station. He was a co-founder of what became American Airlines and a founder of Texas Tech University.

Amon Carter and Dwight D. Eisenhower, 1951

(Courtesy of The Fort Worth Club)

Large immigration from Eastern and Southern Europe to the United States

Fort Worth Club established

Lyndon B. Johnson and Beeman Fisher

(Courtesy The Fort Worth Club)

Oilman Perry R. Bass married Nancy Lee Muse Bass. Their sons, Ed, Sid, Robert & Lee, have followed family tradition (Uncle Sid Richardson was known as second-richest man in America) and built Fort Worth into a modern showplace. Ed, inspired by brothers Sid and Robert's efforts toward the rebirth of downtown with Sundance Square, has continued by creating residential and entertainment complexes, including the Bass Performance Hall.

(Courtesy The Fort Worth Club)

Charles Tandy created Tandy Corporation from his interest in leather goods. Expanding to Radio Shack in the mid-sixties, he built the company into the largest consumer electronics chain in the world. His interest in developing Fort Worth's downtown spurred others to do the same and started a continuing revitalization for the city.

Fort Worth Club Building, built 1926
(Courtesy W.D. Smith, Inc., Commercial Photography Collection, The University of Texas at Arlington Libraries)

The Fort Worth Club

Established in 1885, The Fort Worth Club's purpose was "to provide professional and businessmen with similar interest an opportunity to gather socially while working for the continued growth of Fort Worth". The men were Fort Worth leaders. They met here to have lunch, read a newspaper, or settle a deal -- deals that influenced millions. Businesses were born, from decisions early in the history of Fort Worth that brought the packing plants, to deals that made our city an aviation giant. Men like B.B. Paddock, Burk Burnett, Amon Carter, Sid Richardson dined with presidents, corporate visitors, and entertainers. It has been said that it was a "second home" to Will Rogers; that President Lyndon B. Johnson admitted he "had rather be here than Buckingham Palace"; and that the register was singed by Fleet Admiral Chester Nimitz with the same pen he used to sign the Japanese surrender aboard the USS Missouri. The list of visitors is endless and reads like a who's who, as does the list of Officers, and the Board of Governors from 1885 to the present. The members continue today to honor the heritage of Fort Worth and preserve the integrity of the club that bears this city's name.

excerpts from *The Fort Worth Club - A Centennial Story* by Irvin Farman

WOMEN IN FORT WORTH HISTORY

TELL THEIR STORIES!

Joyce M. Williams

Joyce Williams is a native of Fort Worth with a longtime interest in the city's history. For ten years she served as historian on the staff of the Fort Worth Museum of Science and History

Women have played a vital though often untold part in Fort Worth's history from the very beginning. When Major Ripley Arnold and his men arrived at the bluff above the Trinity River to establish a military post on June 6, 1849 they found Jane Farmer, her husband George Preston (Press), and their infant daughter, Sue, living there in three tents. They had built a log cabin when they had first settled on this prairie land. That cabin had been burned by Indians. We can only imagine what their life must have been like. Surely they were lonely and frightened. We do know that Press became the sutler for the fort. In the next few months Jane and Press's fathers and other family members also settled in what would become Tarrant County. The descendants of Jane and Press have remained actively involved in Fort Worth.

In the summer of 1849 Kate Arnold and her children joined Major Arnold at the fort. Kate had frequently lived on military posts but never one quite so remote and desolate as Fort Worth. She soon became a friend and confidant to the dragoons. When she had her piano brought to the fort she had it installed in the commissary so that all could enjoy it. By the fall of 1850 a fifth child was born. Sadly, Willis and his year -old sister, Sophie, died of cholera. These children became the first to be buried in what would become Fort Worth's first cemetery, now known as Pioneer's Rest.

Jane Farmer and Kate Arnold and their children were true pioneers. When the army closed Fort Worth in 1853, there were only seven women in the community that would become our city.

The cattle drives of the 1870s, the incorporation of the city of Fort Worth in 1873, and the coming of the railroad in 1876 brought people and prosperity to the area. Life in Cowtown in the area known as "Hell's Half Acre" was especially hard on women. Most of the girls there were very young and they lived short and unhappy lives. Many became drug addicts and many died from overdoses and violence. Here are a few of their stories as recorded in the newspapers of the day and by Richard Selcer in his marvelous book, *Hell's Half Acre*:

Dora Doyle, suicide from a morphine overdose, recorded in the newspaper with this comment, "the old story: the lover took a walk and the woman took the poison."

Grace Myers shot herself but fortunately for her, her life was saved by students at the Fort Worth Medical College.

Lulu, suicide, "weary of life, diseased, destitute, deserted, despondent..."

One acre girl with her classic poise and good looks has become the stuff of myth and movies. She was living at Fannie Porter's sporting house in 1901 when she met the handsome Harry Longabaugh. They became an "item" and the next few years of her life were bound to his. Harry and his friends were in town relaxing. They decided to buy some new clothes. They looked so good that they decided to have their picture taken at Schwartz Studio. The picture was so good that Mr. Schwartz put it in the window. A Pinkerton detective saw it and recognized two of the people as members of the Hole in the Wall Gang who were suspected of robbing a bank in Winnemucca, Nevada. Harry, the Sundance Kid, his friend, Butch Cassidy, and the girl, Etta Place, left Fort Worth in a hurry and went to South America. Etta remained there with her husband, Sundance, and Butch for several years until she became ill and returned to the U. S. for surgery. She checked out of the hospital in Denver and disappeared. That much of the story is true. There is a local myth that she returned to Fort Worth under a different name and ran a hotel here until the 1960s, but that part seems to be just myth.

Mary Porter, Jesse Reeves and Josie Belmont were Fort Worth's best known madams. They were in business for many years. Jessie Reeves came to her profession by way of being a circus performer and a monte and faro dealer. Her house at 7th and Main was rumored to be "special" for leading citizens. After leaving Fort Worth she reformed and began a religious lecture circuit tour where she shocked audiences with tales of her former life.

Not all the city's women were involved in the seamy side of our community. Many were teachers, dressmakers, laundresses, homemakers, shop keepers, and business women.

As the city began to grow, education was very important to the citizens. Many women were involved in bringing schools to Fort Worth. When the Fort Worth Independent Schools were formed in 1881 it was a woman, Sue Huffman, who was named superintendent. The schools were reorganized in 1882 and Miss Huffman and Mrs. Clara Peak Walden served as principals. Eleven of the eighteen teachers hired for the first full year of classes were women.

Mrs. Delia Collins, Mrs. L. J. Clayton, Mrs. A. J. Chambers founded a home for single and "fallen" women in 1890. Mary M. Clardy was sent by the Women's Christian Temperance Union to lobby the state legislature to raise the age of consent in Texas for girls from ten to sixteen years. That was in 1891. The efforts were somewhat successful, the age was raised to twelve. In 1884, Belle Burchill, as post mistress, oversaw the first home mail delivery.

When B. B. Paddock and other city leaders wanted to show off the "Queen City of the Prairies", it was the Ladies Auxiliary that raised money, planned events and exhibits and spent many hours decorating the Spring Palace. It was a woman, Ada Large, who was credited with saving the lives of many children when a devastating fire struck the Spring Palace on May 30, 1890. As the wooden building, decorated with dried grasses and Texas produce burned to the ground, she led many to safety even though she was injured.

Daisy Emery became the first woman graduate of Fort Worth Medical School in 1897 and indeed the first woman graduate of medical school in Texas. Daisy, number nine of eleven children had wanted to be a doctor since she was four years old. Following her graduation in Fort Worth she did post graduate work in Washington D. C. She returned to Texas, nursed her ill mother, opened a practice, and taught at the medical school in Dallas. Daisy married Tarrant County native Walter Allen in 1903. The doctors Allen spent their lives practicing medicine in Fort Worth, west Texas, and Oklahoma. As a thirty-seven year old widow with two daughters Daisy taught at the Fort Worth Medical College until it closed in 1917. Her private practice in Fort Worth concerned women and children. She held free clinics, made house calls, and continued her practice for fifty-three years until her retirement in 1950.

In 1912 a west Texas farm girl came to town to attend college at TCU. Upon applying to medical school in 1917 she was told that women were not accepted. She went any way and convinced her professors and classmates that she could do the work. She became a pathologist and returned to Fort Worth in 1921. It was May Owen's research that proved the powder used in doctor's gloves was causing problems. Her work led to the use of safer, powderless gloves. Dr. Owen had a very long and productive life and career in Fort Worth. Dr. Owen and the daughters of Daisy Emery Allen each established loan and scholarship funds to aid others in the medical professions.

Lenora was a five year old girl who joined her mother and other family members in Fort Worth in 1909. Her mother worked as a domestic and later when she and Lenora lived in a shotgun house with no indoor plumbing they did laundry for many prominent citizens of Fort Worth. When the laundry was completed Lenora would walk several miles with it balanced on her head to deliver it. Lenora graduated from Fort Worth Colored (later I. M. Terrell) High School. She worked as a teacher, insurance agent, and as supervisor of a typing pool in Washington D. C. during World War II. When she and her husband returned to Fort Worth she worked as a mortician. Through Lenora Rolla's leadership the Tarrant County Black Historical and Genealogical Society was established.

Lucille Bishop Smith, teacher, author and inventor wrote five vocational training textbooks, produced the nations first hot roll mix and founded Lucilles Fine Foods. Her most famous product today is chili biscuits.

One of Fort Worth's most famous women only came to town to entertain. She was Sally Rand, who was the headliner for the 1936 Centennial Celebration. The Texas Centennial was to be officially celebrated in Dallas. Amon Carter, newspaper publisher and leading Fort Worth booster wanted Fort Worth to have its own celebration. He hired popular entertainer Billy Rose at $1000 per day to produce a show for fun. Casa Mañana and the Frontier Palace were built, and Sally Rand with her fans, and little else, was the headliner. The Woman's Club was asked to be the host for Miss Rand. There was much discussion about that task, but the women decided to do so. Sally Rand took the town by storm. In fact she was honored with a special day and thanked for "bringing culture and progress to Tarrant County."

It was women, led by Mrs. Keeler, who were successful in getting a library for Fort Worth. In 1938 Elizabeth Moncrief, Nenetta Burton Carter, Anne Burnett Hall, and Mrs. W. A. Schmid founded the Maternal Health Center to offer birth control information and materials to women in Fort Worth. Services were expanded to rural areas and during WWII to include women in war industries. In 1949 this organization became the local Planned Parenthood affiliate.

The Fort Worth Council of Administrative Women, led by Ella Smith, Ima Love Kuykendall, Jewell Tillotson, Fanjane Watson, Gladys Miller, Jessica Lloyd, Flossie Kysar, Alma Ray, and Lulu Parker saw a need for a museum for the city's children and established the Children's Museum in 1941. The Museum, now the Fort Worth Museum of Science and History, also benefited greatly from the work of local math and science teacher, Charlie Mary Noble. Her work is remembered today in the astronomy programs conducted in the Noble Planetarium.

During World War II women answered the call to serve in the Red Cross, and to work in the defense plants. One of those plants, Consolidated Vultee, right here in Fort Worth, employed Bess who worked as a silk screener at the plant throughout the war. She was joined by many other "Rosie the Riveters", such as two sisters, Nora and Clara, who worked in the wing and fuselage departments.

When the local Red Cross needed two new trucks transported to Fort Worth for the blood collection drives it was two women, Mrs. Roger B. Owings, chair of the Red Cross Motor Corps and Mrs. W. K. Stripling, Chair of Volunteer Special Services who went after the three-ton olive drab trucks. Apparently they had not considered until they arrived in Indiana that neither of them knew how to drive the trucks. Not to be deterred they soon taught themselves what they needed to know and struck out for home, arriving safely with the much needed trucks.

Clarice Spurlock became Fort Worth's first city councilwoman in 1952. In the 1970s when the city established a Human Relations Commission it was Fort Worth native, school teacher and counselor, Walter Barbour who chaired that committee. Walter later became the first African American woman to serve on the City Council. Of course, recently Kay Granger has been our city's first woman mayor and now the first congresswoman to represent District 12.

All of these women and many more have been a vital part of the history of Fort Worth. Our stories certainly do not end here. You all could add many more stories and I hope you will. As we know women's stories are often left out of the history books, but we know they are out there and it is our job to tell their stories.

St. Patrick's Cathedral construction begins

Saint Joseph's Infirmary opened by Catholic Church; first electric street-car bings (first in Texas and second in all of U. S.); Lake Como built; William Monnig opens department store

Etta Place

Judy Alter

Judy Alter, director of Texas Christian University Press, has received the Spur Award for Best Western Novel (Mattie, 1988) and Best Western Short Story ("Sue Ellen Learns to Dance", 1998). Alter also won the Western Heritage Award and has been honored by the Texas Institute of Letters. Among her titles are Jessie, based on the life of Jessie Benton Fremont and Libbie, Elizabeth Bacon Custer.

Often described as hauntingly beautiful, Etta Place is the most mysterious woman of the nineteenth-century American West. Everyone knows she was the Sundance Kid's girlfriend and that she went to South America with Butch and Sundance, but no one knows where she came from, and no one knows what happened to her after the shootout in Bolivia. Fort Worth claims her as part of its colorful outlaw history, but only one brief visit here is documented. Still it's one of those cases where legend speaks louder than historical truth.

Some stories have her an innocent schoolmarm. In the now-classic movie, *Butch Cassidy and the Sundance Kid* she is, of course, a schoolteacher but one with a taste for adventure and for handsome outlaws. Sometimes she is from Denver, which is cited as her birthplace and where she might have taught music, or she's from New England, where she was educated in proper schools. There's no real theory on how she got from New England to Texas or Wyoming or wherever she met Harry Longabaugh. Where she met him also depends on which theory you believe. Still another possibility is that she was a rancher's daughter, which would account for her extraordinary ability to ride and shoot.

But at least one legend makes Etta Place a Fort Worth girl who worked as a soiled dove in Mary Porter's house and there met Harry Longabaugh, the Sundance Kid. That version puts their first meeting in 1901, which would mean Etta was never on the western outlaw trail, never at Hole-in-the-Wall and never held the horses while the gang robbed banks and trains. She simply followed him to South America right away. Those who accept this theory even identify the building in Sundance Square that once housed Mrs. Porter's establishment.

An entirely separate legend of whorehouse origins places Etta at Fannie Porter's sporting house in San Antonio. Three things about Fannie Porter's are documented: it was at 505 San Saba, it was a favorite hangout of the Hole-in-the-Wall gang, and Fannie Porter was of British origin. In this story, after meeting Sundance in San Antonio in the mid-1890s, she followed him on his adventures (that means bank and train robberies) in the West. The San Antonio story has interesting twists. Some say she was a common prostitute and support their claim by quoting what Butch Cassidy once supposedly told someone: Etta was a great housekeeper, but she had the heart of a whore. In much more complicated versions of the same story, Etta was the illegitimate daughter of an English nobleman who brought her to the English-born Fannie to raise. Never "on the line," she was a companion to Fannie, who saw that she was well educated. This would account for the speech and manners that led even Pinkerton agents to call her "refined."

Harry Longabaugh aka The Sundance Kid with Etta Place, New York, 1900 (Courtesy Pinkerton's Inc.)

Another theory on her origins is almost too complicated to mention here. It also makes her the illegitimate daughter of the English nobleman, but in this version she was adopted by a Utah Mormon family named Thayne. By twists of storytelling, Etta becomes the older sister of Anna Marie Thayne, the first and apparently only wife of Harry Longabaugh. The truth of this was testified to repeatedly by Harry Longabaugh, Jr., who claimed to have a birth certificate and other documents to substantiate his story but never produced them.

At least three other women have been identified as Etta. One of them is Eunice Gray, a prostitute or a respectable boardinghouse owner—which version do you want to believe?—in Fort Worth. The others are famed cattle raiser and outlaw Ann Bassett, and a San Antonio music teacher named Ethel Bishop. Supposedly countless women throughout the West used the name Etta Place.

And are we sure she was so passionately in love and loyal to Sundance? Not at all. Rumors pepper the literature that she had an affair with Butch-before Sundance, while she was with Sundance, even in South America.

But back to Fort Worth. If she was "employed" at Mary Porter's house, Etta met Butch Cassidy and the Sundance Kid on that fateful 1900 trip when the Hole-in-the-Wall Gang had their picture taken by Fort Worth photographer John Swartz. Proud of his work, Swartz posted the photograph of six dapper young men wearing dress suits and derbies on his studio window. A passing Pinkerton agent saw it, recognized the subjects, and the chase was on. Whether this was a first meeting or Etta had come with the boys from Wyoming to Fort Worth, she left with Sundance when most of the gang went south to Fannie Porter's house in San Antonio. From San Antonio, they went to New York, where the one documented photo of Etta was taken. (In other versions, they fled Fort Worth and the Pinkerton Detective Agency in a panic: Butch headed for the Pacific Coast, as a distraction, while Sundance and Etta went east to visit his family and wait for Butch in New York.)

The photo taken in New York is the only real record of Etta Place, beyond a few Pinkerton files which are full of rumor and speculation. In the photo, she and Sundance stand as though for a formal wedding portrait, although there is no indication that they had married. Her dark hair is piled high on her head, her face is flawless and her expression thoughtful. Looking refined and ladylike, she wears a black dress with a white fichu and a small watch-pin. Some stories say that Butch bought her the watch-pin because she had so much admired a similar one owned by Fannie Porter; Sundance, instead of buying her the pin, bought himself a diamond stickpin-another apocryphal story.

In New York, they met Butch—or was he with them all the time?—and the three sailed for South America. Some studies indicate that Etta's presence with the "boys" was not definitely known until they went to South America. No matter where or when she met Butch and Sundance, Etta was the only person to accompany the "boys" to South and Central America. (Or was she?- Fort Worth's Eunice Gray went to South America at the appropriate time, and one student of the history places Ann Bassett there.) Records indicate that in Argentina the trio for some time were peaceful ranchers, well known and loved by their neighbors. When Pinkertons tracked them down again, they may have thought honesty didn't pay. At any rate, they took up the life of crime again, and Etta demonstrated her superb skills as a horsewoman and a shootist as she rode with the boys on their bank robberies. Once again, her story in South America, like that of Butch and Sundance, is no more than conjecture. The movie, of course, showed her in Bolivia, sharing a passionate farewell to the Kid just before the shootout, saying she cannot bear to see him die. The movie closed with a freeze-frame that implied both men died in a violent gunfight.

Today, historical thinking is that Butch Cassidy survived that battle to return to the United States and live out his life as a mostly honorable and peaceful businessman named William T. Phillips, in the State of Washington. Sundance probably died in the shootout- but there is at least one theory that the three reunited some three years later.

And Etta? One story is that she had returned to the United States before the disastrous shootout because of ill health. This legend often has her dying of appendicitis in a hospital in Denver. Remember, in one version Denver was her home town.

But there's another legend, one that has her living in Fort Worth as Eunice Gray. The late Charlie McCafferty, a lifelong resident of Fort Worth's North Side, used to tell the story of walking down the street, as a very young boy, with his father one morning when his father greeted a woman on the porch of her house. The father tipped his hat and said, "Mornin', Miz Gray," and then he urged young Charlie to do the same. As they walked away, the elder McCafferty said, "Son, do you know who that was?" The boy replied, "Miz Gray," but the father said, "No, son, that was Etta Place."

In this version of the legend, Etta Place came back to Fort Worth—a city she had shared with Sundance and learned to love—to run a respectable boardinghouse. She died at age eighty-one in a fire that destroyed the Waco Hotel in January 1962. The twenty-room hotel at 110½ Fifteenth was vacant at the time, except for Ms. Gray's richly furnished apartment According to a reporter for the old Fort Worth Press who interviewed her just before her death, she had plenty of money and was on familiar terms with oilmen, cattlemen and local preachers.

The problem with that story is that Eunice Gray may have run a respectable boardinghouse in her later years, but she is on record for having a house of ill-repute in Hell's Half Acre at the turn of the century. When hellfire preacher J. Frank Norris preached about her, she told him not to worry about her soul; she was closing the house and going to South America. She apparently did just that, which would put her in South America at the right time, but if she was running a house in the Acre, she wasn't robbing trains in Wyoming with Butch and Sundance.

I believe Etta Place met Sundance in San Antonio at Fannie Porter's, followed him west, came to Fort Worth with him when the gang met here, and then accompanied him and Butch to South America, and came back to Fort Worth to spend the rest of her life. It's fun to have her a part of the city's local lore. But you're welcome to believe any version of the story that appeals to you. The trail to the truth is almost certainly now too cold to be followed.

Woman's Club
A BRIEF HISTORY

[Portions reprinted from an article by Marion Day Mullins]

One might say that The Woman's Club of Fort Worth has catapulted into existence in spite of itself. The momentous year was 1923.

The various women's clubs of the town, and several of them were founded before the turn of the century, had been represented by committees that would meet from time to time to discuss the possibility of establishing a mutual meeting place. One club, after the receipt of a modest inheritance from one of its members, went so far as to purchase a lot in the near business section of the town. Some of the husbands who were consulted hastened to point out the expense, not only of erecting an adequate meeting hall but also the constant need for upkeep funds.

In 1923, a handsome property in a substantial residential area, which had been owned by resident aliens and was confiscated by the U.S. Government during World War I, was offered for sale. A philanthropically-minded widow, Mrs. William G. Newby, who was seeking a proper memorial to her banker-husband, learning of the prospect, decided that such a center for the clubwomen of Fort Worth would be a worthy monument to her very civic-minded and community-oriented husband.

Fortunately, there were a number of women in the clubs who were accustomed to managing their own business affairs. One, Miss Anna Shelton, had been a prominent business woman in the community for many years. She was willing to spearhead the movement to unite the clubs in their work for an over-all club which would supply each with a place to meet and at the same time would not curtail their individual activities. So Mrs. Newby bought the property, presented it to the following named clubs, eleven in all: Fort Worth Federation of Women's Clubs, Woman's Wednesday Club, Monday Book Club, Sorosis Club, '93 Club, Shakespeare Club, Penelope Club, Euterpean Club, History Club, College Women's Club (AAUW), Harmony Club. On November 2, 1923, charter members took possession of a building constructed for a family residence and proceeded to convert it into meeting rooms suitable to their diverse purposes.

Anna Shelton Hall
(Courtesy The Woman's Club)

By the end of 1924, there were 1,068 members. Miss Shelton and her Board soon realized that an auditorium was necessary in order that large numbers could meet. Two local architects submitted plans for an auditorium, while the club members began raising money.

With aid of various generous citizens and banks that offered to finance the building at a reasonable interest, in 1925 a hall, designed to seat 350 at tables and 700 in rows, was built.

The Woman's Club meanwhile was continuing to grow, and a number of young women were seeking admittance. Another building was purchased, which made it possible to accommodate them and supply them with their own meeting rooms. However, not all the interest of the Club was centered on building larger quarters.

One of the first departments organized in which all members who were interested might participate was the Art Department. There not only was a course of art study but well known American artists were invited to use the buildings for one-man art exhibits.

Meanwhile various other departments were organized: Bible, Book Review, Current Events, Garden, Creative Writing, Languages, Bridge, Social Service, Lectures, etc. Through the Lectures Department, the entire membership was privileged to see and hear speak scores of famous men and women who toured America on lecture circuits during the last fifty years.

At the time of the depression, in the late twenties and thirties, the members of the Woman's Club were instrumental in performing outstanding community service. The Fort Worth Symphony Orchestra simply did not have enough public support to make it possible for it to survive. The Woman's Club was asked to use its influence, so in 1929 and 1930, the Club and various members helped financially, but that was not enough. In January 1931, the Club voted to undertake the management of the Symphony Orchestra. One of the Woman's Club members, Mrs. C. D. Reimers, was manager for several years.

All these activities called for a growing membership and increasing facilities to house them. Therefore, when the handsome and spacious residence on the right of the Newby Building was offered for sale, it was purchased by the Club, and a small lecture hall was built to connect the two. By this time, the membership had grown to 1,500, and with adequate room to accommodate them more participating clubs were organized. These were made up of women with interests in arts and crafts, gardening, painting and sculpture. Their meeting rooms were equipped to serve their special needs.

The next necessity was a tea room. That, along with a modern kitchen, was built adjoining the large lecture hall, which had been named Shelton Hall. Such expansion meant debt. Many kinds of money-making projects were constantly in progress in order to liquidate the obligation as rapidly as possible. The membership met the challenge with energy and enthusiasm.

In 1952, the only remaining house on the block was offered for sale. The Amon G. Carter Foundation made the purchase by the Woman's Club a reality by the initial payment of $50,000. Generous as the gift was, it was only about one-third of the amount necessary to make the property debt free and to remodel the interior according to the needs of the Club. Since this last building was the most spacious of the complex and since the Junior Club was the fastest growing area, it was immediately decided to move the Juniors into larger quarters and dedicate their former house to the music and fine arts clubs. The acquisition meant increased attention must be devoted to fund raising. This time, as all through the years, annual bazaars, bridge tournaments, antique shows, musical teas, decorated tables and style shows would be often repeated.

As the membership increased, the parking problem became more difficult. The only solution seemed to be to buy land in the area and convert it to that purpose. It so happened that in October of 1952 three lots across the street from the rear of the Club were vacated. They were bought, cleared of their cottages and topped for parking. The area, though limited, helped to lessen the traffic congestion. By 1966, the entire block adjacent to the Club had been purchased, cleared of buildings, drained, leveled, paved and lighted. In 1997, the City of Fort Worth permanently closed the street between the buildings and parking lot and a fence surrounding the Estate was built.

The garden areas of the Club have been so beautifully planted and cared for that several times the Club has been recognized for being the most outstanding in the city. There are three garden areas. One, while shielded from busy Pennsylvania Avenue by a hedge and entered through wrought iron gates, has the appearance of an open garden. Trees shade areas but they are planted near houses that surround it on two sides. In the center is a rectangular lily pool and fish pond, centered by the exquisite bronze figure of the sculptor McMonnies, "Pipes of Pan." Urns and statues emphasize strategic spots in the garden with rose bushes lining the walkway. The second garden, which is slightly smaller and almost square is completely enclosed by buildings, whose entry ways open into it, and walls of brick and ironwork. This garden is shaded by ancient trees, has wide pebbled walkways, ornamental iron benches and assorted shrubs and blossoming plants which make the "Memorial Gardens" an inviting spot to linger for a while. A third garden, the "Texas Garden", features native flowers and shrubs centered by a bronze star.

Community service continues as an important aspect of Club life. Numerous community organizations and charities are assisted by members and participating clubs. Support for individual and community educational programs is provided through volunteer efforts, fund-raising campaigns and by the creation of The Woman's Club Scholarship Foundation, Inc. Financial assistance from The Woman's Club of Fort Worth Historical Preservation Trust helps provide for the preservation, maintenance and repair of the historical and architectural features of the Woman's Club Estate.

It is believed that The Woman's Club of Fort Worth is the only woman's club in the world to have such extensive real estate holdings. Great expense is involved in maintaining and repairing the landmark structures. Four of the buildings bear Texas Historical Survey Medallions.

Right to Left: Junior Woman's Club, Ida Saunders Hall, Bewley Hall
(Courtesy The woman's Club)

The Fort Worth Hispanic Chamber of Commerce

The Fort Worth Mexican-American Chamber of Commerce began in 1973 when a small group of Fort Worth minority business and community leaders recognized the need for effective representation in the local business community.

The organization was chartered August 3, 1974 and became only the fourth Mexican-American chamber of commerce to be established in the State of Texas.

Among the founding members of the chamber were Dick Salinas, who served as its first president; Pete Zepeda, president-elect; Ron Fernandez, vice president; and Manuel Jara, treasurer.

The first chamber office was located downtown in the Sinclair Building and the first meetings were held at various area restaurants. By 1982, interest in the Hispanic chamber grew enough to support a full suite of offices in the historic Stockyards section of the city. The Articles of Incorporation were amended November 25, 1985 and the name of the organization was changed to the Fort Worth Hispanic Chamber of Commerce.

In its first two decades of service, the Fort Worth Hispanic Chamber of Commerce has grown from the original 30 members to more than 500 Hispanic and other businesses, professional leaders and proudly boasts 44 corporate partners.

The chamber strives to serve its membership through business and professional seminars and workshops, various networking opportunities and business procurement assistance through its Economic Development Programs.

The Hispanic Chamber is also a dynamic force in promoting international trade and continued overall development for its membership as well as the area's economic community.

The FWHCC Scholarship Fund has provided education opportunities to more than 100 promising students since 1991 and chamber staff and directors are active throughout the entire community.

The Hispanic Chamber is an excellent entree into local and international Hispanic markets. The chamber has been on the cutting edge of trade relations between Fort Worth's business community and a promising market with our neighbors to the south.

Chamber membership and active participation in its activities, program planning, and business development efforts provides the Fort Worth businessperson with the business and community contacts necessary to compete in a complex and competitive environment.

The Fort Worth Hispanic Chamber of Commerce is proud to serve the business interests of the Metroplex community and will strive to seek opportunity for its membership and achieve economic benefit for all.

Gooseneck Bill McDonald begins political career in National Republican party; moves to Fort Worth five years later and becmoes banker and polictical force

Post Office and Federal Building at Jennings and 11th streets opens; Winfield Scott buys White Elephnat Saloon

Congresswoman Kay Granger presents the Texas Woman's 1997 Power of One Award to Jo Linda Jara Martinez, founder of H.Y.P.E., Hispanic Youth Promoting Excellence.

(Courtesy Jo Linda Jara Martinez)

Jo Linda Jara Martinez

Founder of H.Y.P.E., Jo Linda Jara Martinez "saw that our Hispanic youth were not receiving enough leadership opportunities and didn't have sufficient role models." Since 1993 the HYPE organization, a part of the Fort Worth Independent School District, has helped thousands of children throughout the community prepare for college and develop leadership skills. "More youth are now committed to life-long community service and are aware of the benefits of mentoring one another" says Ms. Martinez. "Not only do they appreciate their own culture, but they have learned to respect and appreciate all cultures."

Mary Jara Wright

Mary Jara Wright has devoted her entire adulthood to working with young people, influencing thousands of children as principal of J. P. Elder School. She has held this position since 1983, and, as far as we know, longer than any current principal has been at a single school in the Fort Worth I.S. D. Here, Mary witnessed with special interest the groundbreaking of a new school built just across the street on the site of Circle Park Elementary. The school was named Manuel Jara Elementary in honor of her father.

Mr. and Mrs. Hinojosa of Monterey Mexico and Congressman Jim Wright greet Jacinta and Manuel Jara at the International Good neighbor convention.

(Courtesy Jo Linda Jara Martinez)

Manuel Jara

Manuel Jara came to Fort Worth when he was nine years old. His father, Alfonso Jara worked for the Railroad and it seems he had always been the spokesperson for the workers. Manuel grew up under the influence of his father's community involvement. Working in the printing business, he still found time to become actively involved at an early age. His awards were numerous, from Boy Scouts of America, the G.I. Forum, and the City of Fort Worth. He was one of the founders of the then Mexican American Chamber of Commerce, now the Hispanic Chamber, and served on the board. Jo Linda Jara Martinez remembers her father was "always ready to do anything and everything in the community to help build understanding between people. He had the ability to make every individual feel important".

Democratic Fund Raiser for L.B.J. in 1964. Left to right: Edna Martin, Jacinta Jara, Mary Bradley. Jo Linda Jara Martinez says "Dad was more visible with his community service, but Mom has been, in her own quiet way, an equal influence on my sister and me."

(Courtesy Jo Linda Jara Martinez)

Bob Schieffer, Manuel Jara, Jacinta Jara, William C. Conner at the 1973 Tarrant County National Conference of Christians and Jews. Manuel was the recipient of the Brotherhood Award for his efforts in improving relations between the communities.

(Courtesy Jo Linda Jara Martinez)

J. Frank Norris

Charismatic preacher of the First Baptist Church from 1909 until his death in 1952. Norris challenged three deacons who sat on a promotion and entertainment committee for a retail liquor dealers convention to quit the church or the committee. They left the church and took with them six hundred members of the congregation. But Norris continued to fill the pews each Sunday. His campaign to shut down Hell's Half Acre brought threats and controversy. In the summer of 1911, he erected a tent that had once been used by Sarah Bernhardt on her national tours, and began a ninety day revival. Under his direction, the First Baptist was the first church to own and operate its own religious radio station and to offer its parishioners transportation to and from services.

J. Frank Norris
(Courtesy Dalton Hoffman, Jr. Collection)

J. Frank Norris shared the bill with John R. Rice at the First Baptist Tabernacle

(Courtesy Dalton Hoffman, Jr. Collection)

Truck used in transporting children in who lived in districts not accessible to trolley car lines

(Courtesy Dalton Hoffman, Jr. Collection)

Laying the cornerstone of the First Baptist Church, northeast corner of 4th and Taylor Streets, Ca 1921

(Courtesy Dalton Hoffman, Jr. Collection)

The Fort Worth Metropolitan Black Chamber of Commerce

Formed in 1979, the Fort Worth Metropolitan Black Chamber of Commerce primarily serves the interests of the African-American business and professional community and communicates those interests to business, civic, industrial and political leaders.

Our mission is to create more jobs, provide more business opportunities, and generate increased spending in our community. The FWMBCC actively promotes an environment which creates equitable and profitable opportunities for minority businesses.

To accomplish this mission, we provide seminars, workshops and technical assistance, which address the special needs and concerns of our members.

We continue to focus our efforts towards creating civic, industrial and commercial ventures that are culturally diverse and reflect the views of the Fort Worth minority community. We feel that this combination of perspectives and talents will help to assure a profitable competitive marketplace.

The FWMBCC, in cooperation with the Business Assistance Program-South, and Small Contractors Development Program played a major role in the planning and development of this document. These programs are available to new business start-ups and contractors dealing with underground utilities, cements paving, and hauling contractors.

The Chamber has a proud record of economic development initiatives. The following are examples of the continuous effort of the Chamber to promote, assist and enhance economic and business development of its members and to create wealth in the communities it serves.

Minyard Grocery Store and Strip Mall at East Berry and Miller Streets

James E. Guinn School restoration

Southeast Training Center in Stop Six

I. M. Terrell School restoration

Special Transportation for southeast residents. Partnered with the "T", the Hispanic Chamber of Commerce and Tarrant County College for residents to attend specialized programs at TCC NW Campus

Evans and Rosedale Near-Southeast Redevelopment project. Collaborated with the City of Fort Worth and KVG Gideon Toal in the successful bid that will result in $9 million dollars in federal funding for redevelopment of that area.

O. D. Wyatt High School Band. Individual members of the Board of Directors of the Chamber answered the call for support of the band's efforts to attend the Fiesta Bowl by making a large contribution to their band fund.

Como Elementary School. The Chamber is an active participant in the education of our youth. We have supported Como Elementary School in the FWISD Adopt-a-School Program for the past five years.

Underground utility contractors. In collaboration with the City of Fort Worth, the Chamber coordinates opportunities for members through its support of several companies, in Fort Worth and Tarrant County, by identifying underground utility contractors. These Chamber members contract to repair or replace the underground sewage lines.

This photo of Bill McDonald is from the December, 1933 issue of The White Man and The Negro Magazine, published by Prof. Phil R. Register of Fort Worth. One was able to subscribe to this publication for $1.50 per year and read about the Knights of Pythias Grand Lodge (Colored) of Texas, or the Powell Hotel and Pleasure Dome of Dallas, and the Eagle Eye Club. The article written by Mr. McDonald discusses the possibilities for the location of the new Negro High School. The magazine stated its purpose was to "promote a better relation between the white and the black races".

William Madison "Gooseneck Bill" McDonald, banker, school teacher, civic leader, Mason official, major influence in early Fort Worth and Texas Black political scene. Founder of The Fraternal Bank and Trust Co., has been called Texas' first African-American millionaire.

(Courtesy Dalton Hoffman, Jr. Collection)

The home of Bill McDonald was located on E. Terrell Avenue

(Courtesy Dalton Hoffman, Jr. Collection)

A group of teachers in front of I.M. Terrell High School, ca 1920s.*(Courtesy Fort Worth Public Library)*

Group photograph in front of St. Johns Baptist Church, May 10, 1931*(Courtesy Fort Worth Public Library)*

Lenora Rolla established the Tarrant County Black Historical and Genealogical Society. She graduated from I. M. Terrell, then the Fort Worth Colored High School, and has been a teacher, insurance agent, and supervisor of a typing pool in Washington D.C. during World War II.

Lenora Rolla visits with Alex Haley, author of Roots. *(Courtesy Fort Worth Public Library)*

Dedication of the Martin Luther King, Jr. Freeway, 1981. *(Courtesy Fort Worth Public Library)*

Fort Worth Jewry: A Sesquicentennial Snapshot

by Hollace Ava Weiner

Hollace Ava Weiner, a graduate of University of Maryland, worked as a journalist with the Fort Worth Star Telegram, leaving in 1997 to complete Jewish Stars in Texas: Rabbis and Their Work (Texas A&M University Press, November, 1999). Weiner's research into Texas Jewry has been published in American Jewish History. She is presently volunteer archivist for Congregation Beth-El.

When 20-year-old Jacob Samuels opened a Fort Worth dry-goods store in 1857, he was the town's only Jewish shopkeeper. A minority of one, he told those who asked about his origins that he was born in a log cabin—neglecting to add that the house of his birth was in Russia.

Samuels' log-cabin imagery was apparently a shorthand code for neighbors who knew little of Jews beyond their Biblical roots. The log-cabin story implied that Samuels, too, came from meager beginnings. He too, had pulled himself up by his bootstraps. He too, could blend into the melting pot. When Civil War fever hit Cowtown, Samuels fought for the Confederacy in a local unit. When a B'nai B'rith lodge formed in 1876, he was among twenty-three Jewish men to become charter members. When he died in 1906, his final resting place became Emanuel Hebrew Rest Cemetery beneath a tombstone etched with the flag of Dixie. A proud, colorful Southern Jew, Samuels' life exemplified the local Jewish community to come: a distinct yet adaptable religious minority conscious of its contributions to the common good.

Like Jacob Samuels, a number of Fort Worth's pioneering Jews came from somewhere else, somewhere foreign to the cowhands, cavalrymen, and dance-hall girls who populated the town in its early decades. Sam Davidson, a rancher, alderman, and "father" of the city parks, was from Prussia. Oscar Seligman, a liquor wholesaler (who sold publisher Amon Carter a warehouse full of whiskey on the eve of Prohibition), arrived in the 1870s with ties to the Rhineland Palatinate. Abraham Luskey, a cobbler who launched the Luskey western wear chain, learned his trade as a bootmaker in the Czar's army. Sam Rosen, another native Russian, built a trolley line to the residential area of Rosen Heights. Polish immigrant L.G. Gilbert, a department store entrepreneur, escorted dozens of relatives from the Old World to the New.

Not all of Fort Worth's Jewish pioneers were foreign-born. Many were first-generation Americans who moved to Texas for a fresh start. Isadore Carb, a Mississippi native whose family lost all in the Civil War, came in 1871 in search of cowboys. The Dahlman brothers, a family of German-Jewish descent, went for broke in 1889 trying to ship refrigerated beef from Fort Worth to Liverpool. Theodore Mack, the city's first Jewish attorney in 1894, was a Cincinnati lad who moved South for his health. Jake and Nat Washer, clothiers whose store endured from the 1880s through the 1960s, moved west from Tennessee and became ranking leaders within the Masons, the board of trade, and the state board of education. Setting the cultural stage were the Greenwall Brothers, Henry and Philip, whose Greenwall Opera House featured Sarah Bernhardt on its marquee.

Most Jewish settlers were peddlers, traders, and shopkeepers dealing in clothing, furniture, tobacco, and groceries. Most were men who arrived alone, with plans to send for extended family. They were the middlemen of the prairie, moving goods from one sphere to another. Jews had developed this commercial niche in Europe, where they were restricted from owning land, attending universities, or joining craft guilds. Buying and selling was among the few trades open. In America, the mercantile field was a natural path to pursue. It required little or no capital because an immigrant Jew could obtain goods on credit from the network of big city Jewish wholesalers. Or a newcomer could gather and sell used goods such as scrap metal – à la Gachman's Metals, a third-generation business launched by a Russian blacksmith.

Home of Ahavath Sholom from 1906 - 1951 on Taylor Street
(Courtesy Fort Worth Jewish Archives)

In 1887, Moses Shanblum, a refugee fleeing Russian persecution, emigrated to New York, then to Fort Worth where an aunt and uncle lived. Borrowing from fellow Jews, 35-year-old Shanblum filled a peddler's backpack with household notions. With his earnings, he bought a cart, then a horse and buggy, and finally, in 1891, a fruit stand at Seventh and Main Streets. By then, his wife and four children had immigrated. So had his brother, a bachelor who borrowed money to fill his own peddler's pack and repeat the pattern.

Ahavath Sholom's third synagogue, at Eight Avenue and Myrtle Place, served the congregation from 1951 until 1980. Sold to All Saints Hospital, the building was later demolished.*(Courtesy Fort Worth Jewish Archives)*

But Moses Shanblum believed that a backpack was not enough. Local Jews needed a place of worship, a synagogue where they could connect with each other and the faith of their ancestors. Shanblum feared that Judaism was becoming a casualty as immigrants adapted to Fort Worth. Already, the local B'nai B'rith Lodge, founded in 1876, had disintegrated. Attempts to launch a religious school had floundered. Picturesque Hebrew Rest Cemetery, an acre at 1400 South Main Street donated by John Peter Smith in 1879, was maintained by a fledgling benevolent society. "When I came to Fort Worth in 1887," Moses Shanblum would recall, "I found only six Jewish families who worshiped in a private house on the holidays."

Leaving his wife, Gutel, to mind the store, Shanblum organized daily worship services in living rooms. On October 9, 1892, he gathered thirty-one Jews at a Calhoun Street home. Lithuanian-born Ben Levenson took minutes in Yiddish, recording the creation of Congregation Ahavath Sholom, Hebrew for love of peace. Shanblum was hardly finished. Dressed in his trademark black coat and derby, he went door-to-door and from peddler to peddler, raising money and convincing fellow Jews "that a synagogue was more important than a new buggy or suit." Within two years, Ahavath Sholom had purchased a $1000 lot at Jarvis and Hemphill streets, twenty blocks from downtown. By 1895 the congregation had a $640-wood frame synagogue, Fort Worth's first Jewish house of worship.

Fundraising continued, with the next goal a building closer to where Jews lived and worked. In 1899, the congregation purchased a downtown lot at 819 Taylor Street. Two years later, the little shul on Hemphill Street was transplanted there, to be replaced in 1906 with a stately brick building financed with a $10,000 bank loan. Fort Worth's Jews not only had a communal headquarters but a visible, institutional presence downtown.

Ahavath Sholom's members were principally Eastern European immigrants, traditional Jews conversant in Yiddish and comfortable praying in Hebrew. Fort Worth's American-born Jews – civic figures such as Isadore Carb, Theodore Mack, and the Washer Brothers – remained unaffiliated with the synagogue. Their families, of German and Alsatian descent, were accustomed to Reform Judaism and translations of Hebrew prayers.

At the turn of the century, Henry Gernsbacher, a prominent kitchen merchant and public servant, moved from Weatherford to Fort Worth intent on organizing a Reform congregation. Initially Gernsbacher helped start a B'nai B'rith lodge in June of 1902 with an organizational meeting at the Knights of Pythias Lodge. Three months later, on September 21, 1902, Gernsbacher called another meeting at the "Pythian Hall," this time to plan religious "services on the reform plan." Fourteen men attended that gathering, with Carb taking minutes on the back of a courthouse circular. They agreed to form a "permanent congregation" called Beth-El, House of God. However, worship services were intermittent. Interest flagged. Beth-El might have disappeared altogether, had not the local Council of Jewish Women stepped in during 1904 to hire a student rabbi for the High Holidays and reorganize the Sabbath school.

The National Council of Jewish Women, founded during the 1893 Chicago World's Fair, energized women to do volunteer work for Jewish and secular causes. Texas' first chapter had begun in Beaumont in 1901. The Fort Worth chapter followed soon after, spurred on in 1902 by the arrival of Cincinnati-born Pauline Sachs Mack, bride of Fort Worth's senior Jewish attorney. While reinvigorating Beth-El, Council launched a temple building fund, raising $500 from public banquets hosted during the annual Fat Stock show. Beth-El's first building, a $6,000 wood-and-stucco synagogue at 601 Taylor Street, was dedicated in 1908. The Council of Jewish Women also launched an Americanization School, holding classes at the County Courthouse to teach immigrants English and "American ideals." In subsequent decades, the Americanization School, begun in 1907, assisted refugees of all races and religions as well as Holocaust survivors and Soviet Jews.

B'nai B'rith also maintained a high profile. The lodge first asserted itself in 1905, coming to the defense of immigrant pushcart vendors. A local association of butchers and grocers were lobbying city hall to ban street vending. Jews were "flabbergasted" to think that their brethren "would not be allowed to earn their bread, even by the sweat of their brow." The B'nai B'rith lodge, then sixty-seven members strong, fought for the greenhorns and won.

Ahavath Sholom's torahs (parchment scrolls containing the five Books of Moses) are covered with ornate mantles and silver filigree indicative of the rich lessons within.
(Courtesy Fort Worth Jewish Archives)

All of Fort Worth's Jewish organizations — from the Wednesday Sewing Group to the Zionist District — rallied to assist refugees who reached Texas via Galveston between 1907 and 1913. The Galveston immigration movement, which resettled 10,000 Jews west of the Mississippi, steered an average of eight immigrants a month to Fort Worth. Those immigrants included Dave Carshon, who opened a butcher shop and café in partnership with M.J. Chicotsky. Both surnames remain part of Fort Worth's wining and dining scene. The Galveston Plan gave rise, in 1907, to the local Hebrew Free Loan Association that paid start-up costs for multi-million dollar enterprises such as Larry's Shoes and Kings Liquors.

In 1921, the Jewish community felt a wave of hatred as the Ku Klux Klan gained political power across Texas. Sol Rosenthal, a restaurant beef supplier, found his cold-storage unit shut off at night and his meat spoiled. Theodore Mack recognized Klansmen among judges and juries and switched to full-time appellate work. At Washer Brothers Clothier, managers who feared a KKK boycott promoted an employee who belonged to the Klan.

In line with the city's infamous outlaw tradition, the Jewish community endured a touch of scandal. Depression-era gangster George "Machine Gun" Kelly obtained his weapons through pawnbroker Jake Klar, who nervously testified at the mobster's Oklahoma trial. In 1913, an embarrassed rabbi rounded-up twenty Jewish prostitutes from Hell's Half Acre. Eighteen were deported.

All in all, Jewish contributions were positive and innovative. B'nai B'rith created a medicine fund to help indigent patients at the county hospital. The lodge also launched a Little Theater troupe that won raves from drama critics. During the decades when Jewish women were excluded from prestigious civic and social clubs, the Council of Jewish Women became the equivalent of the Junior League, launching pilot projects that put its members on boards of high-profile social service agencies. Jews never separated themselves from the larger community. They found ways to contribute and gain recognition.

Simultaneously, Fort Worth Jewry perpetuated institutions of its own, promoting close ties and support networks. B'nai B'rith hosted monthly dances at the Hotel Texas and in 1954 threw a gala honoring presidents of sixteen active Jewish organizations. At annual Presentation Balls, young Jewish women wearing debutante gowns made their bows at the Blackstone Hotel. The busiest site of Jewish activity was the Hebrew Institute, a three-story community center, built on Taylor Street in 1910 with a gym, a stage, club rooms, and after-school Hebrew classrooms.

The Hebrew Institute and Ahavath Sholom's Taylor Street shul were razed in 1951 as the congregation readied to move to a spacious synagogue at Eighth Avenue and Myrtle Place. Ahavath Sholom moved again in 1980 to Hulen and Briarhaven Road in the southwest section of town where a large proportion of the Jewish community now resides. Congregation Beth-El, meanwhile, had left Taylor Street in 1920 for a temple at 207 W. Broadway. The congregation is currently constructing a synagogue at 4900 Briarhaven Road, which will place it back in close proximity to Ahavath Sholom. Both congregations have burial grounds at Greenwood Cemetery, and Beth-El maintains the pioneer cemetery at Hebrew Rest.

As Fort Worth celebrates its sesquicentennial, its Jewish community remains a tiny minority – less than 3,000 Jews comprising 0.4% of the populace. Nonetheless, the group's civic, cultural, and economic contributions are legion. Streets such as Carb Drive, Simondale Drive, and Rosen Avenue are testimony to Jewish participation in the area's early development. The Rosenthal Dome at the Bass Performance Hall and the Dr. Frank Cohen Atrium at the children's hospital are testimony to the diverse ways that this firmly-rooted Jewish community has enriched the region.

Home of Congregation Beth-El from 1908 to 1920 located at 601 Taylor Street.

(Courtesy Beth-El Congregation, from "The Jewish Monitor", 1915.

The six-pointed Jewish star of David, or *mogen david*, was a prized symbol to Erno Fabry, the designer who remodeled Beth-El Congregation's synagogue after a devastating 1946 fire. The designer, a Hungarian immigrant from the Hitler era, recalled how the Nazis had turned the Jewish star into a badge of shame. He wanted it to be viewed as a symbol of beauty and honor. His plans for refurbishing Beth-El's sanctuary called for ten stained-glass windows, each crowned with a golden star of David outlined against a field of blue. The colorful stained-glass was manufactured in Kokomo, Indiana, and the windows were fabricated in Texas by United Glass & Mirror Company on Swiss Avenue in Dallas. The designer's favorite feature in the remodeled sanctuary was a floating Jewish star, carved from wood and suspended from a kidney-shaped well in the ceiling. The giant star was removed during a 1981 renovation and replaced with abstract lights evoking a flock of birds.

(Courtesy Beth-El Congregation Archives - photo by Ralph Lauer)

President Theodore Roosevelt visits Fort Worth

President Theodore Roosevelt on the range — chuckwagon scene from the famous "wolf hunt" in May of 1905. President Roosevelt is in the center with hat, neck kerchief and holding a coffee cup. Among those present were W. T. Waggoner, Major S. B. Young, Tom L. Burnett, Cecil Lyons, Dr. Lambert, Bonnie Moore, Capt. S. Burk Burnett, Chief Quanah Parker, E. M. Gilles, Guy Waggoner, D. P. "Phy" Taylor and Lee Bivens. *(Courtesy Fort Worth Star-Telegram Photograph Collection, Special Collections Division, The University of Texas at Arlington Libraries)* The story goes that there were underlying political reasons behind President Roosevelt's visit to Fort Worth. Samuel Burk Burnett had previously made a trip to see Roosevelt in Washington D.C. to discuss the situation facing Texas cattlemen. Soon after, Roosevelt, who was scheduled to attend a Rough Riders convention in San Antonio, made his first Fort Worth visit. A stop along the way would allow him the chance to hunt for wolf, and meet with Burk Burnett once more. It seems the cattlemen were concerned about the grazing lands north of the Red River they had leased from the Native Americans. When Oklahoma was granted statehood, these lands would be no longer available. During the expedition, Roosevelt apparently agreed to do what he could to delay statehood, allowing the cattlemen a chance to relocate their herds on Texas land.

President Theodore Roosevelt spoke to a record-breaking crowd in Fort Worth.
(Courtesy Fort Worth Star-Telegram Photograph Collection, Special Collections Division, The University of Texas at Arlington Libraries)

President John F. Kennedy visits Fort Worth November 21-22, 1963

President and Mrs. Kennedy's arrival

(Courtesy Fort Worth Star-Telegram, Photograph Collection Special Collections Division, The University of Texas at Arlington Libraries)

John F. Kennedy and Jackie greet the Fort Worth crowd

(Courtesy Tarrant County College - Northeast Campus)

1903

Swift & Company and Armour & Company have grand opening at Stock Show; A. B. Wharton opens auto sales agency

1904

Plans begun for building Thistle Hill; Motor registration established; Byers Opera House opens; Meachams department store opens

Representative Jim Wright, future Speaker of the House of Representatives, introduces President John F. Kennedy while (left to right) Tarrant County State Senator Don Kennard, U. S. Senator Ralph Yarborough, Texas Governor John Connally and Vice President Lyndon B. Johnson wait with the President. (*Courtesy of the Fort Worth Star-Telegram Photograph Collection, Special Collections Division, University of Texas at Arlington Libraries)*

"Against resistance from some of the President's itinerary planners, I held out for a very early, pre-breakfast public appearance on a huge parking lot adjacent to Worth Hotel. On that Friday morning, which today seems an eternity ago, it would have been hard not to feel that the nation and this man who so perfectly symbolized it were in their finest hour.

The events of November 22, 1963, burned themselves indelibly into my memory. The lilting joy of hosting my president and presenting him that morning to my people in my hometown would give way only hours later to the stark trauma of the assassination in Dallas and the unutterable pathos that followed."

Excerpt from Balance of Power, Jim Wright (used by permission)

THE HISTORY OF THISTLE HILL

Ruth Karbach, Curator, Thistle Hill

Thistle Hill overlooked the wealthiest and most fashionable residential neighborhood in Fort Worth, Texas, in the early 1900's. The mansion was planned in 1903 by newlyweds Electra Waggoner and Albert Buckman Wharton. Accustomed to the best, the couple hired the firm of Sanguinet and Staats to design and build their Colonial Revival mansion in the neighborhood known as "Quality Hill".

The home with a carriage house and three-story water tower was completed in the spring of 1904 just as Mr. Wharton opened the first car dealership in Tarrant County. The Whartons actually named the mansion "Rubusmont", which translates Thistle Hill. Though set on one and one-half acres near the southern city limits of Fort Worth, there were a few neighboring homes of "the quality" at the time of construction. By then, the days when this area was prairie land where the thistle bloomed in the early fall and cattle roamed on open range were nostalgic memories.

Mr. and Mrs. Wharton planned their home to accommodate social gatherings, and indeed it was the center of lively parties. It was also home to the Whartons' young sons, Tom and A. B., Jr. At Christmas, 1909, Mrs. Wharton's father, W. T. "Tom" Waggoner, gave each of his three children and his son-in-law, A. B. Wharton, portions of the 595,000 acre family ranch which stretched across six counties in northwest Texas. W. T. Waggoner also stocked the Whartons' new ranch, Sacaweista, with cattle and horses making this remarkable Christmas gift worth over two million dollars (this would be $20 million today). The Whartons decided to sell their first home in Fort Worth and move to a new residence on their ranch near Vernon, Texas.

Two of the honored guests at Thistle Hill parties were Mr. and Mrs. Winfield Scott, a wealthy couple whose numerous business investments were based on a ranching fortune. They purchased the property from the Whartons and hired the firm of Sanguinet and Staats to oversee their remodeling project which cost $80,000.

The Scotts added a teahouse, a pergola, and initiated a formal English-style garden on the grounds. Extensive remodeling was done of the exterior and interior of the house, and it evolved into the elegant Georgian Revival mansion of today.

Mr. Scott died in October, 1911, before the remodeling was completed. His widow, Elizabeth, and their ten year old son Winfield, Jr., moved into the house the next year. Mrs. Scott resided at Thistle Hill until her death in 1938. In 1940, the Girls Service League purchased the property. The League was a charitable organization dedicated to the assistance of young women. The home served as a supervised residence for young ladies until 1968. The formerly well-kept mansion sat empty for seven years and was a sad survivor, surrounded by commercial development, when purchased by a group of concerned preservationists in 1976. The focus soon became restoration of the exterior and interior to the grandeur of the 1903-1920 era. Today, Thistle Hill is a self-sustaining house museum—an on-going restoration project open to the public through tours, exhibits, seminars, youth education programs and other community functions.

(Courtesy Thistle Hill)

1906	1907
February 1, first edition of The Fort Worth Star	*Mount Olivet Cemetery founded*

(Courtesy of Thistle Hill)

ELECTRA OF THISTLE HILL

Ruth Karbach, Curator, Thistle Hill

Electra Waggoner Wharton

On January 6, 1882, the only and beloved daughter of W. T. "Tom" and Ella Waggoner was born on the original Dan Waggoner Ranch, eight miles east of Decatur in Wise County, Texas. She was named "Electra", after her maternal grandfather, Electious Halsell. Two of her four brothers survived childhood: Guy Leslie, the third child, and Edward Paul, the youngest.

When Electra was three years old, three generations of the Waggoner family moved into El Castile. The fine two-story limestone mansion was on a hill at the end of Main Street with a view straight from the courthouse. Sicily Ann and Ella Waggoner, sisters married to a father and son, frequently remained with Tom and Ella's children in the tamer environment of Decatur while Dan and Tom Waggoner traveled to their different ranches at Beaver's Switch, west of Wichita Falls; near Vernon; near Cactus Hill; and in eastern-most Wise County. Today Beaver's Switch is the city of Electra, named in honor of "Miss Electra" for her 18th birthday. Lake Bridgeport now covers Cactus Hill.

Noted a Fort Worth newspaper, Electra was "not the typical cowgirl that one's imagination might picture. When she rode, she wore a smartly tailored habit from a New York shop and her mount was not the Texas cow pony but an animal of fine blood". "Miss Electra" attended Belmont School for young ladies in Nashville, Tennessee. She was a popular and personable young woman whose close friends and family called her "Carbon Copy" because of her similarity in temperament and personality to her father. Among the reasons for her life-long popularity might have been her lack of affectation and her democratic attitude particularly to those less fortunate in an age of decidedly undemocratic tendencies among the wealthy. Her niece and namesake, Electra Waggoner Biggs, the well-known sculptress, remembers her Aunt Electra's love of beautiful objects and her quiet pursuits of painting and stitchery. The world knew another Electra who was both elegant and extravagant.

Electra

(Courtesy of Thistle Hill)

Her spending for beautiful clothes and furnishings became legendary. She is known as the first person to spend $20,000 in one day at Neiman-Marcus, and she returned the next day to spend almost that much—the equivalent of one-quarter of a million dollars today.

At the turn of the century, Electra was regarded as one of "Texas' greatest heiresses . . . a decidedly attractive girl, Gibsonesque in figure and pose, with a wealth of rich brown hair and glorious gray eyes. Her extensive travel and brushing up against the people of the world has given her that cosmopolitan air that sets so well on the American girl" (Beau Monde, 1900). This Texas Cattle Baron's daughter met and fell in love with a young Philadelphia gentleman in the Himalayas when both were on their Grand Tours

Married in June, 1902, at El Castile, at a private ceremony, Electra wore a point de Venice bridal veil for which she paid $1000 during her 1900 trip to Europe. This veil, in the Thistle Hill collection, has been worn by four generations of Waggoner women and will be loaned for future family weddings.

The honeymooners A. B. and Electra visited Chicago and New York before going by steamer to Europe. Though a newspaper report noted that the couple would reside in Philadelphia, A. B. Wharton purchased six and a quarter acres in Fort Worth during a Christmas visit with his Texas in-laws in 1902. On one and one-half acres of this land, construction of the Whartons' Quality Hill home began in May, 1903.

The young couple and their infant son Tom Wharton moved into their new residence in early 1904. Their second son A. B., Jr., was born in Colorado Springs, Colorado, a favorite summer retreat of wealthy Texans.

A socially active young couple, the Whartons had events ranging from a taffy pull in the kitchen to a 4th of July party with a special dance floor constructed on the lawn and with "thousands of dollars" of fireworks. Dances held in the third floor ballroom were restricted to a select group of relatives and friends. Floral decorations for parties, dinners, receptions and dances were lavish; and the favors and game prizes for guests were generous.

After locating their main residence on their ranch Sacaweista in 1911, A. B. and Electra's fortunes increased greatly with the discovery of oil on their property. During the 1910's A. B. and Electra periodically were in residence in Fort Worth at one of the Waggoner homes. They were regulars for the premier society event the Horse Show, and Electra staged the 1917 pageant for that event with the theme of Queen Scheherazade and the Arabian Nights.

As the Jazz Age dawned, A. B. and Electra purchased a Colonial Revival red brick mansion on more than seven acres in newly developed Highland Park, Dallas. Naming the property Shadowlawn, they proceeded with extensive remodeling of this $200,000 home in 1920. Their lifestyle was extravagant and fast-paced, punctuated by roaring entertainments. Their eighteen year marriage ended in divorce in 1921. The next summer Electra married her second husband Weldon Bailey, one of the sons of Senator Joseph Weldon Bailey, a long-time political friend to Tom Waggoner and other oilmen. Nine months later Weldon and Electra sold Shadowlawn and moved to the Bailey Ranch in Arizona. Their marriage ended in divorce in January, 1925.

Electra' s brief marriage to New Yorker James P. Gilmore, the former commissioner of the Federal Baseball League, was initiated on a yacht off Florida and annulled in September, 1925. Within a month, Electra's health deteriorated alarmingly. She tragically died while at her Fifth Avenue apartment, at age forty-three on Thanksgiving Day, 1925, in New York City

A.B. (Albert Buckman) Wharton

(Courtesy of Thistle Hill)

Mrs. Winfield Scott lived at Thistle Hill from 1912 until 1938

(Courtesy Thistle Hill)

QUALITY HILL

At the turn of the century, Quality Hill was the fashionable Fort Worth neighborhood for the "quality" and was a prime location because of its situation on the bluff overlooking the Trinity River. Today, Pennsylvania Avenue represents the southern boundary of the neighborhood and 7th Street the northern boundary. Summit and Ballinger Avenues still run north and south through what was once the heart of the neighborhood (note: South Summit was originally Hill Street). The east boundary varied by as much as two blocks and the west boundary was, more or less, the bluff.

In the 1890's Texas Cattle Barons moved to town and became "capitalists", investing in Fort Worth real estate and establishing businesses and industries. With the opening of the Swift and Armour packing houses at the turn of the century, Fort Worth's population boomed as did business opportunities. Quality Hill became the home of bankers and developers in addition to prominent ranching families. The Quality Hill ladies were civic as well as social leaders. During this era, the Age of Beauty, these women brought the arts, culture, and the library to Fort Worth and were active in promoting city beautification, improving schools and establishing medical programs.

By the thirties the neighborhood began changing, and today is primarily a business and medical district. The grand mansions of Quality Hill at its peak have been lost with a few notable exceptions: Thistle Hill, the Eddleman-McFarland Home and the Pollock-Capps House. These surviving homes evoke a time of gardens and porch furnishings, coaches and early automobiles, and parties from the weekly card clubs to the elaborate costume cotillions. This was also a time of strong family ties with married children living with parents and near grandparents, and aunts and uncles and cousins in the same neighborhood. The people of Quality Hill were not separated by more than a street or two from the grocer and just one or two blocks more from the laundry lady. The residents of Quality Hill were widely traveled and many made frequent European trips and Grand Tours. They spent their summers in the Colorado and New Mexico mountains and in New England generally.

Many prominent Fort Worth and Texas descendants of the Quality Hill families today maintain their roots in the ranching and cattle industry, oil and banking and real estate development. These include the Slaughters, the Reynolds, the Matthews, the Scharbauers, the Waggoner-Biggs-Whartons, the Beggs, the C. O. Edwards, the Ryans (John), and others too numerous to mention.

Thistle Hill in 1911, at the time of the Scott's ownership

(Courtesy Thistle Hill)

Fort Worth annexes the city of North Fort Worth; 2,400,000 head of cattle through the Stockyards

South side fire destroys twenty-six square blocks; W. D. Williams serves as Mayor from April 13 to April 27; In June, W. D. Davis is elected and serves until 1913

The Walter Scott residence, Fort Worth

(Courtesy of Acme Brick)

Elks Club, demolished 1954, was first the home of Burk Burnett

(Courtesy Fort Worth Public Library)

Continued Growth

The Henderson Street Bridge, constructed in 1930; boats and barges were used to span this then-wide section of the Trinity River's Clear Fork

(Courtesy Dalton Hoffman, Jr. Collection)

The Northern Texas Traction Company located their "car barns" on E. Front Street (now Lancaster). This later became the home of the Fort Worth Transit Company. View is to the northeast, looking toward the early home of A. Brandt Upholstering Company. Note: Trolley Cars on left were older vehicles "side lined" at the time of this photograph

(Courtesy Dalton Hoffman, Jr. Collection)

Interior of a saloon located at 100 Houston Street ca. 1900. This saloon operated as both the Kentucky Liquor House and Saloon, and the Tennessee Liquor House and Saloon from the mid 1890's up through prohibition. It is believed that when this shot was taken it was being operated as the Kentucky and managed by Samuel D. Miller who later moved to a saloon around the corner. Note the row of telephones behind the bartender, apparently for patronage use to "phone home". The metal "tray" hanging at the right is advertising Crown Beer made by the Texas Brewing Company which operated in Fort Worth from 1891 to 1918. *(Courtesy of the Dick Ramsey Collection from the Fort Worth Star Telegram photo collection, Special Collections Division, University of Texas at Arlington Libraries)*

Busy Lancaster Avenue at South Main, Ca. 1950. The Al Hayne Monument is at lower left; Frank Kent sold Fords on the corner and the T&P tracks are visible at the right.

(Courtesy Dalton Hoffman, Jr. Collection)

City of Fort Worth, Texas - What's in a Name?

Douglas Harman, CDME, Ph.D.
President and C.E.O of Fort Worth Convention and Visitors Bureau

Fort Worth has "fort" in its name and conveys that image although there are no remnants of the original fort. There have been discussions about the desirability of recreating it.

The early years established Fort Worth as "Cowtown" due initially to the Chisholm Trail route which went through the city, and for many additional years due to the Stockyards which came in the late 1800's and continued up to the 1970's.

During the early years, "Panther City" became a reference first used with Fort Worth suggesting that the city was so dull that a panther was found sleeping on Main Street. This reference was in a Dallas newspaper and added to the competitive spirit between the two cities. Fort Worth responded with humor and made the panther a proud symbol. The panther emblem and name are found in many historical references in the city and is included on the police badge used today. It showed Fort Worth to have a sense of humor about itself. The Panther City reference was often used in the past, and conveyed the image of a sleek, strong-willed cat.

As the city matured in the 1880's , it was referred to as the "Queen City of the Prairie." This was a reference associated with the sophistication, civic improvements and commerce of Fort Worth as it served the surrounding area and as it became a major railroad hub.

The "Tarantula" map of Fort Worth in the late 1800s emphasized this position in which the statement, "all roads lead to Fort Worth", was made. At the turn of the century, Fort Worth was also referred to as the "Gateway to the Great State of Texas", again due to the unique transportation focus of the city.

During the early 1900's, Fort Worth was called a "Modern Metropolis", the "center of the greatest oil fields", and "where the golden west and the sunny southland meet".

At the time of the Texas State Centennial celebration, due largely to the efforts of Amon Carter, Fort Worth had a strong image of being an entertainment city where people could truly enjoy themselves. During this period, Will Rogers apparently said Fort Worth was "where the west begins" and Dallas was "where the east petered out."

The term "Fort Worth, the Way You Want Texas to Be", has been one of the terms used by the Convention and Visitors Bureau as an approach which associates traditional Texas values and images with Fort Worth.

Our city has had distinctive personality characteristics emphasized in its promotion through the years — the connection to the west, its existence as a transportation center, its aviation, technology and cultural features. Fort Worth should always have distinct avenues, because our city does, indeed, have distinctively different personalities.

(Courtesy W.T. Waggoner Building)

1911

Amon Carter sponsors French touring aviators to Fort Worth; Teddy Roosevelt speaks at the Northside Coliseum

1912

St. Andrews Episcopal Church completed; first water filtration plant

A steam-powered pump, the B.B. Paddock - named in honor of the influential publisher, was installed at the Holly Pump Station , Fort Worth's first water purification plant. The pump was still operable in 1953 when it was removed. Photo Ca 1952

(Courtesy Dalton Hoffman, Jr. Collection)

Simon Wilke Freese and John B. Hawley ran "hydraulic jump" experiments in 1924 at the Fort Worth Holly Pump Station
(Courtesy Freese and Nichols)

"LEONARDS DEPARTMENT STORE, "Home of the Famous M&O Subway", downtown Fort Worth, Texas. Leonards Department Store is a giant 2,000-employee retailing complex with over half-million square feet of sales area. It is one of the largest downtown shopping centers in the Southwest and is the owner of the only privately owned subways in the world."

(Courtesy the Quentin McGown Postcard Collection)

"World's first private subway through bluffs of Trinity River to Skyhigh Fort Worth, Texas. This is the first privately owned, department store subway in the world. Two of its five electric cars are seen passing at the entrance. Owned by Leonard Brothers, the vast river level parking lot, subway and cars are free to the public, making the project unique in the annals of downtown business and pleasure."

(Courtesy the Quentin McGown Postcard Collection)

The Leonard brothers, Marvin and Obie, established the downtown department store that bore their name. For a half a decade, Leonard's was the place to shop. You could ride the M&O subway, whose free parking boosted the downtown economy. You could experience the sweet scent of the hot donuts as you disembarked, and enjoy searching the bargain aisle. A downtown Christmas trip was not complete if you failed to visit Monnigs Bears and lunch at the Tea Room. The Leonard's name is gone, but the subway remains. You can ride to the Fort Worth Public Library's underground entrance, shop Fort Worth's Outlet Square, and visit the ice skating rink.

Marvin Leonard was also the founder of Colonial County Club, and started the Colonial National Invitational Tournament; he convinced the United States Golf Association to hold its 1941 U. S. Open (won by Craig Wood) here. Leonard was also responsible for the Colonial having bent grass greens, the first in Texas.

LAKE WORTH

Quentin McGown

Quentin McGown is a fourth-generation Forth Worthian with a life-long interest in history. Director of Gift Planning at Texas Wesleyan University, he served as chair of the City of Fort Worth Historic and Cultural Landmarks Commission and the Tarrant County Historical Commission.

"The largest municipal park in the world!" declared Fort Worth Parks Commissioner Harry Vinnedge, as Lake Worth formally opened to recreational visitors in July, 1917. By the end of that first summer season, nearly 75,000 people, equal to the total population of the city at the time, visited the newest resort in the country. What began as a reservoir to provide an adequate water supply to the growing city, remains today one of the most unique and valuable urban park resources in Texas.

Fort Worth at the turn of the century was a dynamic and vibrant community witnessing an explosive growth. Between 1900 and 1910, the population nearly tripled, from 23,000 to 73,000, and city services strained under the pressure. The city still drew all of its water supply from a series of artesian wells drilled along the western edge of downtown. Even though some city leaders were concerned about the availability of water for the future, the "Fort Worth Record" newspaper in 1907 declared the supply "inexhaustible." Then, in April, 1909, a fire swept across the South Side, destroying nearly three hundred buildings across twenty-six square blocks. The water demand to control the fire depleted the artesian supply, and the city immediately began to explore solutions.

Engineer John B. Hawley was appointed to head a team to locate the ideal site for a reservoir. He had come to Fort Worth nearly twenty years earlier to design the city's first municipal water plant, and had at that time recommended the creation of a reservoir. Following his team's report in 1911 that a dam should be built on the West Fork of the Trinity, about six miles northwest of town , the city spent $1.5 million to acquire the land and construct the dam. As the reservoir began to fill in 1913, the city considered several names for the new lake, including Lake Minnetonka, Panther Lake and Lake Tonkaway, before settling on Lake Worth. The first water spilled over the dam on August 10, 1914.

The demands for recreational use began even before the lake had filled. E.P. Haltom, son of the city's most prominent jeweler, launched his home-built sailboat, the Kingfisher, into the lake in 1913, beginning a long tradition of inland sailing in Fort Worth. It wasn't long before bathers began to appear along the lake shore, taking advantage of the cool waters during the Texas summer. The city administration was criticized for not keeping swimmers out of the new drinking water supply, but, by 1915, buses filled with lake visitors were running from Rosen Heights and the city realized that stopping the public from using their new playground would be impossible. City leaders ordered the lake stocked with fish and began planning a resort development to accommodate the increasing numbers of tourists.

Work began in 1916 on the first leg of the Meandering Road that would eventually encircle the entire lake. Beginning at the dam and running west along the south shore, the road instantly became the preferred Sunday drive in what was usually the family's first automobile. On the northwest shore, where the old wooden Nine-Mile Bridge crossed the river, the city built a $25,000 pavilion, complete with changing rooms, observation decks and diving platforms. 15,000 attended the opening on June 17, 1917. The next month, the city hosted an "aquatic meet" with boat races, water fencing and tug of war. Between June and August, more than 73,000 visited the lake. Lake Worth would remain the centerpiece of the Fort Worth park system for the next thirty years.

While soldiers training at Camp Bowie and the army airfields took advantage of the recreational facilities at Lake Worth, local business leaders raised the money to open the Ruth Lubin Camp for Underprivileged Children, and the Boy Scouts opened Camp Leroy Schuman. Large pleasure boats, including "Miss Lake Worth," "Panther City" and "Alvez" began to operate, taking passengers on leisurely excursions around the scenic park. The last two were destroyed by fire and sank in the lake, but with no casualties. In 1918, the city began issuing leases for campsites around the lake shore. Over the next few years many businesses and organizations developed camps, including Swift, Armour, the YMCA, Travis Avenue Baptist Church and the Panther Boys Club. To meet the demand for public camping, several families began operating small lake resorts including Huffman's, Roach's, Getting's and Shady Grove. By 1926, there were 800 individual campsites recorded around the lake.

Over the years, a handful of large-scale properties were developed along the shores of Lake Worth. On July 4, 1919, the Masonic Mosque opened its doors and welcomed guests to the largest dance floor in the Southwest. The multi-story building, complete with minarets and spectacular stained glass windows towered over the lake at Reynolds Point, later renamed Mosque Point. Hosting special events and Masonic conventions, the building was sold to the Methodist Church and used as a church retreat until it was destroyed by fire in 1927. As the fame of the Mosque went up in smoke,

This Lake Worth Casino and Bath House replaced an earlier, one story structure. It was destroyed by fire ca 1929 and The Casino Ballroom was built on this site.

(Courtesy Dalton Hoffman, Jr. Collection)

another enormous facility took its place. At the site of the old bathing pavilion at Nine-Mile Bridge, the city had given a thirty year lease to the Lake Worth Amusement Company to develop the Lake Worth Casino. The million dollar facility was called "The Coney Island of the Southwest," and featured a boardwalk, a small zoo, amusement rides and a dance floor that could hold 2,000 people. The casino and boardwalk burned in June, 1929, but the property was rebuilt and expanded to include a massive roller coaster.

Also in 1927, local businessman Samuel Whiting began construction of "Iveness," a massive stone house on the South shore of the lake. Built around an old stone cabin dating from the 1860's, the Lake Worth Castle, as it became known, remains one of the most unique properties in Fort Worth. Reportedly using materials salvaged from the Mosque when he began construction, Whiting spent the next ten years completing the castle and five guest cottages. He welcomed the pleasure boaters on the lake to stop at his long stone pier, complete with lighthouse and special fishing enclosure. The castle was for a time used as a recreation resort by Consolidated Vultee, and hosted actor Jimmy Stewart during his filming of "Strategic Air Command."

Amon Carter opened his famous Shady Oaks Farm on 900 acres on Lake Worth in 1923. Over the next thirty years, Carter would host virtually every major dignitary who visited Fort Worth, including several presidents. The famous "Frontier Bar" is described in the WPA Guide to Fort Worth: "Immediately beyond the farm house is the Frontier Bar, with a sign 'Howdy Stranger' over its front; this was the gateway to the 1936 Fort Worth Frontier Fiesta...Scattered over the walls are crude signs reminiscent of early Texas such as: 'No shooting, check your pistol.' 'No checks cashed not even good ones.' 'Dallas passport must be okayed.' On the walls are mounted specimens of native longhorn steers, one of which entertains with ribald songs including a humorous tirade against Dallas, Texas and during its rendition, the steer symbolic of Carter's hatred of Fort Worth's sister city will emit snorts and smoke from its nostrils." Nothing remains today of the famous farm except a few foundations and the small stock pond.

Lake Worth

(Courtesy Freese & Nichols, Inc.

Lake Worth spillway under construction, 1912. (Courtesy Freese & Nichols)

Aeroplane View of Beach and Casino, Lake Worth, Fort Worth, Texas. Lake Worth Casino, built at a cost of more that $1,000,000, is Fort Worth's open air playground. Boating and bathing are popular sports and a wide variety of carnival attractions are offered.

(From the collection of Quentin McGown)

Lake Worth and Mosque *(From the collection of Quentin McGown)*

Nine Mile Bridge at Lake Worth, Bath House and Beach in distance, Ca 1918.
(From the collection of Quentin McGown)

In 1943 several sea planes from their bases along the Texas coast sought the safety of Lake Worth when a hurricane threatened
(Courtesy Fort Worth Star-Telegram Photograph Collection, Special Collections Division, The University of Texas at Arlington Libraries)

In 1934, the city commissioned the nationally renowned Kansas City landscape design firm of Hare and Hare to develop a comprehensive design for the city's parks, including Lake Worth. The firm developed a plan for the lake that would create picnic areas, sheltered pavilions and long vistas. The plans became a reality with the opening of Camp 1816 of the Civilian Conservation Corps. Between 1934 and 1937, the men of the CCC constructed roads, built bridges, and completed most of the recommendations in the Hare and Hare plan. Twenty stone picnic areas were built, along with restroom facilities and water fountains. Rocks cut from the cliffs along the lake shore decorated drainage culverts and nature trails and were used to build magnificent shelter houses and lookouts. A monument in the Fort Worth Nature Center chronicles the tremendous work of the CCC.

Other milestones in the lake's history include the founding of the Fort Worth Boat Club in 1929 and the Lake Worth Sailing Club in 1935. In 1928, with help of Fort Worth Congressman Fritz Lanham, the federal government opened the largest fish hatchery in the Southwest just below the dam. Today the facility is managed by the Texas Parks and Wildlife Department. The lake froze over in January, 1930, allowing people to drive across the ice. In 1943, dozens of seaplanes were flown onto the lake from their bases along the Texas coast to protect them from a possible hurricane. Shortly after the war, a bomber crashed into the hillside across the lake from the Convair Plant. During the Cold War, the hills surrounding the lake were dotted with missile silos to protect the military operations in Fort Worth.

Lake Worth was once the premier park in the Southwest. Its popularity as a destination declined with the development of municipal swimming pools, air-conditioning, television and the distractions of modern life. As Fort Worth grows to surround this urban park, its treasures will again attract visitors to the natural settings and the magnificent landscapes so carefully designed and painstakingly executed. A drive around Lake Worth today is as inspirational as it was when the first cars rolled along Meandering Road and Fort Worth families discovered the wonders of nature in the city's own backyard.

Dam and Spillway, Lake Worth
(From the collection of Quentin McGown)

A few brave souls drove their cars onto frozen Lake Worth in January of 1930, while others attempted to ice-skate. To prevent any unforeseen tragedies, the Fort Worth Police cleared the lake of the fun-seekers.

Courtesy Fort Worth Star-Telegram Photograph Collection, Special Collections Division, The University of Texas at Arlington Libraries

Area Lakes

Trolley lines were run to both of these "resort" spots in an attempt to promote suburban growth

Lake Erie, later known as Lake Arlington

Lake Erie, Handley Park, Ca 1907.

Lake Como, Arlington Heights, Fort Worth, Texas. These Beautiful Amusement Grounds are located in the center of Arlington Heights Property.

Pavilion and Lake at Arlington Heights, Fort Worth, Texas. (1908)

(Postcards from the collection of Quentin McGown)

Fort Worth Boat Club. The Club house, storage and harbor facilities are shown in this view of the Fort Worth Boat Club at Eagle Mountain Lake, Ca 1967

(From the collection of Quentin McGown)

Many times a post card would be artistically enhanced as was this night scene with the addition of a moon and clouds.

(Courtesy of the Quentin McGown Postcard Collection)

Looks Like Bad Weather . . .

Trinity River Flood of May 1949

Not all weather is bad. According to the NOAA (National Oceanic and Atmospheric Administration), there was a White Christmas in 1841; reports show the residents of Bird's Fort (later Birdville and now Haltom City) "tracked a bear on Christmas day in six inches of snow". And although the 1875 hurricane at Indianola was fierce enough to wipe out that city, it brought no ill effects to Fort Worth. But NOAA records show a damaging hail storm in the year of 1891, and the following September, the Great Galveston Hurricane killed 6000 citizens of the coastal city, and the resulting storms dumped ten inches of rain on Fort Worth. The Trinity flooded, and again in 1908, 1922 and 1932. Then came the flood of 1949. These photographs indicate the extent of the damage.

(Fort Worth Public Library)

7th Street became a river that May day

(Courtesy Dalton Hoffman Jr. Collection)

Water rose to the second floor of the Montgomery Ward's building on West Seventh in 1949.
(Courtesy Tarrant County College, Northeast Campus)

The flood of April 1922 killed thirty-seven people and drove 1500 from their homes. Almost one mile of the Trinity's levee system was washed away, as well as railroad lines. The electric power plant shut down until emergency service could be "borrowed" from Waco via a connecting "high-tension" line. Thousands of livestock were lost and over three million dollars in damage sustained.

Farrington Field looked like a swimming pool

(Courtesy Tarrant County College, Northeast Campus)

(Courtesy Fort Worth Public Library)

(Courtesy Dalton Hoffman, Jr.)

Excessive rains were not the only problems dealt Fort Worth. In 1916, both freezing and 100 plus temperatures were recorded in March. The next year a severe dust storm "blocked out the sun for most of the day". The Trinity flooded once again in 1949 but repeated summer droughts meant hot and dry weather. In 1961, after a brief snow in January, Hurricane Carla spawned local thunderstorms and flash floods. The big news of 1978 was the extended freeze, repeated in 1983 with more than two weeks of below freezing temperatures. The tornados, hail, high winds and flooding of 1989 were forgotten by 1991 when when the records show it was the wettest year ever. In May of 1995, however, the Great Mayfest Hail Storm sent 10,000 dashing for cover. El Niño affected Fort Worth beginning in 1998 with rain and floods, then dry and warm weather moved across Mexico and smoke from out-of-control fires restricted our visibility for days. This was followed by hail, more rain, high winds, heat waves and drought, only to end with a wet fall and an icy December. It seems Fort Worth fits right in with the "Texas Weather" adage - if you don't like the weather, wait a minute".

(Courtesy The Paris Coffee Shop Collection)

On campus of the Southwestern Baptist Theological Seminary, snow blankets the automobiles parked in front of Fort Worth Hall, 1975

(Courtesy Southwestern Baptist Theological Seminary, photo by R. Langley)

April 1942
Marine Creek Flooded

(Courtesy Fort Worth Public Library)

United States declares war on Germany; Camp Bowie established ; Hicks, Everman and Benbrook airfields open

W. D. Davis elected Mayor, serves until 1921

Civic Buildings

The City Hall, Ca 1907
(Quentin McGown post card collection)

City Hall, Ca 1940

(Quentin McGown post card collection)

The Civil Courts building, built in 1958, received a tromp l'oeil facelift in the 1980's

(Quentin McGown post card collection)

Tarrant County Courthouse

Above left, Tarrant County's first perminent courthouse was destroyed by fire in 1876. *(Courtesy Fort Worth Star Telegram Photogrpahic Collection, Special Collections, The University of Texas at Arlington Libraies)* Above right, the second courthouse, built after the 1876 fire, stood until county commissioners authorized construction of the present courhouse. *(Courtesy Fort Worth Star Telegram Photogrpahic Collection, Special Collections, The University of Texas at Arlington Libraies)*

Fort Worth won a questionable contest against Birdville to become the seat of Tarrant County. The story goes that both cities were providing free whiskey for voters; as luck would have it, Birdville ran out of whiskey about the same time Fort Worth gained an extra barrel. It has also been speculated that many Wise county voters cast their ballot that day in 1856 as residents of Tarrant. As a result of the shenanigans a new election was held. Fort Worth leaders offered to finance a new courthouse, thus swaying the vote. The new courthouse was constructed, but burned in 1876. The photo to the left shows the crew a-top the current courthouse,completed 1893.

(Both Photos below Courtesy Fort Worth Public Library)

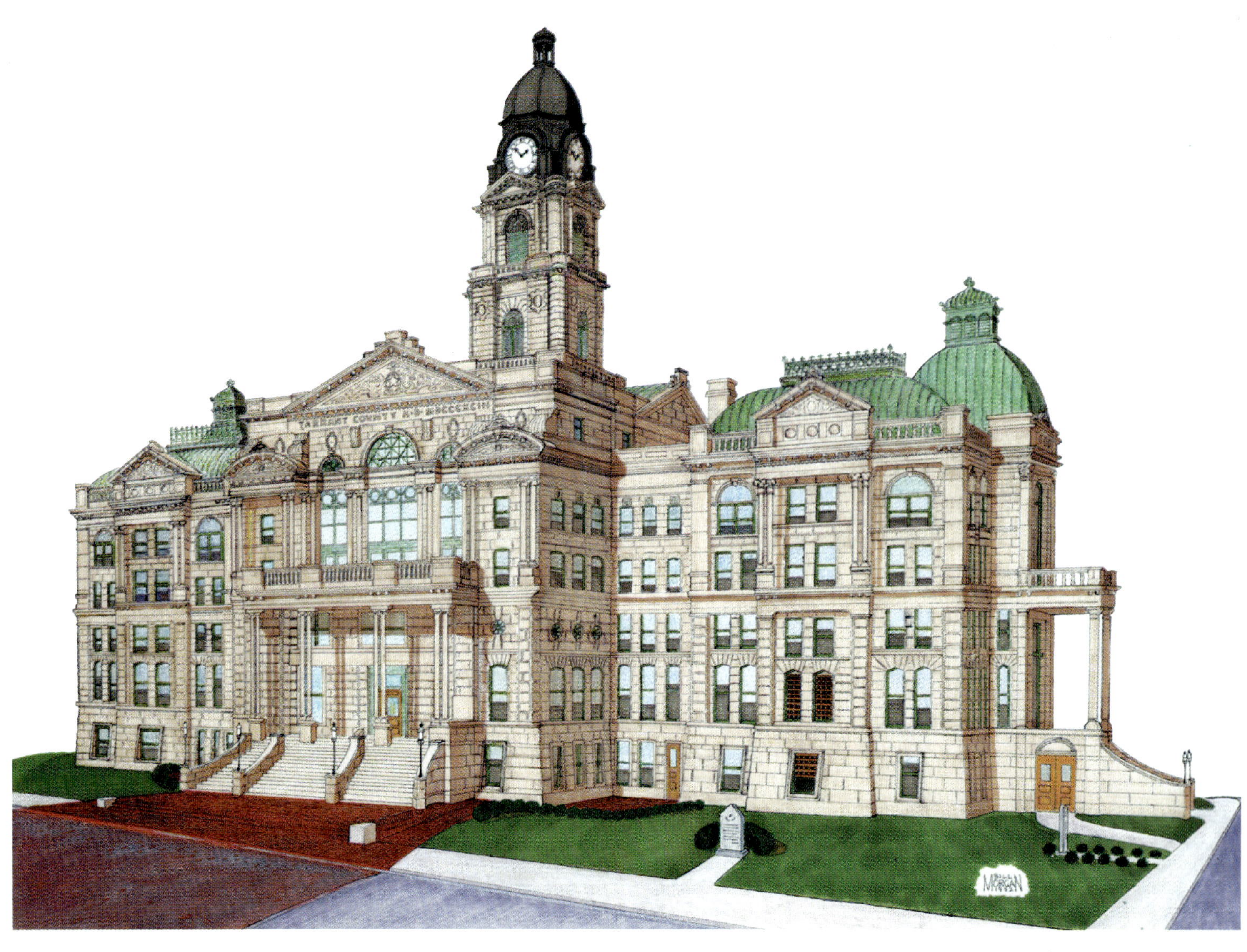

In a period when Texas architects were designing some of the nation's greatest public buildings, Tarrant officials went to Missouri for their architects. Louis Curtiss and Frederick Gunn formed a partnership that became a pioneer in the use of concrete and structural steel, and the Tarrant commissioners were pioneers themselves - going for a much larger building than they needed, in anticipation of future growth. The 1893 courthouse was finished in the same red granite used on the Texas Capitol, its lines suggest a sort of mini capitol, a condensed version of one of the most graceful public buildings in the state. The granite and marble blocks and columns were quarried in Burnet County, in the Hill Country. The stone was hauled to the construction site where it was chiseled to exact specifications by stonemasons making $1.50 a day. When the building was inspected in 1970, after more than 75 years of exposure to the elements, there wasn't a crack to be found in the exterior.

Bill Morgan

Bill Morgan is a fourth generation Texan who began his professional career in journalism working with Texas newspapers such as the Fort Worth Star-Telegram, The Dallas Times Herald, Dallas Morning News and Lufkin Daily News. The artist's interest in courthouses resulted in a career change, and in 1991 he began traveling Texas to paint those imposing edifices. Bill is the author of Old Friends: Great Texas Courthouses,Landmark Publishing, 1999.

HISTORY OF THE FORT WORTH POST OFFICE

Duane Gage

The first official mail to arrive in Fort Worth apparently came by way of Dallas, for Major Ripley A. Arnold, founder of the military camp that became a city, wrote to Maj. Gen. Roger Jones on June 2, 1649: "I have located a new post on West Fork Trinity River. My address will be 'Dallas, Dallas County Texas,' a town about thirty-five miles east of me." A weekly dragoon express brought letters, newspapers and parcels from Dallas; later, before the post was abandoned in 1853, the military mail came from Waco, which was the post office for Forts Graham and Worth.

In 1850, to provide postal service to the civilians who had begun to move to Fort Worth, mail was sent by pony from Dallas and distributed at a general merchandise store operated by Henry Daggett and Archibald Leonard. The village continued to grow and on February 28, 1856, an official United States Post Office was established; Julian Feild, a merchant who was one of the first five civilian settlers in Fort Worth, was appointed the first postmaster by President Franklin Pierce. The post office was in a one-story wooden building located on the west side of Main Street, between present day Second and Third Streets. Mail was distributed whenever the stage arrived from Dallas. The postal receipts for the first year were $91.99.

In 1875, the post office was moved from the original location on Main Street to 109 W. Weatherford. Around 1884, during the administration of Postmaster Belle M. Burchill, the first free delivery service of mail was inaugurated and the post office was moved into a two-story building on Main Street between 5th and 6th Streets.

The red sandstone turreted post office and federal building located on Jennings at 11th was completed in 1896. For thirty-six years, this building was used as Fort Worth's post office and as the federal court building. During that period postal revenues expanded significantly (from $75,510.45 in 1900 to $1,650,682.11 in 1930) and a much larger facility was needed.

The Fort Worth Post Office located on the southeast corner of Jennings and Lancaster Avenue in downtown Fort Worth is an impressive structure that was needed because of the community's growth and the need for expansive facilities to meet the city's postal service needs. In 1931, the federal government purchased a tract of land from the Texas and Pacific Company for $200,000, on which to construct the new post office building. Its location, adjacent to the Texas and Pacific Railway Station, was expected to improve service since most of the incoming and outgoing mail would be handled by the railroads using that station.

Post Office, Jennings at 11th Ca 1914
(From the collection of Quentin McGown)

Groundbreaking for the planned $1,245,000 building took place on August 11, 1931, by Ralph Sollitt & Sons, a Chicago, Illinois contracting firm. Tom Archer and Company, a local concern, was awarded the contract for the excavation work. The building was designed by the firm of Wyatt C. Hedrick, a nationally known architect/engineer. The Renaissance Revival style building is ornate with solid bronze fittings and solid marble columns. The lobby's twenty-five foot ceiling is covered with Renaissance gold leaf. The exterior features include sixteen massive three foot diameter solid turned limestone columns on its front. These columns and the pilasters on the building sides are topped with eclectic Corinthian capitals of special design involving longhorn cattle—a unique feature characterizing the colorful southwestern setting of the structure.

The formal opening of the post office building occurred on February 22, 1933, George Washington's birthday. A few weeks later, on April 9, 1933, a unique dedicatory ceremony held by Julia Jackson Chapter #141, United Daughters of the Confederacy, received special attention. That date was chosen for its historical significance, being the sixty-fifth anniversary of the date that General Robert E. Lee surrendered his Confederate forces at Appomattox, Virginia. A tablet placed inside the front northwest entrance of the building states: "Dedicated to the Confederate Veterans by the UDC and SCV, Fort Worth, Texas, 1933."

For nearly fifty years the Fort Worth Main Post Office Building has served the growing municipality. Postal receipts showed steady and impressive growth, from $1,524,036 in 1940; $4,511,019 in 1950; $9,274,501 in 1960; $17,230,279 in 1970; and $44,532,957 in 1980. The post office building, which was designed to take care of the needs of Fort Worth for decades, was outgrown in twenty years. In late 1979, Postmaster Jack D. Watson announced plans to build a major mail distribution facility in northern Fort Worth, near the intersection of I-820 and I-35, a facility that would provide space for mail distribution services that were housed in the Main Post Office.

The future of the structure on Lancaster became clouded when in 1979 there leaked word that the Texas State Highway Department was drafting tentative plans to widen the elevated Interstate 30 Highway that paralleled Lancaster Avenue, bringing a widening freeway to within twenty feet of the majestic 1933 structure. Preservationists immediately began to seek an alternate plan that would spare the building from the hazardous encroachment of the traffic artery. The historic Fort Worth Main Post Office Building now stands as a symbol of the difficulties encountered when a dynamic growing city is energetically involved in both progress and preservation.

Post Office, Fort Worth, Texas. This fine building is constructed of white Texas limestone, Texas granite trim with Tennessee marble wainscoting and large green columns of Grecian marble in the lobby, the upper section of which is trimmed in bronze. Cost, a little over $1,000,000.

(From the collection of Quentin McGown)

Longhorn cattle were used in the design of the Post Office on Lancaster Avenue

(Landmark Staff Photo)

The Ole Tyme Postique of Fort Worth, Texas

This unique museum is a must for those interested in the history of Fort Worth. Located in the Post Office on West Lancaster and Jennings, you will discover more than Postal History. Pass along the Italian marble hallway and look for the old-fashioned sign on the door .

Jeanette Hodges, window clerk, adds the personal touch to your tour. Ms. Hodges' mother and father also once worked for the U. S. Post Office. Jeanette will tell you about the double-dial, double-lock safe; show you the Colt 38, standard Post Office gun issued about 1884.

The photos that line the walls tell their own stories, while the badges, scales, hats and uniforms tell another. Learn of the danger involved for the railway carriers who "exchanged" mail at non-stop stations. These men leaned out and hooked the mail sack to an extended "arm" and were fortunate when the transfer went without mishap.

Stop by and check the time on the 1897 New Bundy clock, while those of you who are philatelics pick up the latest issues. Postique hours are Monday through Friday, 10 a.m. until 1:30 p.m. and 2:30 until 6:00 p.m. Oh, by the way, you can also mail a letter.

East Lancaster Post Office Interior

(Landmark Staff Photo)

Carnegie Public Library. Above, Ca 1910. Below, under construction

(Photos Courtesy Fort Worth Public Library)

Fort Worth Public Library, Ca 1940's

(Photos Courtesy Fort Worth Public Library)

The Fort Worth Public Library opened its new building in October of 1999. Designed by architect Dave Schwarz, the new building was constructed over the subterrainian library that was built in 1978. Partial funding for the new building was from the Fort Worth Public Library Foundation

(Courtesy Fort Worth Public Library)

1921

Grand Opening of The Texas Hotel; First Fort Worth radio station - WBAP

1921

E. R. Cockrell elected Mayor, serves until 1924

Masonic Orphans' Home

(From the collection of Quentin McGown)

Masonic Temple, Forth Worth, Texas. This majestic building was erected at a cost of $1,000,000.

(From the collection of Quentin McGown)

FORT WORTH FIRE DEPARTMENT

by Jim Noah

Jim Noah is a retired Battalion Chief of the Fort Worth Fire Department and has spent several years compiling and documenting the history of the department. He was featured as "Fireman Jim" on the 1959 television program, "Ranger Jim's Cartoon Clubhouse".

For almost a quarter of a century there was a Fort Worth, but absolutely no organized fire fighting. From 1849 to the time of the incorporation of the city, if a citizen suffered a fire it was "do the best you can".

By early 1873 the railroad boom had turned Fort Worth into a flammable town of four square miles, a burgeoning city crammed with flimsy wood buildings and even a tent city all heated by fireplace and wood stoves. Destructive blazes were common. When the Texas Legislature enacted a bill incorporating Fort Worth into a city, the newly-seated city council gave top priority to a call for "better protection of property from fire..." Fort Worth's fires might have well continued to rage uncontrolled if not for Captain B.B. Paddock.

Captain Paddock rode into Fort Worth in October 1872 as if by appointment. A veteran Confederate officer, self-taught lawyer and literary wit, he was one of those flamboyant talents – like Amon Carter in a later era – who seemed to have been brought by destiny for the betterment of Fort Worth. Captain Paddock wasted no time in mounting a single-handed campaign for fire protection. He took over as editor of the town's lone newspaper the day he arrived; and by early 1873 the Fort Worth Democrat was issuing ringing calls for a volunteer fire brigade. He privately extracted promises from many of the town's leading citizens to meet him on the courthouse steps to organize a volunteer fire company. As luck would have it a "blue norther" blasted into town that evening, and Paddock found himself alone on the freezing steps. After continued prodding from Captain Paddock, fifty men gathered to organize Fort Worth's first volunteer fire company. On May 2, 1873, Hook & Ladder Company No. 1 was officially born.

Protection Engine Company Number One — Organized 1876. Ben U. Bell — Foreman... earliest known photo of the Fort Worth Volunteer Fire Department. *(Courtesy Jim Noah)*

To raise cash for their first piece of firefighting apparatus, a hand-pulled hook and ladder wagon priced at $600.00, the resourceful volunteers staged a contest to select the most popular woman from among the town's beauties. They charged 10 cents a vote, and Miss Sallie won not only the popularity contest but the right to name Fort Worth's first fire company. Miss Johnson renamed Hook & Ladder No. 1 the M. T. Johnson Hook & Ladder Company after her father Col. Middleton Tate Johnson. Meanwhile the still unpaid for hook and ladder wagon was delivered by rail to Dallas, the nearest depot.

Original Central Fire Station, built in 1883, was used until 1899 when New Central was built. Note Bell Tower in rear at the extreme left. N.C. Hall Jewelers' sign can be seen at extreme right. Notice the horsedrawn ladder truck with tiller. This photo was made about 1898-99, and the station was located on Main Street between 11th & 12th.*L-R:* Petersmith Hose Company Driver, F. Massingale, Capt. Jerry O'Brien, Pat Noonan, O. Tronbridge, M.T. Johnson. Hook & Ladder # 1 Driver Frank Bishop, Capt. W.E. Bideker, Peter McGrath, Charlie Sneed, Geo. Kaywood, W. Kinkle, Oscar McCain-Tiller.*(Courtesy Jim Noah)*

May 1st, 1883. Volunteer Fire Department Wagon decorated for "May Fest" Parade downtown, Fort Worth, Texas.

(Courtesy Jim Noah)

Triumphant volunteers trooped to meet it, then pulled it some thirty miles to Fort Worth. When additional money-raising efforts failed to produce the cash needed to pay off the wagon, the volunteers reluctantly sold it to the city for $1000. The city council, however, met stiff rebuff from the firemen when it sought the power to appoint their company officers as a condition for allowing firefighters to use the hook & ladder. Fort Worth's volunteers, poor but unbowed, had already devised a firefighting system possibly unique in firefighting history.

Still, the volunteers faced a serious problem – the lack of a reliable water supply. Although the Democrat launched an impassioned campaign for a public water works, it would be four long years before Fort Worth would have even a minimal firefighting supply.

With the coming of the railroad to Fort Worth, and a second bigger boom, generating phenomenal growth, the city became a hub for both rail and stage lines. But the city's lone volunteer fire company with its primitive equipment remained the only defense against fire. City fathers ignored all calls for improved equipment until three major fires proved that Fort Worth had outgrown its hook & ladder phase.

The story goes that in 1904 there was to be a "pumping" contest among the area Fire Departments. Fort Worth's Fire Chief gave his permission for his men to participate, but they had to take the old reserve truck, in case the newer one was needed. The men felt the truck downright ugly, and asked the city to paint it; they even received a bid on doing so, but the city said "no". Undaunted, the men passed the hat and paid the Lennox Carriage Works to spruce up the old girl. Fort Worth won the day, and the old reserve truck was the envy of all -- with its fresh white paint and gold trim. Since then, all Fort Worth Fire Department Trucks have been painted in these winnings colors. Recently, the new chief added a sleek blue stripe.

Courtesy Dalton Hoffman, Jr. Collection

In the small hours of the morning of March 22, 1876, the county courthouse was found on fire and burning fast. Despite the best efforts of the M. T. Johnson Company and citizens who joined the fight, the flames consumed the courthouse, destroying all county records. Before Fort Worth had recovered from that loss, a fire that started in the Prairie House Hotel on September 22, 1876 burned to the ground not only the hotel but a sizable section of the business district, including a saloon, stores, and homes. Only a month later, the town jail was badly damaged when a prisoner tried to escape by burning it down.

Amid public outcry, the city council at last agreed to order a steam pumper for Fort Worth's firefighters provided citizens would raise $1000 toward its price. A Silsby steam engine was ordered, dubbed the Panther Engine, at the cost of $6,250. The city refused to pay for horses to pull the engine or to fund cisterns to provide a water supply, but a determined group of volunteers formed Fort Worth's second volunteer firefighting company, the Panther Engine Company No. 1 and in 1876, the two companies merged to form the city's first true "Fire Department".

On January 23, 1877, the Department moved into quarters in the new City Hall, built at Second and Rusk streets on land donated by former Mayor Burts. Fire Hall No. 1, the town's first fire station – occupied the first floor, under the city offices.

The city adopted a system of renting horses to pull the engine and finally, in 1877, the city council allocated money for the construction of three cisterns – one near the railroad, one behind City Hall and one on the Courthouse Square. These provided Fort Worth's major supply of water for firefighting until 1882 when the city's first water mains were laid. The 1880's brought significant improvements and fostered a spirit of pride among the volunteers. The city had five fire stations by 1889 and was soon to face its greatest challenge.

The Texas Spring Palace - a structure that was "built to burn". Constructed in 1889 of pine from east Texas, covered with wheat, oats, corn, Spanish moss and every other organic material available to make it, as Captain Paddock described it, "easily the most beautiful structure ever erected on earth." Unfortunately, the great civic pride generated by the building was soon to turn to tragedy. On the night of May 30, 1890, as 7000 people were dancing on the second floor, a fire broke out. Within eleven minutes, the entire building was alive with flame as visitors leaped for their lives from second floor windows. Despite their preparation, firefighters proved no match for the tremendous inferno. Al Hayne was the only fatality, but the fire made it painfully clear that further improvements needed to be made in firefighting equipment and personnel. Even with new equipment and new fire stations, the members of the city council began to take a harder look at the idea of a full-salaried fire department.

As the century turned, the department comprised six stations, four hose companies, one ladder company, and one chemical engine, plus the steamer. Firefighting was a wild affair. Responding to a call,

Fort Worth Fire Station No. 1

(Courtesy Jim Noah)

1909 Central Station. Chief Ferguson, Driver Jim Pope, Fire Chief Bideker (far right) with a 1909 Maxwell Auto, the first motorized vehicle owned by the city of Fort Worth

(Courtesy Jim Noah)

Texas & Pacific Station fire, 1904
(Courtesy Fort Worth Public Library)

horses raced through the dirt streets at break-neck speed. Trucks frequently leaned over on two wheels as they careened around the narrow street corners. In 1902, Dick Rockett became the first firefighter killed in the line of duty when he fell off of the ladder truck and was crushed under the wheels. Since the city offered no compensation to the families of those killed, firefighters joined together in 1901 to establish the Fireman's Relief Association. Each member of the department agreed to contribute one dollar each month to aid injured firefighters or the relatives of those who laid down their lives in the course of their work.

A major change came in 1905 with the appointment of Chief William Edward Bideker. Chief "Bill" inherited a fully horse-drawn department, with thirty-eight men and seven stations. After fourteen years of his administration, the department had grown to 100 firefighters, and thirteen stations, but perhaps most significantly, Bideker oversaw the departments transformation from horse-drawn to motor-driven apparatus, and a two-platoon system. A plain speaker and fair-handed dealer, Bideker fought for labor reform while at the same time instituting tough disciplinary actions upon those firefighters who did not measure up to his standards of professional behavior and ability.

Aftermath of the disastrous "south side fire", April 3, 1909

(Courtesy Jim Noah)

In 1907, the old original Fire Hall was demolished and a new No. 1 built on the site. Several new hose wagons and a new aerial truck were ordered. A change in the firefighters work schedule came, and with an annual budget that now exceeded $75,000, Fort Worth fire officials considered the department fit to cope with even the worst kind of catastrophe. On the windy afternoon of April 3, 1909, that catastrophe occurred.

The South Side Fire started shortly before 1:00 P.M. as two barns were reported to be burning. As the clouds of black smoke began to cover the downtown area, the fire spread from roof to wood shingle roof over a wide area. The fire, assisted by a strong gale from the southwest, quickly outdistanced the companies. The intense heat melted the copper telegraph wires and the Chief called a general alarm from a telephone. Dallas responded to a call for assistance by dispatching a special train, an engine with a boxcar for the horses, a flatcar for a steamer, and a caboose for the firefighters. Fort Worth's Engine No. 8 crashed while veering to avoid a pushcart peddler on the way to the blaze. Hose Co. No. 5 was lost as a horse slipped on the brick pavement and broke a leg. Company No. 1 arrived and prepared to attack the wall of fire, but the radiating heat of the blaze set the hoses on fire before firefighters could get water in them. The Dallas engine unloaded their steamer at the Texas & Pacific Depot only to learn they were to return to Dallas where they were needed at their own conflagration.

Within three hours the fire consumed everything in its path. The only thing that stood between the inferno and downtown was the Texas & Pacific railroad "reservation" with their roundhouse and shops. The structure formed a natural barrier, with little to burn. As the depot was consumed, the firefighters gained control and breathed a sigh of relief. The city's downtown had been spared and the Department had fought "the big one". The toll was staggering, but by no means as bad as it could have been. Only one life was lost but more than 290 homes and businesses lay in smoldering ashes over an area that extended twenty-six square blocks. The fire's cause was ruled accidental. Two boys, about eight years old, had apparently been experimenting with smoking in one of the barns.

In 1909, when Fort Worth annexed North Fort Worth City, the two North Fort Worth Fire Stations became No. 11 & 12. That same year, the city made a purchase that moved the Fire Department into the young decade in style.

The Fort Worth Fire Department, along with the American people, joined the motorized world with a car for Chief Bideker, two combination chemical and hose wagons and the American LaFrance truck. In 1917, many Fort Worth firefighters took leave to fight in World War I; they returned to a city that had grown from a meat packing town to a booming center for oil speculation. By 1919, the transformation from horse to motor-driven apparatus was complete. The city purchased eight new LaFrance trucks and the last sixteen horses and wagons along with all harness were sold. The modern Fire Department had truly begun.

A 1911 fire consumed the horse and mule barns during the annual Stock Show, resulting in the construction of the fireproof "mule alley" barns in the Stockyards.

Courtesy Dalton Hoffman, Jr. Collection

In 1945 the Worth building burned at 7th and Main Streets

(Courtesy Jim Noah)

By the end of the 1920's the department had expanded tremendously. In 1930, the First Aid team was formed. Operating throughout the depression and the Second World War under the command of Battalion Chief Johnny O'Brien, the team became the forerunner of today's Emergency Medical Technician. Perhaps the most significant development for Fort Worth Firefighters during the period came with the institution of Civil Service regulations. Before 1925, there were no standardized entrance requirements for incoming firefighters. After July 25, 1925, the regulations insured a higher level of professionalism and competence in both the Fire and Police departments.

The severe economic depression of the 1930's cast a dark pallor over the spirit of America. Some citizens, fearing the repossession of their homes because of their inability to meet mortgage payments burned their homes for the insurance money. By the mid-30's the department received four to five such calls per day. The tragedy of economic collapse cut deeply and directly into the personal lives of the firefighters. Short on funds, the city government began to pay firemen in promissory warrants rather than in negotiable checks. While some banks agreed to cash the warrants, most charged three percent of the notes as a service fee. At the same time, across-the-board pay cuts affected every Fort Worth municipal employee.

By the mid-1930's, the winds of change had begun to blow in Fort Worth. In 1931, Jack Bostick,

The first 65 foot "Snorkle" truck for Fort Worth. This photo was taken in 1960 on the Chambers Street bridge at I 30 (now demolished) with the Fort Worth skyline in the background. Driver is Alvie Lee Pruitt.

(Courtesy Jim Noah)

a young idealist intent upon going to law school joined the department. A natural leader with a talent for organizing and negotiation, Bostick rallied rank-and-file support for the creation of a Firefighters Union. As pressure grew for the right of firefighters to collectively bargain, department employees petitioned the International Association of Fire Fighters for a charter. The petition was granted by the authority of the American Federations of Labor on August 29, 1935. The charter of the new Fort Worth Fire Fighters Association granted local firemen the right to collectively bargain and instituted a system for the orderly presentation of grievances. However, state law forbade the City of Fort Worth to even recognize the association, and any gains were made only after many frustrating tries. Bostick became the secretary-treasurer of the new organization. He was elected president of the group many years later. From its beginnings, the association strenuously campaigned for the passage of a series of legislative acts designed to improve firefighters pay, job security and working conditions. Late in the 30's the Association succeeded in having a bill introduced into the Texas Legislature setting an increased minimum salary for firefighters in Texas' four largest cities. The Fort Worth Fire Fighters Association was instrumental in forming the Texas State Association of Firefighters, the legislative voice for the states firefighters which is based in Austin. Jack Bostick served forty-five years on the Fort Worth Fire Department. When he retired in 1977, he left behind a legacy of successful activism that will long be remembered and appreciated. His devotion and unselfishness brought firefighters throughout the state of Texas, as well as the nation, a dignity and purpose unknown to them before him.

World War II brought a bomber plant to Fort Worth and workers flocked to the assembly lines. By 1941 the municipal limits of the city had expanded to cover 100 square miles. Despite twenty-one Fire Stations, the department found itself barely able to keep up with the demands upon its services. As soon as the war ended, the department was able to purchase the equipment it desperately needed. Numerous fires plagued the city in 1945, and in November of that year, hundreds of gallons of anti-freeze exploded at the Jno. Miller Auto Supply Company. The combined efforts of fifteen companies were required to bring the four-alarm blaze under control.

In 1954, the "Sparky Fire Department", conceived by Captains L. E. Koch and W.S. ("Fireman Bill") Pierce, began presenting demonstrations at local schools. Created with the specific intention of educating children to the dangers of playing with matches and other flammable substances, Bill's programs won many accolades for its color and substance. Bill became a legend in his own time because of his ability to catch the attention and imaginations of the children.

Fire Safety Education Division was created within the Bureau of Fire Prevention in 1956. Captain Luther E. Koch, an assistant arson investigator whose hobby was the study of fire prevention methods, pioneered efforts to bring fire education to the residential and industrial community.

In 1959, KFJZ-TV debuted "Ranger Jim's Cartoon Clubhouse". The locally televised spots featured "Ranger Jim" Pratt and "Senior Clem" Candilera, with "Fireman" Jim Noah as a weekly guest. The show was designed to reach pre-school children; Noah drew cartoons, talked fire-safety, conducted poster contests and live firefighting demonstrations on the back lot. The program reached throughout the state as well as into neighboring states via Channel 11.

In 1959, citizen James R. Pirtle received the first Alfred S. Hayne Courage Award for saving the lives of an unconscious man and woman in their smoke-filled, flame-engulfed home.

Despite the spirited emphasis placed upon fire prevention, spectacular blazes continued to plague the city. In 1957, the Carpenter Paper Company's abandoned warehouse collapsed as firefighters battled the three-alarm blaze. Sixty-five firefighters and fifteen pieces of apparatus were called to the fire. Four men were hurt, two (Lieutenant E. W. McAlister and Rookie Donald Peacock) seriously, and one truck severely damaged. Although the fire was extinguished in four hours, smoke continued to curl over the city for most of the evening.

As the increasing number of high-rise fires became a primary concern for fire departments throughout the United Sates, the Fort Worth Fire Department took an experimental step toward combating the problem when it purchased the first "Snorkle" in the state of Texas. The 1960's saw major advancements in emergency medical rescue techniques and equipment, as well as improvement in firefighter

"Fireman Bill", Captain William S. Pierce, entertained and enlightened thousands of Fort Worth's school children with his Fire Safety Program

(Courtesy Jim Noah)

1966, a car wreck brings the Emergency Medical Technicians into play as a resuscitator is used to assist a victim while EMT's work to free the other trapped passenger.

(Courtesy Jim Noah)

training. L. P. Cookingham conceived the idea of "Squad 2", the forerunner to Fort Worth's Emergency Medical Team. Today, all members of the department are certified E.M.T.'s . In 1961, Bob Gibson organized the departments Diving Team.

Perhaps the most significant improvement in Fort Worth fire service training came with the opening of the Fire and Police Training Center in 1967, a result of the intensive campaign by District Chief J. D. Allison under Chief H. A. Owens. The center proved to be an immediate success, setting an example which continues to be studied by municipalities nationwide.

The effectiveness of the improved training programs underwent several severe tests in the late 1960's – a four-alarm fire devastated the old Curtis Mathis plant, the Tandy Mart & Bowling Alley, the blaze in which eight people died at Lucky's Grave on West Vickery Blvd., and the Fort Worth Star Telegram building that burned in 1968. This fire marked the first day that a newspaper was not published in the city for more than a half-century. A push to revitalize the department resulted in a drastic surge in fire equipment purchases between 1960 and 1969.

From Fire Station No. 4, 1973, "Blossom" rides with Pvt. Louie Hobbs

(Courtesy Jim Noah)

In 1981 the Rivercrest Country Club burned

(Courtesy Jim Noah)

Two spectacular blazes marked the 1970's – November of that year, a the driver of a truck loaded with 9,600 gallons of propane failed to negotiate the East Lancaster exit on the Martin Luther King, Jr. Highway (then called the Poly Freeway). As the truck tumbled, its tank ruptured and exploded igniting a fireball that was seen more than fifty miles away. The tank dropped down onto the incoming lane of the freeway and the end catapulted like a rocket into the night air. Airborne for an estimated four city blocks, the tank crashed into a three-story masonry building at the Pat Crow Forge Company. The driver was killed instantly, but no one else was seriously injured.

Few firefighters will argue that the most tragic fire of the 70's took place in July, at the abandoned Leland Hotel on Commerce Street. This four-alarm blaze took the life of Engineer Travis Jackson, of Ladder 5, who repeatedly entered the smoke-filled building.

In 1972, the department formed the "Bomb Squad", and by 1973, the 100th anniversary of the Fort Worth Fire Department, the first phase of a plan to renovate the communications division began. The 80's brought the Computer Assisted Dispatch (CAD) system and improvements continued well into the 90's.

Today the sophistication and scope of the Fort Worth Fire Department far exceeds that wildest dreams imagined by Captain Paddock as he sat alone on the steps of the courthouse that night in 1873. Yet, despite the modernized equipment, rapid communications, and decentralized fire station system, it is the people who have made the Fort Worth Fire Department the pride of the South. In the future, the department promises to continue the commitment to excellence begun over 120 years ago by the Hook and Ladder Company No. 1.

Firefighters who have lost their lives in the line of duty:

Dick Rockett — Jan 1902
John Bennett — July 1911
Harry Slate — April 1914
L. E. Ferguson — July 1914
J. E. Sadler — July 1916
Frank Bishop — May 1925
Frank Massengale — June 1927
B. O. Keeton — Dec 1928
O. H. Redden — Jan 1929
J. F. Powell — Oct 1932
G. E. Wilson — Oct 1932
Lee Payne — Dec 1932
John O'Donnell — Jan 1937
O. W. McCain — Sept 1938
Eddie Westmoreland — Sept 1938
V. B. Murphy — Nov 1939
T. J. O'Brien — Nov 1939
W. H. Bargsley — April 1941
H. H. Williams — July 1951
Earl Warren — July 1961
Hubert Barham — Nov 1969
M.E. Kays — May 1972
Travis Jackson — July 1973
Joe Buswold — Jan 1981
C. L. Smith — Dec 1982
R. L. Keen — Jan 1985
Brian Collins — Feb 1999
Phillip Dean — Feb 1999

A gasoline transport had just taken on a full load when an auto collided with the truck at 28th Street and North Sylvania. The resulting fire spread quickly and gas entered the sewer system, creating the blaze from the manhole

(Courtesy Jim Noah)

Firefighters Will Gregg (left) and Mike Wynne rescue a woman who drove her car into Sycamore Creek.

(Courtesy Jim Noah, photo Dale Blackwell)

Fort Worth Police Department Milestones:

1873 The first police force has four sworn officers, but is disbanded one month later.

1873 First jail is constructed at 2nd & Commerce behind Fire Hall # 1 at a cost of $493.00

1876 Jim "Longhair" Courtwright is appointed as the city police officer, with two officers under him

1883 First detective and first traffic officer are appointed; traffic officer works at intersection of 3rd & Main on Trade Days

1887 First permanent police force is created, consisting of two mounted officers, two patrolmen, one jailer, and two sanitary officers (to clean streets); often prisoners escape log jail due to poor construction

1889 Set of regulations are adopted and standard uniform is designed; hours are 12 hour days, seven days a week.

1905 Fort Worth joins the Texas State Bureau of Information

1907 First woman is hired to serve as police matron

1909 First motor vehicle goes into service; a 5 hp Indian Motorcycle; first traffic ticket; Henry Lewis was first motorcycle officer; he patrols the 100 block of W. 7th St.

1911 First motorized patrol wagon is put on line

1914 First patrol car is placed in service

1923 First STOP sign - located at 13th and Jennings

1925 Police Department is placed under Civil Service

1933 Halloween night, first police car is dispatched by radio; a report of pranksters throwing rocks; Sgt. Rip Burks sends out the call on his radio, which can only transmit

1939 First two-way radio is installed

1943 First policewomen – ten women officers are working Traffic Detail

1947 The Fort Worth Star Telegram reports: "Gone are the days when a rookie cop walked about with a veteran for a few days, then was handed the badge; today's policemen are put through an intensive school with lectures on every phase of the law."

1948 Police Officers Association is formed

1949 Department issues capshield, badge and ticket book – officer buys all other equipment

1954 First Radar speed check

1956 First teletype machine is added to the department

1959 First one officer patrol unit

1960's First Wrecker & Ambulance ordinances are drafted; first radar in Texas; first Helicopter in Texas

1961 Police Crime Laboratory opens and the Rehabilitation Center near Lake Worth opens

1965 Texas Legislature creates minimum standards for police officers

1968 First community relations unit is formed

Chiefs

Cato Hightower	1953 - 1969
T. S. Walls	1969 - 1976
A. J. Brown	1976 - 1979
H. F. Hopkins	1979 - 1985
Thomas Ray Windham	1985 - present

1925	1925
Debut of Fort Worth Symphony Orchestra; Fort Worth receives air mail - first in Texas	***Fort Worth Club moves into its new Seventh Street building; H. C. Meacham elected Mayor, serves until 1927***

Fort Worth Motorcycle Officers pose for a group photo in fornt of Will Rogers Memorial Center

(Courtesy of Fort Worth Police Department)

Motor Officer Bob Armstrong, 1931

(Courtesy of Fort Worth Police Department)

1927

Charles Lindberg lands in Fort Worth; William Bryce elected Mayor, serves until 1933

1929

Cook Memorial Hospital opens; Rose Hill Burial Park, later Shannon Rose Hill, founded; Blackstone Hotel built

In June of 1951, the Fort Worth Police Department welcomed General McArthur and his wife, shown here escorted by Officer Jim Stout upon arrival

(Courtesy of Fort Worth Police Department)

(Courtesy Fort Worth Police Department)

The following members of the Fort Worth Police Department lost their lives in the line of duty:

Frank Coffey	June 1915
George G. Gresham	April 1920
John D. Bell	Aug 1924
Frank Maco	Dec. 1926
George Turner	May 1928
W. O. (Dub) Whatley	Aug 1949
Henry C. Cleveland	Feb 1952
Namon L. Cox	June 1952
Charles W. Hoffman	June 1952
James L. Dowdy	June 1956
Claude H. Harmon	Oct 1957
Loy H. Walton	May 1959
Hal C. Stephenson	Oct 1968
Edward M. Belcher	Oct 1971
Wm. Vernon Welch	May 1973
H. Paul Malloux	Nov 1975
Ludwig Bruno	Mar 1977
Randy L. Fletcher	Aug 1977
Jesse R. Parris	Sept 1977
Jimmie F. Chadwell	Dec 1978
James C. Gaul	Jan 1979
Ken W. Pendergraft	April 1980
Darrel G. Moon	July 1980
Robert F. Camfield	Nov 1983
Walter S. Taylor	Oct 1988
Brent D. Wilson	Sept 1992
Donald J. Manning	June 1993
Alan F. Chick	Dec 1993
Jesse D. Moorman	Mar 1994

(Courtesy Fort Worth Police Department)

Education

This school, built in 1879, was relocated from Marine Creek. It is the oldest standing school in what was originally the North Fort Worth Public School System

(Landmark Staff Photo)

Special thanks to Mr. Billy W. Sills who provided the photographs from the Fort Worth Independent School District Archives, along with much of the text for this section. Mr. Sills retired from the Fort Worth Independent School District after forty years of teaching Social Studies at Meadowbrook and Eastern Hills. He also served as Social Studies Consultant for the Fort Worth Independent School District, and lead the efforts of the Tarrant County Historical Commission in rallying the children of the county in supporting the rededication of the Horse Fountain located on the lawn of the Tarrant County courthouse.

The Fort Worth High School, called the "finest school building in Texas" by some, opened to students for the district in 1891 as its first permanent high school. It was located on South Jennings between Jarvis and Daggett Streets, and it also served as the system's administration building. It burned December 2, 1910.

(Courtesy of the Billy W. Sills Center of the Fort Worth Independent School District Archives)

1930

Harris Hospital opens

1930

Sinclair Building completed

Old Fort Worth University, 1891. In 1918 Central High School was built on this site facing Cannon Street. Later the new school would become Paschal High School and eventually Trimble Technical High School

(Courtesy Fort Worth Public Library)

Central High School was renamed for a former principal, R. L. Paschal

(Courtesy the Quentin McGown Postcard Collection)

1930
Public Market completed

1930
Lake Worth freezes

Built in 1905, North Fort Worth Public School was later known as M. G. Ellis School
(From the Quentin McGown Postcard Collection)

Fort Worth High School, 1910-1918, was later known as Jennings Avenue Jr. High
(From the Quentin McGown Postcard Collection))

Miss Lily B. Clayton in this late 1890's faculty meeting in the high school's library is the only lady on the left not wearing a hat. Mr. Ernest Parker, for whom the first junior high school was named, is the first man from the left.
(Courtesy of the Billy W. Sills Center of the Fort Worth Independent School District Archives)

Superintendent E.E. Bramlette is seated at the center with some of the 1897 staff in this picture just outside the high school building. R.L. Paschal is second from the left of the five men standing in the top row just below the ladies in the center *(Courtesy of the Billy W. Sills Center of the Fort Worth Independent School District Archives).*

First Ward School, one of two almost identical frame buildings, was built in 1883 at East Second Street and Crump for the new Fort Worth Public Schools. Later it would be named the Crockett Elementary School.
(Courtesy of the Billy W. Sills Center of the Fort Worth Independent School District Archives).

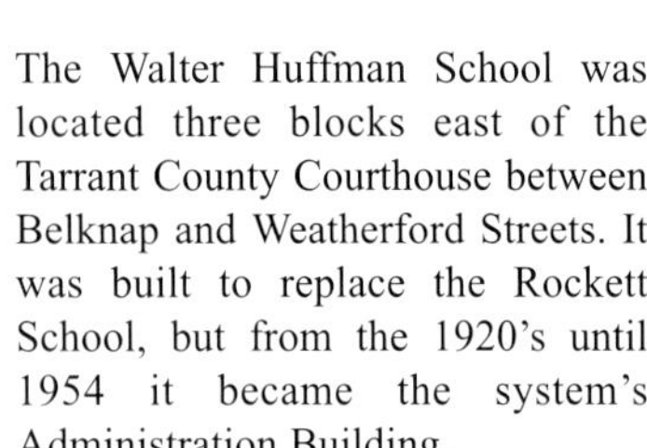

The Walter Huffman School was located three blocks east of the Tarrant County Courthouse between Belknap and Weatherford Streets. It was built to replace the Rockett School, but from the 1920's until 1954 it became the system's Administration Building.
(Courtesy of the Billy W. Sills Center of the Fort Worth Independent School District Archives.

The Ninth Street Colored School, a frame structure built about 1884, was located at Ninth and Pecan and was the first Fort Worth Public Schools building constructed to house black students in the district. It was often referred to as Professor Terrell's school.
(Courtesy of the Billy W. Sills Center of the Fort Worth Independent School District Archives.

The Fort Worth Colored High School, the first brick high school for black students opened May, 1910, at East Twelfth and Steadman. In 1921 it was renamed to honor former principal, I.M. Terrell. In 1942 its name became George Washington Carver School and, before it closed, it was known for several years as the Carver-Hamilton Elementary School.
(Courtesy of the Billy W. Sills Center of the Fort Worth Independent School District Archives.

Charles Nash Elementary School. A 1946 view of this unique architecture as seen from the corner of Samuels Avenue and Peach St. Located at 401 Samuels, the school was built in the 1930s.

(Courtesy of the Billy W. Sills Center of the Fort Worth Independent School District Archives.

North Side High School, late 1930's

(Courtesy the Quentin McGown Postcard Collection)

1933

U. S. Post Office opens on W. Lancaster; R. E. Cox store opens

1934

Fort Worth Botanic Gardens established; Last Interurban electric train runs between Fort Worth and Dallas

This was Arlington Heights High School from Ca 1920's until the school moved to the building now known as W. C. Stripling

(Courtesy of Acme Brick)

This is a view of Polytechnic High School, built in the 1930's

(Fort Worth Public Library)

Trinity Valley School, known for academic achievement and innovative learning approaches, is located on an eighty-five acre property in a rapidly growing suburban area.

(Courtesy Carter & Burgess)

Following are only a few of the prominent local athletes, the Fort Worth schools they attended, and their achievements

Name	Schools	Achievements
Herman Clark	North Side TCU	High School Coach, Poly, North Side. Paschal, Tremble Tech, Arlington Heights, and others; FWISD Athletic Director
Darrow Hooper	North Side Texas A &M	Olympics Bronze Medal winner in shotput and Texas A &M discus; won state in the late 40's, became multiple Southwest Conference champion in both weights;
James Cash	Terrell TCU	Harvard Professor; first black basketball player in the Southwest conference
Julius Truelson	Oakcliff (Dallas) TCU	Coach Carter-Riverside; Arlington Heights; Principal; Superintendent FWISD
Walter Day		Coach Terrell' Principal O.D. Wyatt, author
Richard O'Neal	Poly TCU	Board of Educators; top scorer and rebounder on championship TCU basketball team in mid 50's; very active in civic and school business; orthodontist
Lon Goldstein	Poly TWC	Pro basketball; Coach Carter-Riverside; Athletic Director FWISD
Tommy Thompson	Paschal University of Tulsa	Pro quarterback Philadelphia Eagles (Champs)
Frank Ryan	Paschal Rice	Quarterback with Cleveland Browns; he and King Hill alternated as quarterback in Rice SWC championship season in mid 50's
Yale Lary	North Side Texas A & M	All pro with Detroit Lions; excellent punter at Northside, top defensive back, Texas A & M
Jack Billingsley	Paschal TCU	coach, Assistant athletic director, athletic director, assistant superintendent Fort I.S.D.
Jim Shofner	North Side TCU	pro player & coach; TCU coach NFL coach
Turner Gill	Arlington Heights Nebraska	Assistant Coach Nebraska

(Information provided by Jack A. Billingsley and Bill Morgan)

Farrington Field, Fort Worth, Texas. *(Quentin McGown postcard collection)*

Texas Wesleyan University

The Polytechnic Methodist Church, built in 1909, today houses the Texas Wesleyan University School of Fine and Performing Arts
(Courtesy Texas Wesleyan University)

(Courtesy Texas Wesleyan University)

Texas Wesleyan University, founded in 1890 in Fort Worth, Texas is a United Methodist institution with a tradition integrating the liberal arts and sciences with professional and career preparation at the undergraduate level and in selected graduate areas. Founded as a private school by the church, Wesleyan is the oldest continuously operating university in Tarrant County.

Believing that the primary goal of education is the development of students to their full potential as individuals and as members of the world community, the University strives to give students opportunities to grow intellectually and spiritually. Texas Wesleyan is committed to the principles that each student deserves personal attention and that all members of the academic community must have the freedom to pursue independent thought and to exercise intellectual curiosity. To this end, the University actively seeks and employs faculty with commitment and education to teaching and inspiring students and staff who provide a wide range of support services. The University also accepts its responsibility to the community by providing leadership and talent through programs that improve society.

With the advantages of a small student body, the University serves a diverse student population drawn from the Fort Worth/Dallas metropolitan area but with a significant number from national and international sources. Texas Wesleyan supports the variety of ages and the cultural, ethnic, and socio-economic backgrounds of its students.

The purpose of the University is to create a learning environment where personal attention provides each student an opportunity to pursue individual excellence, to think clearly and creatively, to develop a spiritual sensitivity and commitment to moral discrimination and action, and to develop a sense of civic responsibility. In its undergraduate programs, Texas Wesleyan fosters an appreciation of the role of arts, sciences, and humanities in students' cultural development and prepares students to use their knowledge in productive careers. Whether in its undergraduate or professional programs, the University endeavors to produce individuals who become informed, responsible, creative, and articulate citizens.

(Courtesy Texas Wesleyan University)

Dan Waggoner Hall, designed by Sanguinet and Staats and built in 1917 houses the School of Education

Texas Wesleyan University

(Photos Courtesy Texas Wesleyan University)

Texas Christian University

Nestled in the heart of Fort Worth, amid tree-lined streets, purple and white flowered gardens, buff-yellow brick buildings and bustling students, lies Texas Christian University. This acclaimed Fort Worth institution has grown from a small school on the cattle frontier to a major center of independent higher education located in a dynamic city.

Brothers Addison and Randolph Clark dreamed of establishing a lasting institution dedicated to education, diversity, creativity, objectivity and rationality. Thus, the groundwork for TCU was laid in 1873 in Thorp Springs, Texas - forty miles southwest of Fort Worth. In 1885, the college moved to Waco, but a 1910 fire destroyed the campus. That year, Fort Worth promised the college $200,000 and fifty acres on which to begin again.

Throughout the years, Fort Worth has realized a solid return on its original investment. It is estimated that TCU's current annual financial impact on the community is $700 million. With an endowment of approximately $800 million, Barron's has listed TCU as a "best buy" among American colleges and universities.

TCU is defined in many ways by its location and friendly atmosphere. The university is affiliated with the Christian Church (Disciples of Christ), a denomination that embraces openness, tolerance and unity. TCU's spirit and style proclaim inclusiveness and individuality. A strong sense of independence and community, as well as a "just-right" size, are accurate reflections of the city of Fort Worth.

With an enrollment of approximately 7,000 students, TCU offers more than 100 undergraduate and graduate areas of study in addition to six doctoral programs. It features eighteen NCAA sports as a Division 1-A college, the highest level of college athletics. And it is a university with global reach through international activities - the university recently opened the TCU London Centre.

Growth is not confined to students' outlook and education. The school itself is constantly developing. Under Chancellor William E. Tucker's reign from 1979 to 1998, the university doubled the size of the library and added several buildings, including the Charles Tandy Hall housing the M. J. Neeley School of Business, the Winthrop P. Rockefeller Ranch Management Building, the Walsh Complex for Weight Training and Rehabilitation, the Dee J. Kelly Alumni and Visitors Center and the Mary D. and F. Howard Walsh Center for Performing Arts.

TCU is embarking into the next millennium under the leadership of Dr. Michael R. Ferrari, a respected university administrator with a reputation for one-on-one student relationships and a vision for future accomplishments.

From its inception, TCU has been about people, education and opportunity, That commitment to individual excellence will continue through the next hundred years and beyond, on the campus, in the city and throughout the world.

1937	1938
W. J. Hammond elected Mayor, serves until 1938	*Franklin D. Roosevelt approves $165,000 for WPA to build Farrington Field; R. H. W. Drechsel serves as Mayor from May to July; T. J. Harrell is then elected and serves until 1940*

Early shot of Texas Christian University Campus
(Courtesy Texas Christian University)

(Courtesy of the Quentin McGown Postcard Collection)

Texas Christian University Alumni Center

(Courtesy Freese & Nichols, Inc.)

Texas Christian University

(Courtesy of the Quentin McGown Postcard Collection)

Davey O'Brien
. . . excerpts from Spring 1978 "This is TCU"

No single name is more synonymous with TCU athletics than that of David O'Brien. The diminutive "Little Davey" caught the nation's attention in the late 1930s as the giant-killer quarterback who led the Horned Frogs to the 1938 national championship - and its only undefeated, untied season - and became the first and only man to win the Heisman, Camp and Maxwell trophies in the same year.

A winner not only in collegiate foot-ball but also in his years in professional ball, as a special FBI agent and later in private business, he was a "living legend" dedicated to service to others. On a plaque presented him by Philadelphia Eagles owner Bert Bell at the close of the 1940 National Football League season, he was described as "The greatest player of all time . . Small in stature with the heart of a lion . . . A living inspiration to the youth of American . . ."

The spirited, little firecracker's exploits in the Purple and White uniform set records that have stood for almost 40 years. After playing as a sophomore behind Sammy Baugh in 1936, Davey became the signal-caller the next season and was a four-way threat - running, punting, passing and playing the secondary - in an era when specialists were almost nonexistent. During his senior season he paced the team to 11 straight wins, including a 15-7 victory over Carnegie Tech in the Sugar Bowl, as it amassed 290 points to its opponents' 90 and the "No. 1 in the Nation" title.

Davey, who earned a B.A. degree with a major in geology in 1939, played in every game for three seasons. Never taking a time-out for an injury, he was nicknamed "The Oaken Knot" by sportswriters. In a Dallas Morning News interview, he recalled that the only two injuries he ever received were during his growing-up years in Dallas - a sprained ankle when he was on the Gaston Avenue Bulldog teams and a shoulder injury as a Woodrow Wilson High all starter.

Record books take note of the fact that he actually handled the ball in 562 plays on passes, punts, runs, punt and kickoff returns and interceptions - an average of 56 times per game - - in the 1937 season he fielded and ran back 63 punts and punted 24 times for a game record. His career statistics show no fumbles, most touch-down passes in one season, only four interceptions in 194 attempts while stacking up 1,457 passing yards and a 30-year record of 21 career touchdown passes. The record goes on to list his being conference leader in five different departments, 18 career interceptions, a three-year varsity total of 1,123 yards on punt returns and, as humorously recalled by the record-setter, being the shortest football player ever honored by a Wall Street ticker-tape parade.

Davey O'Brien *(Courtesy TCU Athletics)*

"He was everything," according to his former coach L. R. "Dutch" Meyer. "He was the best play selector, the greatest field general I ever saw. When he started to run I thought he would get killed. But, you know, every time he got hit he bounced up like a rubber ball and started helping big guys to their feet. A 155-pounder helping 250-pound tackles get up. Man, I loved that."

While his gridiron feats were making him a unanimous choice for 13 all-America teams, he found time to be active in other campus activities such as the Bryson Club and the baseball team.

Earning a degree didn't end his athletic career. Instead his reputation followed him into professional football, where he signed with the Philadelphia Eagles for a then-impressive $12,000 bonus and a two-year contract that included a percentage of the gate receipts. As a rookie in 1939, he passed with such precision that he earned first-team honors as quarterback on the National Football League all-star team. During his two-year professional career, he set a record that still stands and earned all-pro recognition.

All of Davey's exciting experiences were not limited to the athletic field. On the final day of the 1940 NFL season, he and L. B. Hale, teammates in high school and at TCU, entered the Federal Bureau of Investigation. The two later were firearms instructors at Quantico, Va. Ten years with the FBI brought him into contact with the entire spectrum of criminal activity.

As a businessman, Davey became a part of the Texas oil industry in 1950. He was associated with the Hunt Oil Company, Gibbons Oil Well Servicing Company, the Dresser-Atlas Industries of Dallas and headed his own Fort Worth firm.

Whatever demands his vocation made on his life, Davey found time to fill many roles of leadership and service. With a lifelong interest in the development of youth, he served on the Metropolitan Board of the Fort Worth Young Men's Christian Association and played key roles in YMCA membership drives and capital campaigns. He served his alma mater as president of the TCU Alumni Association in 1957-58 in addition to other offices and in 1965 headed the Frog Club. He was chairman of the Tarrant County Democratic Party in 1956-61. Formerly a deacon in Northway Christian Church in Dallas, he and his family were members of University Christian Church.

Just as his accomplishments brought recognition to the Southwest during his playing days, memories of those actions by the spirited player with the impish grin brought personal awards to Davey. He was named to the Texas Sports Hall of Fame, the TCU Lettermen's Hall of Fame and the National Collegiate Football Hall of Fame. He donated his Heisman Trophy to the Texas Sports Hall of Fame for its permanent display.

In 1968 he was one of 25 men selected to receive Sports Illustrated's Silver Anniversary Award. Open to anyone who played senior varsity football, the award was based not on athletic prowess but on success in life in the 25 years following graduation.

The following year the TCU Alumni Association presented him the Frog o' Fame award during spring homecoming activities.

In his honor, the Fort Worth Club named its annual sports award the Davey O'Brien Trophy. The first presentation of the award, designated for the Southwest's top college athlete, was made to Earl Campbell, 1977 Heisman Trophy winner from the University of Texas at a formal banquet on Feb. 2.

"What I remember most from our first meeting was the man, Davey himself, real and human in his own eyes," said Dr. A. M. Pennybacker of University Christian Church, who conducted the O'Brien service. "I suspected that that was a maturity among all the honors not easily come by. But that first memory of mine has often been confirmed in the sharing of these recent years. After a seven-year battle with cancer that only a giant-killer could face and endure with optimism and words of encouragement for others, Davey died in November of 1977, following a five-month hospitalization.

"Let his legacy of accomplishments on the field and off, his devotion to the University he served in so many ways, his gratitude for our country and his service in its life, his endeavors in business, his national honors . . let them be a rich heritage."

Dedication of the Davey O'Brien Hall of Fame, February, 18, 1985. Left to right: Mrs. Richard Flutie, mother of winner Doug Flutie; Darren Flutie, brother of Doug Flutie; past winners Steve Young, Jim McMahon, Earl Campbell, Todd Blackledge, Mike Singletary, and former Cowboys Coach Tom Landry, guest speaker for the award dinner

(Courtesy Fort Worth CLub)

Southwestern Baptist Theological Seminary Chronological History

1901 Theological Department at Baylor University, Waco, Texas, was established.

1905 Baylor Theological Seminary founded from the Theological Department.

1908 March 14th, Southwestern Baptist Theological Seminary was founded as a separate entity from Baylor University. Original faculty include: B. H. Carroll (founder). Calvin Goodspeed, A.H. Newman, J. D. Ray, J. J. Reeve, L. R. Scarborough, and C. B. Williams.

1910 SWBTS moved to Fort Worth, Texas, and occupied Fort Worth Hall which was completed in October. W. T. Conner elected to the faculty.

1911 C. T. Ball elected to the faculty

1913 W. W. Barnes elected to the faculty. C. B. Williams elected as Dean.

1914 The building later designated Barnard Hall was constructed for the Women's Missionary Training School.

1921 The schools of Religious Education and Gospel Music were created to join the work of the School of Theology.

1925 Control of the Seminary passed from the Baptist General Convention of Texas to the Southern Baptist Convention. Jeff Ray elected as Chairman of the Faculty.

1930 W. W. Barnes elected as Chairman of the Faculty

1948 Groundbreaking for the Memorial Building (including Scarborough Hall, Truett Auditorium, the Rotunda, and Fleming Hall).

1949 The Memorial Building was completed and opened for classes.

1982 Construction completed on Roberts Library.

1995 Dr. Tommy Lea elected as Dean.

Fort Worth Hall, 1912

(Courtesy Southwestern Baptist Theological Seminary)

Rotunda, Southwestern Baptist Theological Seminary, 1959
(Courtesy Southwestern Baptist Theological Seminary photo by Floyd Craig)

Aeiral view of the campus of Southwestern Baptist Theological Seminary, 1953

(Courtesy Southwestern Baptist Theological Seminary Ralph D. Churchill, Barnes Aerial Surveys)

All Saints Health System History

In 1906, All Saints Episcopal Hospital, the first Protestant hospital facility in the city, celebrated its completion (Fort Worth's first hospital, Saint Joseph, a Catholic institution had opened in 1889). Located at the corner of Magnolia and Eighth Avenue, the brick structure housed 24 beds and a school of nursing. An adjacent dormitory housed the student nurses who comprised the bulk of the hospital staff. Registered nurse Alice Taylor was All Saints' first administrator, and physician services were supplied primarily by medical professors from Fort Worth's now bygone downtown medical school.

The chain of events leading to the establishment of All Saints actually began in 1896. A group of fifteen women, members of Trinity Episcopal Church, identified the need for additional hospital facilities to accommodate Fort Worth's rapidly growing population. Known as the "Comfort Band", the group applied for a hospital charter. Today, these founding women are considered All Saints' first Auxiliary group. The hospital charter was granted in 1900, and construction began soon after. The hospital was originally to be called "The Maria Hospital" in recognition of Comfort Band President Maria Beggs. It was then decided to place the hospital under the auspices of the Episcopal Church, and as a result of that affiliation, the hospital was renamed All Saints Episcopal Hospital. The dedication ceremony, conducted by Bishop Alexander C. Garrett, was appropriately scheduled on All Saints Day, November 1, 1906.

The hospital thrived as it served the city's rapidly growing population and in 1914 underwent its first expansion that brought the total number of beds to fifty. In those early years, the nursing school flourished as well.

In 1918, a new Nurses' Home was constructed. A maternity ward was added in 1921 to meet the increasing demand for hospital births. By the end of the 1920's All Saints had delivered over 500 newborn Fort Worthians. A three-story center section was built in 1926 that increased capacity to 62 beds, and added new surgery and delivery rooms, a new kitchen and boiler, and for the first time, elevator service. By 1928, the modern and efficient hospital was considered state-of-the-art, boasting two operating rooms, a combination emergency room/orthopedic room, and a fully equipped radiology department.

This period of growth for the hospital ended abruptly with the onset of the Great Depression. In 1929 patient admissions dropped from their 1928 high of over 2000, to less than half that number. Hospital-based medical care had rapidly become a luxury affordable only to the most affluent citizens. Compounding the effects of the Depression, the construction of three new Fort Worth hospitals, the Methodist Hospital, the Baptist Hospital, and Cook Hospital, was completed by 1931. In addition, St. Joseph's bed capacity was doubled during this same time period. As patient admissions declined, the financial stability of the community's hospitals began to falter.

By 1937, the All Saints Board of Trustees reluctantly resolved to close the hospital, however, a board committee negotiated a management contract with Dr. Truman C. Terrell. The contract required Dr. Terrell to furnish X-ray and laboratory services on a percentage of gross fees basis; rehabilitate and refurbish the hospital; and, underwrite its operating expenses for a reasonable period of time. Dr. Terrell fulfilled these obligations, and within two years the hospital was again operating profitably.

The end of the Depression heralded All Saints' second phase of significant expansion. In 1939, with Terrell's leadership and financial support, 33 more beds were added by converting the old nursing school quarters. In 1945, a fourth floor was added, bringing total bed capacity to 110.

As the city prospered, All Saints began yet another period of expansion to accommodate the growing population. In 1952, the All Saints nursing school revised its curriculum and was accredited as the first licensed school of vocational nursing in the city. Impetus for a new building program was first provided by a donation from Mr. and Mrs. A.E. Duncan in 1947. Mrs. Dora Roberts of Big Spring, Texas arranged for a generous donation to the hospital in her will. When she died in 1953, All Saints was able to purchase a site for a new hospital.

In 1952, responding to the acute shortage of hospital beds, local businessmen joined forces to create the Greater Fort Worth Hospital Fund, an organization designed to raise funds for all area hospitals. The campaign goal was set and solid progress was made with the help of substantial contributions from Amon Carter, Sid Richardson and W.A. Moncrief. All Saints' share of these funds was set at 21.5% of the total. Shortly after, plans for the new hospital were completed and ground breaking took place on July 18. The new All Saints Episcopal Hospital, an eight-story 365 bed facility, was dedicated on All Saints Day, November 1, 1959.

In the 1960's Fort Worth continued to grow and change. For All Saints, the following decades were heavily influenced by the socio-economic trends. In addition, American health care was subject to a dramatic proliferation of medical and technological advances. Determined to keep abreast of these developments, the hospital demonstrated a pattern of consistent response to the changing needs of Fort Worth and its residents. Work began in 1964 to increase bed capacity to 427. Demonstrating its progressive commitment to providing employee child care, the hospital dedicated the Sid W. Richardson Child Care Facility in 1970. All Saints completed the Moncrief Annex in 1973, increasing the total bed capacity to 533. Longtime supporters, Mr. and Mrs. W.A. Moncrief funded the hospital's acquisition of a computerized tomography (CT) scanner in 1977. In 1979, the Moncriefs celebrated their 61st wedding anniversary with a $2.5 million donation to All Saints that provided for the establishment of the Moncrief Radiation Center.

On November 1, 1981, in recognition of its 75th anniversary, All Saints held re-dedication ceremonies on All Saints Day. The 1980's represented a period of significant growth and expansion. All Saints extended its geographical scope in 1981 when it assumed management of the 100 bed Bishop Davies Center, an extended care facility located in suburban Hurst. In 1983, the Moncriefs again generously provided funding designated for All Saints' purchase of a nuclear

1906 — All Saints also opened the first school of nursing in Fort Worth.
(Courtesy All Saints Hospital)

magnetic resonance scanner. That same year, All Saints assumed management responsibility for a second suburban facility in nearby Haltom City.

All Saints achieved a first in 1984 when it recognized the need for quality home health services and established All Saints Home Care Services. By 1985 two new services were added to meet the outpatient needs of the community: the expanded Carter Rehabilitation Center, and the Moncrief Ambulatory Care Center. A third suburban hospital, All Saints Cityview, was opened in 1987.

For All Saints, the 1990's have witnessed a continuation of the trend toward more advanced and comprehensive services. All Saints opened The Heart Center, a full-service cardiovascular care facility, in 1991. Other special programs and centers include the All Saints Behavioral Health Center, the Wound Management Program, and All Saints' Lymphedema Center. By 1995, the organization began to expand throughout the metroplex with the establishment of All Saints Medical Associates. Primary care practices were opened in the Mid-Cities and in Springtown, and Parker County. In 1995, All Saints opened a new facility on its Eighth Avenue campus to accommodate astounding growth in outpatient services made possible by advancing technology. A concurrent expansion of the Carter Rehabilitation and Fitness Center doubled the size of the existing facility. The centerpiece of All Saints' Eighth Avenue campus was dedicated on All Saints Day, 1995.

All Saints is committed to providing the residents of Fort Worth and North Central Texas with state-of-the art medical care. In the process, All Saints' progressive facilities assist in the training of physicians, nurses, and medical technologists. All Saints is the home of the Terrell Center for Medical Technology, and continues to supply the area with licensed nurses by offering opportunities for clinical training in partnership with area colleges and universities.

Today, All Saints continues to play a pivotal role in offering quality health care, medical facilities, and health-related educational opportunities to the citizens of Fort Worth and beyond. All Saints Medical Associates, a network of primary care practices, has expanded to fifteen locations in three counties. It joins two acute care hospitals with a multitude of medical programs, to serve well over 100,000 people in our community each year. More than 900 staff physicians in dozens of medical specialties work daily to improve the health of our families, friends, and neighbors.

All Saints Hospital incorporated in 1983 as All Saints Health Care, Inc. (later changed to All Saints Health System), and implemented a new infrastructure to support the future growth and development of the system.

Like the first auxiliary group, the "Comfort Band", volunteerism continues to play an integral role in supporting and enhancing the professional services offered by All Saints Health System. Each month, over 300 active community members contribute more than 3,000 hours of their time to assist the patients and staff of All Saints, and in 1997 the All Saints Auxiliary opened a Guest House within the hospital, an innovative hotel for families of patients and the only one of its kind in the area.

All Saints will celebrate its one-hundredth anniversary in 2006, a milestone that few institutions in Fort Worth can claim. It is a history rich with civic support, medical advances, and lives restored by physicians and staff. Exemplifying the true spirit of community, what All Saints gives to its city, its city eagerly returns in kind.

All Saints Episcopal Hospital/Fort Worth, 1999
(Courtesy All Saints Hospital)

Cook Children's Medical Center More than 80 Years of Caring

It is not far, in terms of distance, from the current Cook Children's Medical Center, with its blue peak roofs and peaceful grounds, to the site where pediatric health care first began to take shape in Fort Worth more than 80 years ago.

Those years, however, have witnessed many remarkable changes in medical science's ability to care for children. And for more than 80 years, Cook Children's has grown steadily, expanding and adapting its services to meet the changing needs of children in Texas.

Looking Back

In 1918, a former postmistress, Ida L. Turner, stirred concerned individuals into taking the decisive steps to found the Fort Worth Free Baby Hospital to care for the sick and injured children of the area. Her interest grew from a chance encounter she had in November 1917. While she waited for a street car, a young doctor walked up carrying a sick infant who had been abandoned. The doctor was taking the child home while trying to find appropriate care. When Mrs. Turner offered to help, she soon discovered no facility for children's care existed in the city.

Mrs. Turner mobilized the City Federation of Women's Clubs, and activity progressed at a rapid pace. On March 21, 1918, 350 people attended the opening of the 25-bed Fort Worth Free Baby Hospital at 2400 Winton Terrace West.

More than a decade later, on January 17, 1929, the W. I. Cook Memorial Hospital opened its doors, adding to the growing strength of pediatric health care in Fort Worth. Matilda Nail Cook of Albany, Texas, honored the memory of her husband and daughter by providing generous shares of her oil royalties to build the 30-bed facility at 1212 West Lancaster Street. The Cook board of trustees decided in 1952 to serve children exclusively.

Fort Worth's last two giant strides toward pediatric health care as it is today came with the 1985 merger of Cook and Fort Worth Children's Hospitals and the 1989 opening of the current 181-bed Cook Children's Medical Center at 801 Seventh Avenue.

Today and Into the Future

In recent years, Cook Children's Medical Center has formed the foundation for a comprehensive Cook Children's Health Care System. The system also includes Cook Children's Physician Network, the largest physician network in Texas, and Cook Children's Home Health.

Today, Cook Children's Medical Center is designed to meet a full range of children's health care needs, from general medicine and rehabilitation services to advanced specialized care for conditions such as cancer, traumatic injury, heart disease, lung disease, and complications at birth.

Taking care of children, though, involves more than responding to illnesses and injuries. It also means working to prevent these from occurring. Cook Children's has become increasingly involved in advocacy issues related to children's health and safety and has become a leading voice in the campaign to ensure that all children have access to medical care.

Through the years, what has not and will not change, is the mission of Cook Children's to provide quality pediatric health care to all children in the community, regardless of a parent's inability to pay.

(Courtesy Cook Children's Hospital)

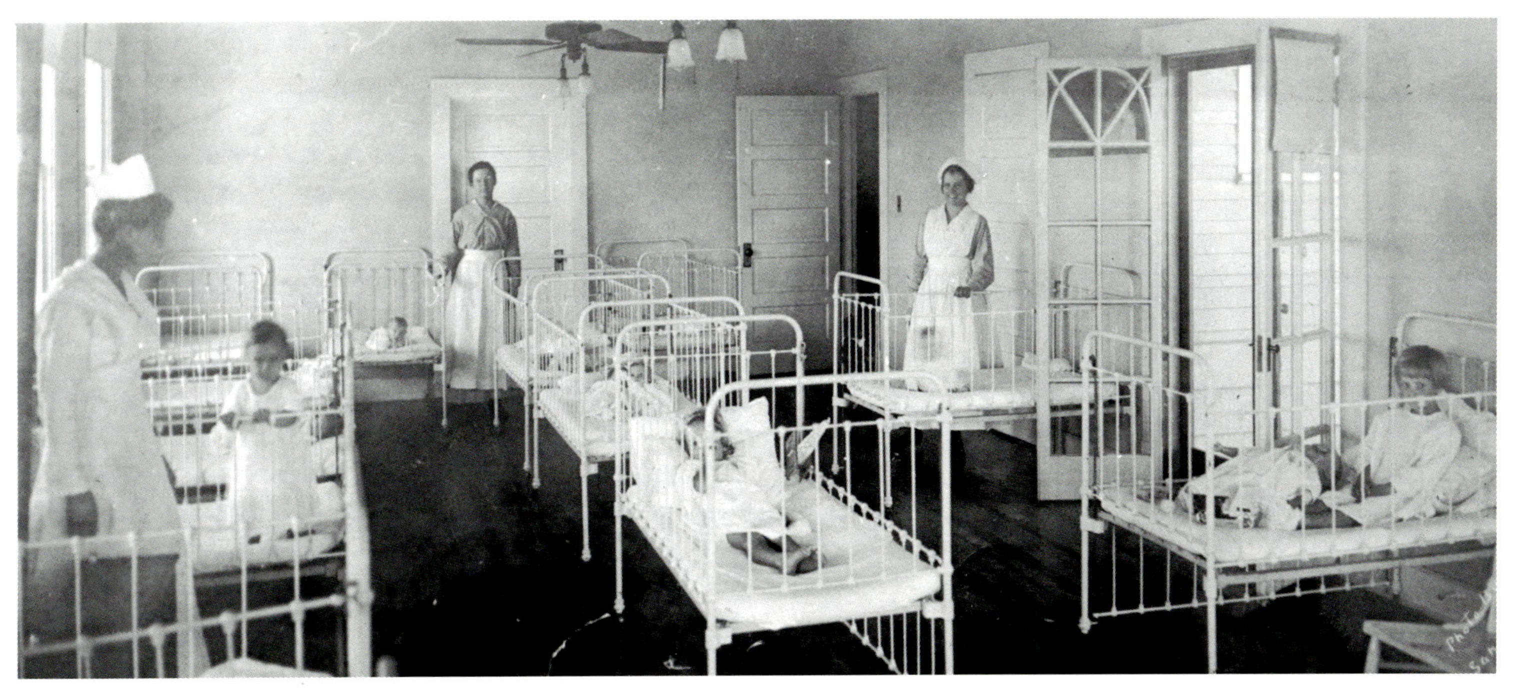

Cook Children's Hospital

(Courtesy Cook's Children's Hospital)

HARRIS METHODIST FORT WORTH HOSPITAL HISTORY

In 1912, Charles Harris opened a 50-bed hospital and nursing school at Fifth Avenue and Rosedale and furnished it with the finest equipment, including the first X-ray installed in Fort Worth. This clinic is where Methodist Hospital's roots lie.

In 1919, Harris approached a group of Methodist ministers about Fort Worth's need for a public hospital and offered his clinic as the foundation for the project.

In 1921, to appease the medical community's desire for a larger, more centrally located hospital, Harris trustees purchased the T. B. Yarbrough homestead at 1300 Cannon Street. Trustees paid $25,000 for the lot on which the hospital would be built.

Construction of Methodist Hospital began in 1923, but a lack of funds in 1926, left the building unfinished. The Rev. C.Q. Smith, hospital commissioner in 1927, obtained a loan to resume construction. Local businessman A.P. Barrett oversaw an additional drive in 1929 to furnish the new hospital. On March 3 1930, Methodist Hospital opened with accommodations for 100 patients and many unfinished floors.

Financial burden and a depressed economy caused the hospital to declare bankruptcy in 1937. Within a month, hospital trustees bought back the hospital for $253,000, made possible by a generous $53,000 gift from Harris as well as his guarantee of the balance.

In June 1937, the Board of Trustees approved a merger of Harris' institution and Methodist Hospital.

Methodist Hospital, as it was initially named, opened on March 3, 1930, more than 10 years after Dr. Charles H. Harris proposed the idea of a new hospital to a group of Methodist Church leaders. In the beginning, Methodist Hospital occupied one city block and was the largest hospital in Fort Worth.

The Methodist church maintained ownership and asked the surgeon to be the hospital's director for the next 20 years or until his death. The facility's name changed to Harris Memorial Methodist Hospital, in memory of Harris' father. In 1948, at the age of 79 and 11 years of service, Harris retired and transferred management to the Central Texas Conference. At that time, the Board of Trustees changed the institution's name to Harris Hospital, in honor of Harris and his service. Harris later moved into the hospital's rooftop apartment, where he lived until his death in January 1958.

The organization of the School of Medical Technology at Harris in 1939 was only the beginning of the hospital's education program. In 1942, the Charles H. Harris Trust Fund was established to fund the Harris College of Nursing. In 1946, the Harris College of Nursing became the first Texas nursing school and one of two Southern schools to receive national accreditation. The same year the nursing school became affiliated with Texas Christian University.

The Harris Methodist Fort Worth Hospital Auxiliary was founded April 17, 1940. Mrs. J.K. Wilkes served as first president of the Auxiliary.

Today, over 300 members strong, members of the Auxiliary greet patients and visitors at the information desks, while they answer the patient information telephone lines, operate the 5th Avenue Gift Shop, and provide numerous educational scholarships to area high school students.

In 1942, one of the first surgical recovery rooms in the country was developed at Harris.

In the 1950's, Harris Hospital also established an infant recovery room, the first in Fort Worth and the second in Texas.

Technological advances continued in 1958, when Harris Hospital opened the first intensive care unit in Fort Worth.

A team of 12 physicians, headed by Dr. Clive Johnson, made medical history in 1959 when they performed the first open heart surgery in Fort Worth.

Harris Hospital continued to enhance its services and make medical breakthroughs throughout the 1960s and saw rapid growth and numerous innovations, one of which was the opening of the Fannie M. Harris Hall for nursing students in 1960.

The hospital introduced a new radium storage and handling cart in 1962. The cart, the first of its kind in the nation, was used to transport radium supplies to patients in surgery. This same year, philanthropists Mr. and Mrs. O. C. Armstrong dedicated Armstrong Auditorium, located on the first floor of the Harris Building.

Made possible by a gift of the Jesse Jones Foundation of Houston, the Mary Gibbs Jones Building opened in 1963.

In 1989, the Helen McKee Ryan Birthing Center was opened on the first floor of the Mary Gibbs Jones Center for Women and Infants' Health. This birthing center, with the most modern design, facilities and the latest in technology was made possible through the generosity of the John P. Ryan family of Mr. Ryan's mother, Helen McGee Ryan, who was a beloved and distinguished citizen of Fort Worth. The center is officially dedicated to the health and well-being of all the mothers and their children who the department are privileged to serve.

Today, the Mary Gibbs Jones Center for Women and Infants' Health is considered a Level III (high risk) maternal and newborn referral center and over 5,000 babies are born here annually. The center also provides sensitive, individualized care for women needing surgical care/services during and after the childbearing years.

In addition, the building includes a newly remodeled state-of-the-art neonatal intensive care unit which provides optimal development and family-centered care to sick and premature newborns in order to maximize outcome potential. The spacious unit offers two private breast-feeding rooms, three rooming-in accommodations for families with full-size beds and private baths, a private consultation room, an abundance of glider rockers and uplifting and calming artwork.

A spacious reception/check-in area has been created and there is a comfortable lobby area, along with a private family lounge area.

Throughout the 1990's, the readers of Fort Worth Child magazine named HMFW the best place to have a baby. In 1996, Self magazine, a nationally-known women's health and fitness magazine, named HMFW as one of the top ten hospitals in the nation to have a baby.

Knowing the hospital's foundation is the Methodist church, Administrator at the time, Willard P. Earngey, Jr., and the hospital staff were pleased in 1966, when Harris became the first hospital in the metroplex to be accredited by the Association for Clinical Pastoral Educators as a training center for clinical pastoral care education.

Harris Hospital, Ca 1954.

(Courtesy Harris Hospital)

Education remained an important focus in 1970, when Harris established the first Respiratory Therapy School in Texas.

In 1971, Harris acquired a renal dialysis unit to treat patients with kidney disease. The unit's first treatment occurred in 1972, which is also when the hospital's beds capacity reached 606 beds and 98 bassinets.

Also in 1972, a new intensive care unit and the first intermediate intensive care unit opened. The intermediate unit featured four telemetry system devices, a gift from the Auxiliary, which allowed patients to be monitored while in bed or moving about the hospital. Harris Hospital was the first Fort Worth hospital to have equipment that permitted heart patients to be ambulatory.

The addition of a Cardiovascular Physiology Department expanded the hospital's cardiac treatment capabilities in 1976. Staff members performed the first heart catheterization the same year. By 1979, Harris was handling 83 % of all heart catheterizations in the county.

In 1988, the hospital dedicated Earngey Mall to honor Earngey's allegiance. The mall is an atrium walkway that connects the three main buildings found on the campus today.

With a $4 million gift from the Sid W. Richardson Foundation, Harris Methodist Fort Worth made new strides in patient care when it opened the Sid Richardson Pavilion, a six-story facility which included 18 surgical suites designed and created to help ensure that patients and visitors receive quality service. Today, the pavilion is home to 22 surgical suites and numerous private patient rooms.

The Castleberry Memorial Chapel, Harris Fitness Center, Plaza Café, Industrial Rehab Clinic and the Mabee Rehab Center are all located on the Pavilion's Plaza Level. The Industrial Rehab Clinic is home to the Commission on Accreditation of Rehabilitation Facilities (CARF-accredited) Work Trax Program and the Chronic Pain Management Program. The Rehab Center houses the CARF accredited Brain Injury Transitional Services program, occupational and physical therapy, speech/language pathology, and a hand clinic staffed by certified hand therapists and hand specialists. The Rehab Center includes a large gymnasium complete with computerized therapy equipment and the M.J. Neeley Pool, which is a large, heated therapy pool equipped with a wheelchair lift.

In 1995, the doors of the Klabzuba Tower opened to the public at 1300 West Terrell Street. Today, this tower houses the Klabzuba Cancer Center, the Doris Kupferle Breast Center, bone marrow transplant program, outpatient chemotherapy services, a cancer resource library, radiation therapy, cancer registry and research department, and a genetic risk assessment and counseling program.

Opened in 1990, the Doris Kupferle Breast Cancer Center is dedicated to the memory of Doris Kupferle, an elementary school teacher, who lived as a breast cancer survivor for 15 years. The Breast Center is equipped to screen, diagnose, treat and rehabilitate women with breast disease. A high-quality clinical staff and multidisciplinary "breast cancer care team," including education and support groups, are available to meet the needs of patients, families, and the community. The Breast Center is known for its mammography services, which include three in-house mammography units and two mobile mammography units, which travel to under-served areas to provide screening services and educate women about the importance of early detection of breast cancer.

Harris Methodist Fort Worth *(Courtesy Harris Hospital)*

The Harris Methodist Occupational Health Clinic, now located on Pennsylvania Avenue, provides businesses with programs aimed at reducing medical costs as well as improving and maintaining the health and well-being of the company's employees.

The Pavilion's mezzanine houses the W. H. McFadden Center for Digestive and Pulmonary Disease, a clinic for endoscopic procedures. The center was made possible by an endowment from Ella C. McFadden.

The third level features an 11-bed CARF accredited rehabilitation unit and a 19-bed skilled nursing unit. Here, patients have access to a community day room and an outdoor sun deck. Patient care rooms occupy the Pavilion's top three floors. Each room is comfortably furnished to offer the patient the most pleasant environment possible.

The Pate Helipad, located on the Clay J. Berry Parking Garage roof, allows quick access to the hospital's emergency and trauma departments. Made possible by Aggie M. Pate Jr., Joyce Pate Capper and Sebert L. Pate, the helipad can accommodate three CareFlite helicopters at once, if necessary.

Emergency transport by air can be traced back locally to 1965, when a Harris Hospital team joined forces with two Bell Helicopter pilots to air rescue a Hico patient with a blood disorder.

In 1999, CareFlite celebrated 20 years of service to the community with a simple message, "Twenty years of making precious minutes count".

Harris Methodist Fort Worth Hospital has a team of highly-trained personnel with specially equipped services to offer excellent emergency and trauma treatment. The 50-bed emergency department specializes in trauma, cardiac care, major medical and surgical cases, on-the-job injuries, minor emergencies, and obstetric, gynecological and orthopedic cases and more. Harris Methodist Fort Worth Hospital's Emergency department treats more than 65,000 patients annually. Dr. John Geesbreght has served as the department's medical director since 1974.

Recognizing that the citizens of Fort Worth had limited access to trauma care services, Harris Methodist Fort Worth Hospital began seeking trauma center status in 1984. Harris was designated as a trauma receiving facility by the Emergency Physicians Advisory Board (EPAB) in 1989.

To help provide a more comfortable atmosphere for patients and families, the emergency department has a separate minor medicine area away from the hustle and bustle of trauma. The minor medicine area houses ten private rooms.

In 1995, the Emergency Department received the prestigious Quality Cup Award in the Not-For-Profit category. This is a national award given by the National Institute of Technology and USA Today newspaper.

In 1999, construction began on a 98,000 square-foot, five-level brick veneer Critical Care Tower, which will centralize services needed for critically-ill patients. This $31.5 million project will build a tower at the corner of Cooper Street and Fifth Avenue on the south side of the hospital campus near the emergency entrance. The tower will house 64 critical care beds for trauma, neuro-science and medical-surgical ICU patients. Officials are doubling the patient room size to accommodate the increased technology now available and tripling support service space, and adding additional areas for family support and comfort. In addition, four additional ER "fast track" beds are being created.

Hospital officials wish to acknowledge the generosity of so many who have contributed of their time and financial resources over the years. Major benefactors include the Beatty, Carter, Castleberry, Davidson, Fuller, Jones, Klabzuba, Kupferle, Mabee, McFadden, Neeley, Pate, Richardson, Rowan, Ryan, Walsh and Ward families.

As Harris Methodist Fort Worth Hospital continues to grow and expand its services to meet the needs of the patients it serves, the residents of Fort Worth and area communities will surely benefit.

JPS HEALTH NETWORK HISTORICAL PERSPECTIVE

October 17,1877- John Peter Smith deeded land (5 acres) on South Main Street in Fort Worth "where the indigent of Fort Worth and Tarrant County could have the best of Medical Care."

1906- First city county hospital established as an affiliate of Fort Worth Medical College.

1913- Voters approved $200,000 bond issue for construction of new city county hospital at 4th and Jones adjacent to medical school.

1918- Medical College dissolved, property transferred to Baylor University.

1921-No longer have medical school students to staff city county hospital; paid medical staff hired; beds in operation increased from 25 to 80; outpatient clinic moved to building vacated by medical school.

1931- Facilities in use are "inadequate to meet present needs, "; 80 of the city's leading doctors give their services gratis; the hospital was built to house 80 patients and 108 are now housed there.

1937- New city council, mayor and city manager realize medical care in existing hospital is substandard; bonds in the amount of $137,000 issued to match Public Works Administration grant of $225,000 for construction of new hospital on South Main.

(Courtesy JPS Health Systems)

1938- Construction of 166 bed hospital begins on So. Main site donated by J. Peter Smith in 1877.

1939- New hospital is occupied.

1954- Name of hospital changed to John Peter Smith Hospital to honor man whose vision had provided site for the hospital.

1955- Hospital expanded to 195 beds with addition of third floor.

1959- inadequate financing has now resulted in inadequate health care for the indigent; election in April allows for creation of Tarrant County Hospital District.

1962- Outpatient clinics remodeled and expanded; Multi-phase renovation program begun.

1968- Phase I of construction plan completed including new emergency and radiology facilities, power plant, space for new cafeteria.

1969- Phase II included the finishing of dietary and cafeteria areas as well as new clinical and anatomical laboratory facilities, blood bank, pharmacy and laundry.

1971- Phase III, an eleven story tower completed on the exterior and the interior of five floors was completed and ready for occupancy.

1974-1976-Financial crisis hits district, major service reductions take place to avoid bankruptcy, beds closed, staff reduced; "loan" from county obtained to keep hospital open.

1982-New Outpatient Clinic Building dedicated.

1984- TCHD Board of Managers obtains permission from Tarrant County Commissioner's Court to hold general obligation bond election to provide major renovation and construction on hospital campus. Voters approve $49.5 million general obligation bond package.

March 1985-1986-1991 - Bond funded construction program included expansion of outpatient clinic building, floors 3 and 4, family care center, medical library, medical records

Since 1991 major expansion of community-based services have included the construction or renovation of health centers in neighborhoods throughout Tarrant County and the opening of programs in schools. the development of a new service location for obstetrical and gynecological care at the JPS Health Center for Women. JPS has also established special health fund to support development and operation of community services, and adopted JPS Health Network as the name of all operational units. JPS opened the Institute for Health Career Development, which includes School of Vocational Nursing, School of Radiologic Technology and career development and continuing education components. Residency training programs in psychiatry and podiatry have been added. A psychiatric evaluation center and skilled nursing unit were opened and JPS created a HIV/ AIDS treatment service including outpatient, same day care and inpatient services known as Healing Wings. JPS recently received licensure for subsidiary HMO, MetroWest Health Plan and became designated as Level II Trauma Center.

St. Joseph's Infirmary, under the auspices of the Roman Catholics, is one of the latest and finest of the public buildings erected in Fort Worth. The management and citizens are justly proud of this institution, which is said to be one of the best appointed and up-to-date hospitals in the south. (1907)

(From the collection of Quentin McGown)

St. Joseph's Infirmary, Ca 1935

(Courtesy of Acme Brick)

City-County Hospital, Ca 1935

(Courtesy of Acme Brick)

University of North Texas Health Science Center at Fort Worth

The University of North Texas Health Science Center is one of the nation's distinguished academic medical centers, dedicated to the advancement of all three disciplines of medical science —education, research, and patient care.

A 15-acre, $71 million medical complex located in Fort Worth's Cultural Arts District, the health science center injects some $244 million into Fort Worth's economy annually. In addition to the 1,145 people directly employed by the health science center, another 1,155 jobs in the Metroplex are supported through the center's presence here.

The health science center's educational components are the Texas College of Osteopathic Medicine (TCOM), the Graduate School of Biomedical Sciences, and the School of Public Health, with a combined faculty of more than 190, a staff of 900 and a cadre of some 300 volunteer community physicians.

TCOM is Texas' only college of osteopathic medicine, and one of only 19 in the nation. Roughly three-fourths of the almost 2,000 physicians it has trained since 1970 practice primary care, such as family medicine, internal medicine, obstetrics/gynecology and pediatrics. This is the highest proportion among the state's eight medical schools and one of the highest in the country. Since primary care is the linchpin of the medical managed care system now evolving, it is likely that most of our 449 current medical students will also pursue primary care careers, although their training prepares them to aspire to any specialty, from aerospace medicine to heart transplant surgery.

Since 1993, the graduate school has offered masters and doctoral degrees in the biomedical sciences, with specializations in anatomy and cell biology, molecular biology and immunology, pharmacology and integrative physiology.

In January 1999, a School of Public Health received state approval and will soon award Master of Public Health (MPH) degrees and Doctor of Public Health (DrPH) degrees. A Doctor of Philosophy (PhD) degree in epidemiology is planned for the near future.

In 1997, the health science center launched its first undergraduate program, offering a bachelor of science degree with a major in Physician Assistant Studies.

The center is also home to the Gibson D. Lewis Health Science Library, where virtually the entire wealth of the world's current medical knowledge is accessible to the public seven days a week through sophisticated information search networks and computer databases. In keeping with the center's location in Fort Worth's Cultural District, the campus also boasts a public art gallery.

Faculty members of the center's medical school constitute the Physicians & Surgeons Medical Group, Tarrant County's largest multi-specialty medical group practice. These 110 doctors practice in 24 medical and surgical specialties and subspecialties, including allergy/immunology, cardiology, neurology, oncology, pathology, sports medicine and neuro-surgery. More than 188,000 patient visits are logged each year to the health science center's network of 24 clinics and laboratories by patients seeking everything from pre-natal to geriatric care. A new 135,000-square-foot Patient Care Center opened on campus in 1997.

In keeping with its commitment to research, the health science center has created several Institutes for Discovery — the Geriatric Education and Research Institute, the Cancer Research Institute, the Cardiovascular Research Institute, the North Texas Eye Research Institute, the Substance Abuse Institute of North Texas, and the Physical Medicine Institute.

Through the Office of Clinical Trials, faculty physicians participate in some 20 clinical research projects seeking improved treatments for disorders such as high blood pressure, migraine, ulcers, arthritis and diabetes. The health science center is also home to the premier DNA identity testing laboratory in Texas.

The health science center is an active partner in scores of community endeavors. Among these is a leadership role in establishing MEDTECH, Fort Worth's medical and technology business incubator. This singular project holds promise of creating new businesses and new jobs in and for the city of Fort Worth.

A collaboration between the health science center and a development corporation will result in Fort Worth becoming the hub for one of the largest sites in the nation for research, treatment and prevention of Alzheimer's Disease. The Fort Worth site, called Heritage St. Joseph Gardens, is expected to bring together the largest patient base for Alzheimer' s Disease research in the world.

1950

Bell Helicopter opens in nearby Hurst; Korean War begins
General Motors opens in Arlington

1951

U. S. sends military advisors to Vietnam; J. R. Edwards serves as Mayor until 1953

University of North Texas Health Science Center at Fort Worth

(Courtesy of University of North Texas Health Science Center at Fort Worth)

Places of Worship

Beth-El Congregation

Beth-El Congregation will meet here at the Broadway synagogue which was built in 1920 until the completion of the new building on Brairhaven Road.
(Courtesy Beth-El Congregation Archives, Photo by Ralph Laueer

Ahavath Sholom

Ahavath Sholom is located on Briarhaven Road at Hulen. This building was constructed in 1980
(Courtesy Fort Worth Jewish Archives)

Broadway Baptist Church

Broadway Baptist, ca 1920
(Courtesy Fort Worth Public Library)

Midtown Church of Christ

(Courtesy Midtown Church of Christ)

Three individual congregations have worked together to create the Midtown Church of Christ.

Diamond Hill saw its humble birth in 1913 with the assembling of eight members in a home. Only a few months earlier that had met in a potter's home, sitting on pews of timbers supported by clay vessels. Eventually, Diamond Hill was to occupy a modern facility adequate to the demands of the times.

Of similar origins, Riverside to the east was born in 1920. Twenty members began worshipping together as a result of a gospel meeting held in a tent. A simple frame structure on Belknap Street was followed in 1947 with a modern stone edifice and congregational growth brought about additional expansions.

Eastridge's birth was from the motivation of the people at Riverside to establish a congregation for the needs of the community in the newly-developing Haltom City area. In 1953, the Riverside congregation divided itself and built a new site on NE 28th Street.

Although each individual congregation worked diligently, the separate results were not satisfying enough when compared to the potential existing if the three worked as one.

The Midtown Church of Christ is an 1100 member congregation located on a seventeen acre tract of land adjacent to Interstate Highway I-35 W, just three and one half miles from downtown Fort Worth. It is located in the Northeast portion of the city in the Oakhurst section. The three groups met as the Midtown Church of Christ officially for the first time on Wednesday night, December 16, 1970 when 977 persons met for a devotional service of praise and thanksgiving. The group worshiped on the Lord's Day first on December 20, 1970.

Ministers at Midtown today include: Jack Roe, full-time Elder and Staff Administrator, Jim Hackney, Pulpit, David Rogers, Congregation Care, Chuck Roe, Children, Rus Hooper, Spiritual Formation.

Mt. Gilead Baptist Church

In September of 1875 a group of 40 former slaves organized the Mt. Gilead Baptist Church in Ft. Worth, Texas. Mt. Gilead Baptist Church is considered one of the oldest African-American churches in the Southwest and the pioneer African-American church of the region. The church has produced two former presidents of the National Baptist Convention, three presidents of the State Baptist Convention, and three college presidents.

The first church structure was built in 1876. The second church structure, built in 1882, stood a few blocks east of Main Street in downtown Fort Worth. The church stood in the middle of what was then called "Hell's Half Acre," a red light district that had been a part of the city since its early days as an army outpost. A new location for the church was necessary, and the church worked to raise the $10,000 needed to purchase the present downtown church site on 5th and Grove Street. The new church was built at a cost of $51,000, and the members made the march from the old church to the new on August 31, 1913.

Designed by the famous Fort Worth Architectural Firm of Sanguinet & Staats, the present structure is one of the premier Neo-Classical style churches in the Southwest. The building has a columned pedimented entrance, and a stained glass dome ceiling in the sanctuary. Over the years, the building has been altered somewhat with the last major renovation completed after extensive hail damage was sustained by the structure in May of 1995, but the church still features red brick and many of the original stained glass windows.

Mt. Gilead Baptist Church
(Courtesy Fort Worth Public Library)

First Christian Church, Throckmorton St. Fort Worth's oldest congregation

(Courtesy Fort Worth Public Library)

Central Methodist Church, now the Southside Preservation Hall, Lipscomb Street

(Courtesy the Quentin McGown Postcard Collection)

The First Baptist Church of Fort Worth

In 1867, the Reverends W. W. Mitchell and A. Fitzgerald established Fort Worth Baptist Church. The small church struggled with a frequent turnover of pastors. By 1873, only twenty-six members met to worship. Reverends J. R. Masters and W. M. Gough challenged this small congregation to commit themselves to building the church. On September 12, 1873, the congregation changed their name to the First Baptist Church of Fort Worth. Land was donated by Hyde Jennings to build the church's first building.

In 1886, First Baptist Church extended a call to Reverend J. Morgan Wells, a brilliant orator, a tireless worker, and an outstanding fund-raiser. Reverend Wells accepted money for the Lord's work from church members and gamblers alike. The growing attendance, dust, and odors resulting from cowboys driving their cattle by the church to the railhead for shipment to Kansas, prompted the church to sell the Jennings Avenue building to the City of Fort Worth and build again on the corner of Third and Taylor Streets.

In 1891, the church hosted the Southern Baptist Convention. The preliminary work for the establishment of the Baptist Sunday School Board was completed during this session, and is still in effect today.

In 1909, "The Home of the Cattle Kings", as the church had become known, extended a call to 32 year old J. Frank Norris. With his acceptance, Dr. Norris brought with him ownership of The Baptist Standard. In 1911, Dr. Norris began a campaign to shut down the notorious Hell's Half Acre. He was repeatedly threatened with hanging, shooting, and being run out of town. February 4, 1912, the church was destroyed by an arson fire. The church rebuilt at Fourth and Throckmorton. In the early 1920's, the Southern Baptist Convention passed a resolution denying recognition of the First Baptist Church. As a result, Dr. Norris founded the Independent Baptist Fellowship and his own seminary, the Fundamental Bible Baptist Institute. Under Dr. Norris' leadership, First Baptist was the first Church to own and operate its own religious radio station and to offer its parishioners transportation to and from services. At its height in the mid 1920's, the church had 12,000 members. The church building burned again in 1929. Upon rebuilding, Dr. Norris was instrumental in leading the church to contribute $45,000 to the Southwestern Baptist Theological Seminary.

With Dr. Norris' passing in 1952, Homer Ritchie became pastor. Under his leadership, the church relocated to Fifth and Penn in 1965. In 1979, Dr. Ritchie relocated the church to its present location at 5001 NE Loop 820. Two years later, Dr. Ritchie approached Rolling Hills Baptist Church with the prospect of merging the two congregations. Dr. Ritchie retired and Johnnie Ramsey became pastor, followed by his son Bill Ramsey in 1984. Reverend Bill Ramsey led the church to rejoin the Southern Baptist Convention.

In 1997, Donald J. Wills became pastor of First Baptist. The church has been blessed with growth and a vision for the future. Through God's grace, and for His Glory, the First Baptist Church continues to minister to the City of Fort Worth.

Former 5th and Penn Street location of the First Baptist Church, Ca 1970
(Courtesy of the Quentin McGown Post card Collection)

First Baptist Church of Fort Worth
(Courtesy Fort Baptist Church of Fort Worth)

First Presbyterian Church of Fort Worth

The Fort Worth Presbyterian Church was organized in 1873 with ten charter members. Affiliated with the Presbyterian Church, U.S. ("Southern"), the congregation built a frame sanctuary on Jones Street between 1st and 2nd. In 1886 the name was changed to First Presbyterian Church of Fort Worth, and a new stone structure was built at 4th and Calhoun in 1890.

A Fort Worth congregation of the Cumberland Presbyterian Church was formed in 1878. Located at Fifth and Taylor Streets, it was renamed Taylor Street Cumberland Presbyterian Church in 1888. When the Cumberland Presbyterian Church affiliated with the Presbyterian Church, U.S.A. ("Northern") in 1906, the word Cumberland was dropped from the local Church's name.

Desiring to work together to serve the community with worship and missionary programs, the two Fort Worth congregations united in 1916 to form a federation, the first such union in Texas. The members met together and shared one pastor, but maintained separate national affiliations. The congregation erected a new edifice at Penn and Texas Streets, opening it on December 23, 1956. The "Southern" and "Northern" denominations united in 1983 to form the Presbyterian Church (U.S.A.).

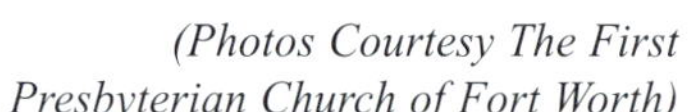

(Photos Courtesy The First Presbyterian Church of Fort Worth)

First United Methodist Church of Fort Worth

(Courtesy First United Methodist Church)

The actual beginning of the First Methodist Church in Fort Worth was at the December 27, 1852 meeting of the Texas Annual Conference. Here John W. Chalk was appointed to the Red Oak Mission, which included Tarrant County. By 1856 the growth of Fort Worth and surrounding territory and the number of Methodists had grown sufficiently to warrant the creation of a Fort Worth District.

Prior to 1874, there was no Methodist church building in Fort Worth. At the beginning of 1866, the city was the only pastoral charge in Tarrant County. That year, the first session of the Northwest Texas Annual Conference, which included the present Central Texas Annual Conference, was held in Waxahachie on September 26, 1866 with Bishop E. M. Marvin residing. The Fort Worth Circuit was one of seven pastoral charges placed in that district. With the annual conference of 1869, the Fort Worth Circuit was moved from the Waxahachie District into the newly created Weatherford District.

A significant milestone in the history of this church came at the annual conference of 1873. R.H.H.Burnett was appointed by Bishop Kavanuagh to the Fort Worth Station. For the first time in the twenty years of this church's existence, it now had the full-time service of a minister, one who did not have to divide his time among several churches. Meetings were held Sunday afternoons in the old Masonic Hall on Weatherford Street. A lot was purchased at Fourth and Jones Streets for the first Methodist church building.

In 1887 it was decided that the Fourth Street church would be moved to the rear of the lot. This made room for a new brick structure, which was erected at a cost of about $16,500. In 1890, the official name of Fourth Street Church was changed to First Methodist Church.

By 1903 enlarged facilities were greatly needed. A building committee was authorized to purchase a lot at the corner of Seventh and Taylor Streets. When this building was completed in 1908, it was thought that the edifice would provide adequate facilities for its membership for at least fifty years. Soon skyscrapers were enroaching upon the church grounds and the membership grew so rapidly it was necessary to secure space in office buildings located in the vicinity. By 1928 the building committee began to consider either enlarging the facilities or moving to a new location. Efforts were made to secure the balance of the block then occupied by the church. Failing in this, the committee selected the site at Fifth and Florence. The property at Seventh and Taylor was sold and on October 5, 1930, the corner stone of the new church was laid.

The opening services of the Fifth Street church were held in the sanctuary in June, 1931. At the general conference held in 1968, the official name of the denomination, which included First Church, was changed. With the union with the Evangelical United Brethren Church, it became the United Methodist Church. In this same year, a dedicated group of church members purchased and gave to the church the remainder of the property in front of the church building. This included the area between Seventh and Fifth and between Henderson and Macon. The most beautiful part of this is the esplanade down the center, which was formerly Florence Street. This street was closed by the City of Fort Worth at the request of the church, and in the center of the esplanade is a marble statue of Christ.

First Methodist Church, corner of Seventh and Taylor (1908 - 1930)
(Courtesy Fort Worth Public Library)

Saint Patrick Cathedral

(Courtesy Fort Worth Public Library)

Prior to 1876 the few Catholic families in Fort Worth were visited each month by a priest who would say Mass in the residence of one of the families.

In 1876 Fort Worth Catholics received their first parish priest, Father Thomas Loughrey. The parish then built their first church, St. Stanislaus Church, on the site of the present rectory. It was a small frame structure and was used until the present St. Patrick Cathedral was finished. After that, it was used as a school for boys until it was torn down in 1908 and replaced by the present Rectory.

Father Loughrey was replaced by Father Jean Marie Guyot in 1884. Father Guyot was a native of France and was determined to build a beautiful stone church like the ones in his native country. The cost of the church was estimated at $80,000. The cornerstone was laid October 14, 1888, and the church was dedicated July 10, 1892.

The Cathedral is Gothic Revival in style. It is built of native limestone which has had to be water-proofed through the years because of deterioration. The columns on the inside are solid granite. Although the original design called for twin towers, they were never added - -either from lack of money or the fact that the weight of the bells plus the weight of the towers, themselves, could not be supported by the church. The architect was J. J. Kane.

This magnificent building is a lasting monument to Father Guyot, who now lies buried beneath its main altar. At the time it was built there were no other churches of such grandeur in the Catholic communities - not even in Galveston, which diocese had sent Father Guyot to Fort Worth.

The Cathedral Complex is entered in the National Register of Historic Places and is also listed as a Texas Historical Landmark. In May of 1999 approximately 1700 families were registered as members of St. Patrick's.

Interior St. Patrick Cathedral. 1206 Throckmorton Street, Fort Worth Texas. Parish was established in 1870. The Cathedral is an historical monument.

(W.D. Smith Inc., Commercial Photography. Courtesy St. Patrick Cathedral)

Saint Andrews Episcopal Church

(Courtesy the Quentin McGown Postcard Collection)

Our Lady of Victory Academy, Fort Worth, Texas. (1912)
(Quentin McGown post card collection)

Gustavus Adolphus Swedish Lutheran Church. Fort Worth

(Courtesy of Acme Brick)

TRAVIS AVENUE BAPTIST CHURCH

In 1908, a Mr. Ellis (perhaps Ellison) organized an independent and non-denominational afternoon Sunday school at the Prairie Chapel School, located about 125 yards west of Hemphill Street near Biddison Street and Travis Avenue. When leadership passed to R. B. Kirven, then a member of College Avenue Baptist Church, this church agreed to sponsor the mission project.

R. W. Langham, the first pastor of the mission, came as a student to the new Southwestern Baptist Theological Seminary. Under his leadership, on January 15, 1911, the mission was organized as the South Side Baptist Church. In October, 1911, J.L. Price became the pastor. During the summer of 1912, a small wooden church building, costing $250, was constructed on a lot loaned by Mrs. W. P. Biddison. In October, 1912, Langham returned as pastor. The church then purchased two lots located on the northeast corner of Berry Street and Travis Avenue. The warranty deed shows the date of August 21, 1913. One Friday in October, 1913, volunteers dismantled the old wooden church building and used horse-drawn wagons to move the lumber. The church building was reassembled in one day's time at the new location facing Berry Street.

The next pastors of the church were J.L. Mahan (June, 1914-June, 1916), W. W. Barnes (June, 1916-January,1918), S.H. Frazier (Jan-Sept., 1918), A.C. Gustavus (early 1919-June, 1919), and A. S. Harwell (July, 1919 - Sept., 1922).

On March 10, 1920, the South Side Baptist Church voted to change its name to Travis Avenue Baptist Church.

In September of 1922, Dr. C. E. Matthews was called as pastor. Church membership grew from 209 to 6073 members by 1946, when he resigned to become Evangelism Director for the Baptist General Convention of Texas. The buildings now designated "A" and "B" were constructed during his ministry. Building "A" was considered the most modern one-unit church and Sunday school plant in America when it was completed in 1925.

Dr. E. L. Carnett became pastor in 1946, and the progress of the church continued as the Sunday school was graded and Building "C" was erected. He resigned to become president of Buckner Benevolences in June, 1952. Dr. Robert A. Baker, Professor of Church History at Southwestern Baptist Theological Seminary, was called as interim pastor.

On October 14, 1952, Dr. Robert E. Naylor became pastor of Travis Avenue Baptist Church. Two Sunday morning worship services soon became necessary, one at 8:30 A.M. and the other at 11:00 A.M. with Sunday school in between. Groundbreaking took place on October 13, 1957, for a new 3,200 seat sanctuary. At the time of completion in April, 1959, it was the largest sanctuary in the Southern Baptist Convention. In 1958, Dr. Naylor resigned to become President of the Southwestern Baptist Theological Seminary. Dr. Robert A. Baker again served as interim pastor.

In October, 1959, Dr. James E. Coggin was called as pastor. With an emphasis on evangelistic outreach, including a bus ministry, the church experienced excellent attendance, and baptisms more than doubled. In 1973, Building "A" was totally remodeled into more educational space and a small chapel on the ground floor. On October 16, 1983, Dr. Coggin retired after twenty-four years as pastor of Travis Avenue Baptist Church. Dr. Jimmy Allen became interim preacher in November, 1983, with Dr. Bill Pearson, Minister of Music, named as the staff coordinator.

Dr. Joel Gregory became pastor on June 1, 1985. During his ministry the church acquired property on Hemphill Street and a former Safeway store building near the southwest corner of Hemphill and Berry Streets. The remodeled building, now called the "South Complex", contains educational space, a kitchen and church dining room, a gym, storage space, and a library. Dr. Paul Powell was called as interim pastor on March 3, 1991, upon the resignation of Dr. Gregory, who was called as pastor to the First Baptist Church of Dallas.

Dr. Michael Dean became pastor of Travis Avenue Baptist Church on September 1, 1991. Dr. Bill Pearson, who had served as Minister of Music for thirty-one years, retired in 1995, and John B. Lee was called to assume that leadership role. Presently, Dr. Dean conducts a worship service every Sunday morning at "The Gathering" in the South Complex at 9:30 A.M. as well as the 11:00 A.M. worship service in the Sanctuary. Travis Avenue Baptist Church now has a membership numbering 8,870. An emphasis on both ministries and missions is evidenced by the church's slogan, "Contagious Christianity: Knowing Love, Showing Love: "

by Grimes and Rachel Fortenberry

Travis Avenue Baptist Church. Building A (right) completed 1925, building B (left) completed in 1937

(Courtesy Travis Avenue Baptist Church)

This air shot of Travis Avenue Baptist Church was done in 1986. Note downtown Fort Worth skyline in background.

(Courtesy Travis Avenue Baptist Church)

Cemeteries of Fort Worth

Ahavath Sholom Hebrew Cemetery on North University Drive was created in 1909 from a section purchased from Greenwood. Here, you will find the monument to the millions of Jewish victims of the Holocaust.

Emanuel Hebrew Rest Cemetery, located on South Main, was founded in 1879. The oldest grave is that of a child, Leah Kaiser, who died in 1879.

Forest Hill Cemetery, on Forest Hill Drive is the resting place of Press and Jane Woody Farmer, early pioneers of the area.

Greenwood Cemetery, located on White Settlement Road is the final resting place of Amon Carter, Ben Hogan, Marvin Leonard, Davey O'Brien, to mention of few of the city's elite. There is also a section for the Royal Flying Corps pilots who were killed during training here in Fort Worth.

Isham Cemetery, on John T. White Road, is the burial site for Joe Works, one-time producer of Mississippi Riverboat plays.

Laurel Land Cemetery, on Crowley Road, was founded in the 1920's as Parkland and became Laurel Land in 1942.

Mitchell Cemetery, NE 28th at Decatur Avenue is one of Fort Worth's pioneer cemeteries that has not survived; however, records indicate that one who rested here was a veteran of the Mexican war, Seaborn Gilmore, who was also Tarrant County's first elected county judge.

Mount Olivet Cemetery, on North Sylvania Avenue, was founded in 1907. The former homestead of Charles B. Daggett. In addition to the members of the Daggett family, you will find influential Fort Worthian, B. B. Paddock, and U.S. Congressman William Pinckney McLean.

Oakwood Cemetery, on Grand Avenue, was created in 1879 on twenty acres donated by John Peter Smith and was known simply as "City Cemetery" for the first few years. A section of the East Oakwood portion, known as "Soldier's Row", was for Confederate veterans and their wives. The cemetery now contains over 60 acres and features a small chapel at the north gate which was built in 1912. Among those famous Fort Worthians buried here are Burk Burnett, W. T. Waggoner, Major K. M. Van Zandt, John Peter Smith, Alfred S. Hayne, Bill McDonald, "Jim" Courtright, Luke Short. Major Horace S. Carswell, Jr., was relocated from Carswell Air Force Base in 1993.

Pioneer's Rest Cemetery, located on Samuels Avenue, is the resting place of Major Ripley Arnold, and two of the Arnold children. Also buried here are General Edward H. Tarrant; Charles Turner, Texas Ranger; and E. M. Daggett.

Polytechnic Cemetery, Avenue C, has a Masonic Home section and is the burial site for Paul Hollis, inventor of Poly-Pop.

Shannon Rose Hill Cemetery, is located on East Lancaster and was founded in 1929 as Rose Hill Burial Park. In 1984, the Shannon family, a Fort Worth institution since 1906, bought this east side cemetery and it became Shannon Rose Hill. The cemetery is probably best known as the burial site of Lee Harvey Oswald, however, among those resting here you will find several prominent Fort Worthians, including members of the Pate family, and Major Handley, founder of Handley, Texas.

Oakwood Cemetery
(Courtesy of Oakwood Cemetery)

Oakwood Cemetery Chapel
(Landmark Staff Photo)

Pioneer's Rest Cemetery
(Courtesy Tarrant County College, Northeast Campus)

Casa Mañana

The story of Casa Mañana began in 1936. Amon G. Carter, publisher of the Fort Worth Star Telegram, paid Billy Rose $1,000 a day for one hundred days to produce the "show of shows" for the city's celebration of the Texas Centennial. In only 110 days, a forty acre cow pasture was transformed into a midway of Broadway-style entertainment. The complex included a dance hall, a burlesque show, a musical rodeo and a nightclub with dinner, dancing and a stage show that ran twice a night.

The nightclub was named Casa Mañana — "House of Tomorrow." The open-air theatre had the largest revolving stage and cafe in the world. The floor level provided dinner seating for 1,000 guests and was surrounded by tiers of balconies for guests who came just to see the show. The stage was surrounded by a 600,000 gallon moat, where gondolas with singing gondoliers floated until show time. The stage and its surrounding moat prevented the use of a traditional curtain. Instead, an illuminated wall of water created by high-shooting fountains were used to mask the stage.

The 1936 Centennial shows played to full houses for the next five months. These shows were so successful that Carter decided to open the theatre again and again, with shows presented each year from June through September. For four consecutive years, the wonders of Broadway were brought to Fort Worth.

In 1940 the chance of war in Europe delayed planning for the summer shows. In early May, the Casa Mañana shows were canceled and never returned. Most of the theater's structure was eventually dismantled to provide metal and other materials for the war effort.

With memories of the grandeur and success of live theatre in the 1930's, a citizen's committee organized a bond drive to raise $500,000 to rebuild Casa Mañana But the bond could not be retired in 1943, and the funds lay dormant for a dozen years.

In 1956, Melvin O. Dacus, the General Manager of the Fort Worth Opera, and oilman James H. Snowden, President of the Opera Association, began looking for a way to raise money for the organization. Dacus and Snowden requested to use the bond funding to build and operate a theatre-in-the-round, primarily for the production of Broadway musicals. The Fort Worth City Council approved the project on the stipulation that the summer musicals would be separate from the opera. Dacus and Snowden resigned their positions with the opera and took similar positions with the newly formed, not-for-profit Casa Mañana Musicals, Inc.

The project was approved by the Fort Worth City Council on January 14,1958, and construction began two months later, on March 13. After a record-breaking 114 days, the theatre opened its first season that brought five Broadway musicals to Fort Worth and introduced "musicals-in-the-round" to the Southwestern United States. Casa Mañana made national theatrical headlines with its black-tie opening July 5, 1958, and has been making them ever since.

Today, Casa Mañana produces and presents shows year round. These shows include locally produced Broadway musicals and the best of Broadway's national touring shows. Casa Mañana also presents several Children's Playhouse performances each year and operates one of the largest acting schools for children in the United States. The silver-dome theatre is still Casa's home. However, several national touring shows and other locally produced performances are also presented at the Nancy Lee and Perry R. Bass Performance Hall and Will Rogers Auditorium.

With its dedication to present the highest quality live theatre and with the overwhelming support of the community, Casa Mañana continues to realize the meaning of its namesake — "House of Tomorrow."

Interior and backstage of Casa Mañana (1937)
(Courtesy of the Quentin McGown Post Card Collection)

Casa Mañana January 1937
(Courtesy Fort Worth Star Telegram Photograph Collection, Special Collections Division, The University of Texas at Arlington Libraries)

Lone Star Ensemble – Last Frontier. Fort Worth, Frontier Centennial "Casa Mañana" of the Fort Worth Frontier Fiesta, Fort Worth, Texas (1937).
(Courtesy of the Quentin McGown Post Card Collection)

Singers and dancers in Billy Rose's production at Casa Mañana, Fort Worth, 1936.
(Courtesy of the Quentin McGown Post Card Collection)

Sally Rand's "Dude" Ranch

(Courtesy Dalton Hoffman, Jr. Collection)

Casa Mañana's geodesic dome was designed by R. Buckminster Fuller
(Quentin McGown post card collection)

1961

Amon Carter Museum opens; John Justin elected Mayor and serves until 1963

1961

John F. Kennedy elected President

Entertainment!

Hippodrome Theater, Ca 1917
(Courtesy Jack White Photograph Collection, The University of Texas at Arlington Libraries)

Ideal Theater – shown here in the 1930's. Later, this was one of the first integrated theaters in Fort Worth.
(Courtesy Jack White Photograph Collection, The University of Texas at Arlington Libraries)

Liberty Theater
(Courtesy Jack White Photograph Collection, The University of Texas at Arlington Libraries)

Palace Theater, formerly Byer's Opera House
(Courtesy W.D. Smith, Inc., Commercial Photography Collection, The University of Texas at Arlington Libraries)

Majestic Theater, circa 1920's
(Courtesy Fort Worth Star-Telegram Photograph Collection, Special Collections Division, The University of Texas at Arlington Libraries)

John Glenn, Jr. becomes the first American in orbit

Marvin and Obie Leonard open the M & O Subway

The Worth Theater was Fort Worth's largest in the late 1920's and early 30's. This shot was taken Ca 1932

(Courtesy of the Dalton Hoffman, Jr. Collection)

The Worth Theater World Premier of *The Westerner,* starring Gary Cooper, September of 1940, was an Amon Carter accomplishment. Note Roosevelt headquarters.

(Courtesy of the Dalton Hoffman, Jr. Collection)

John F. Kennedy visits Fort Worth and is assassinated the following day in Dallas; Lyndon B. Johnson assumes Presidency

Bayard H. Friedman elected Mayor and serves until 1965

Local celebrity, the late Bill Camfield, AKA "Icky Twerp", entertained many Fort Worth children as host of Saturday's Slam Bang Theater which spotlighted The Three Stooges as well as cartoons. (Photo courtesy Dave Naugle and Jim Noah)

Exterior shot of Ridglea Theater December 17, 1951
(Courtesy W.D. Smith, Inc., Commercial Photography Collection, The University of Texas at Arlington Libraries)

Rose Theater on North Main Street will live again as a part of the city's Mercado Project
(Courtesy Jack White Photograph Collection, The University of Texas at Arlington Libraries)

Advertisements of the day proclaimed
“moving pictures are your best entertainment!”

Isis Theater
(Courtesy of the Quentin McGown Post Card Collection)

(Quentin McGown post card collection)

“Cottage City” first motel in Fort Worth, Texas, 1927 – 6200 block of Camp Bowie

(Courtesy Betty Porter Walther)

The Interurban, Ca 1912
(Quentin McGown post card collection)

Popular radio entertainers, The Light Crust Dough Boys, who broadcasted for the Burrus Mill & Elevator Co. of Fort Worth, Texas, millers of Light Crust Flour.

(Courtesy of the Quentin McGown Post Card Collection)

Cowtown Jamboree, Panther Hall, Fort Worth, Texas. Bob Wills - Leon Rausch and the Texas Playboys.

(Courtesy of the Quentin McGown Post Card Collection)

LA GRAVE FIELD
FORT WORTH, TEXAS
"Home of the Fort Worth Cats"

The Fort Worth Cats

Bobby Bragan, catcher for the baseball team, served as player-manager from 1948-1952. The team won two Texas League Championships during those five seasons. Bobby is also co-author, with Jeff Guinn, of When Panthers Roared: The Fort Worth Cats and Minor League Baseball, Texas Christian University Press, October, 1999. The photographs presented here are from the Bobby Bragan Collection, now archived at Texas Wesleyan University

Top Row - GEORGE BROWN, GINO MARIONETTI, GEORGE SCHMEES, CHRIS VAN CUYK, GENE COSTELLO, GEORGE DOCKINS, DEE FONDY
2nd Row - DICK WILLIAMS, IRV NOREN, EDDIE CHANDLER, BOB BRAGAN Mgr., MERV DORENBERG, HOMER MATNEY, JOHN LEGROS
Front Row - JOHN PRIMM, Road Sec., WALLY FIALA, JACK LINDSEY, BOB AUSTIN, WILLIE RAMSDELL, DWAIN SLOAT, ALEX THOMAS, Trainer.
Bat Boys - BURCH COATS and EVERETT ROBERTS

L-R: In uniform, Wayne Belardi - first base, Steve Lembo - catcher and manager, Bobby Bragan greet Al Gionfriddo, reassigned to Fort Worth Cats. Al Gionfriddo (Brooklyn Dodgers) made the "miraculous" catch of a Joe Dimaggio (New York Yankees) drive in the '47 World Series that was labeled as one of the greatest catches in the World Series History.

Left to Right, players of 1951 in the dugout at LaGrave Field: Ray Moore, pitcher; Joe Torpey, second base; Peter Mondorf, pitcher; Ben Taylor, first base; Bill McCahan, pitcher; and Bobby Bragan, player-manager.

Left to Right: Fort Worth Cats outfielder, Bill Sharman, Rex Barney, who pitched a "no-hitter" for the Brooklyn Dodgers, on reassignment to the Fort Worth Cats, Bobby Bragan, player and manager, and Billy Hunter, shortstop who played for three big league teams — St. Louis Browns, Baltimore Orioles, and New York Yankees, who later managed the Texas Rangers, greet the newcomer at LaGrave Field.

Bobby Bragan with "The Yankee Clipper", Joe Dimaggio

Martin Luther King, Jr. and Robert Kennedy are assassinated; Tarrant County Convention Center opens

Richard Nixon elected President

History of the Fort Worth Zoo

The oldest continuous Zoo site in Texas, the Fort Worth Zoo opened in 1909 with one lion, two bear cubs, an alligator, a coyote, a peacock and several rabbits. Today, the Zoo houses a collection of more than 5,000 exotic and native animals and is dedicated to the conservation of all wildlife. The Zoo is consistently ranked as one of the top Zoos in the nation by the Los Angeles Times and by Family Life and Southern Living magazines.

During the first ten years, the Zoo's collection of animals grew to include a pair of panthers, beavers, cinnamon bears, monkeys and prairie dogs. In the early 1920s, two American bison and a zebra were purchased partially from coin donations at the Zoo. This began a long tradition of citizen involvement in improving the Zoo.

In 1923, the Elephant Fund was established to solicit donations for the purchase of the Zoo's first elephant, "Queen Tut." To accommodate the popular Asian elephant, the Zoo's first permanent shelter was built, which serves as part of the Koala Outback exhibit today.

As the Zoo's popularity grew, Zoo Commissioners began plans for additional permanent exhibits including an octagonal monkey house and a row of cat and bear cages.

With the reorganization of the Work Progress Administration (WPA), several WPA projects led to improvements which included the Alligator Pond, the Monkey Island, a bird house and some smaller exhibits. In 1934, a combination rock shelter, a comfort station and a concession stand were built.

In 1939, the Zoological Society was organized under non-profit status to raise money for Zoo improvements.

In 1940, Elephant Club donations funded the purchase of a second elephant, named "Penny" to commemorate the many pennies donated by the public.

For several years, World War II interrupted additional Zoo improvements. Then in 1945, a postwar municipal bond passed designating $85,000 for Zoo improvements. Through a 1946 fund sponsored by the Fort Worth Star Telegram, a baby hippopotamus named "Bluebonnet Belle" was purchased. The popular hippo was the first of its kind in the state and was housed in a new shelter complete with a heated pool, paid for with bond funds.

"Queen Tut" and "Penny". "Queen Tut" traveled all the way from Lancaster, Missouri on a flatbed train to become the first elephant at the Zoo. "Penny" was purchased in 1940 and given her name to commemorate the donations of pennies given by children visiting the Zoo *(Courtesy of Fort Worth Zoo)*

This exhibit by the WPA is under construction, becoming a home for the seals. The one in the water doesn't seem to mind that it used to be the home for many monkeys. Today, it is the Zoo's Gator Swamp.

(Courtesy of Fort Worth Zoo)

In 1950, the Zoological Society decided to gain official status and became the Fort Worth Zoological Association, a non-profit organization. In June, the Association bought Fort Worth's first two giraffes, "Topper" and "Goldy."

In 1953, the Children's Zoo was completed, receiving more than 200,000 visitors the first year. The same year, Amon Carter Jr. presented a check for $50,000 to construct a "bang-up aquarium." The James R. Record Aquarium was completed in 1954, with more than 100 tanks featuring more than 400 species. It was decided that an admission fee would be charged at the aquarium to raise funds for future improvements. Also in 1954, a terrifying incident occurred, "Pete the python" escaped during the night. This 18-foot python was on the loose making world-wide headlines for seventeen days. "Pete" was finally found in the monkey house. Several Zoo staff members used a six-foot pipe and loop to catch him and return him to his cage. Amazingly, a few months later "he" gave birth to 50 giant white eggs. So, "she" was immediately renamed "Patricia the Python."

In 1960, the fourth indoor exhibit was built. At its opening, the Herpetarium housed the largest collection of reptiles and amphibians in the world.

In 1971, McFadean and Everly, nationally recognized Zoo planners, completed a master plan for the Fort Worth Zoo. The plan described a contemporary Zoo of approximately 100 acres.

In 1975, a new cafe and gift shop were opened to generate funds for improvements. The following year, an exhibit for hoofed animals was renovated with new fencing and a new barn for blackbuck antelope, axis deer and Asian cranes. A premier Great Apes House was opened in 1979 for gorillas, chimpanzees and orangutans.

An infant care facility was opened in 1981, providing housing for small mammals, birds and orphaned Zoo babies. Also in 1981 came the expansion of the Sidewalk Cafe, more sidewalks, and the beginning of a major landscaping effort throughout the Zoo.

In 1985, the $1.25 million Asian elephant breeding facility was opened, and is still considered one of the best elephant exhibits in the nation. The next year, a walk-through, free-flight bird exhibit was constructed on the site of the old Children's Zoo.

The Fort Worth Zoo Association assumed management of the Zoo from the City of Fort Worth in October 1991 after more than 50 years of support.

Once it began managing the Zoo, the Zoo Association immediately began renovations and improvements. The Zoo held its "grand reopening" in April 1992 featuring two new premier exhibits: World of Primates and Asian Falls, along with dozens of small exhibits. When the new exhibits and improvements were unveiled, Zoo attendance soared to more than one million visitors in 1992. The Zoo's attendance has surpassed one million visitors per year since then.

In 1993, Raptor Canyon and Asian Rhino Ridge helped maintain high attendance. The Zoo continued making new additions in 1994 with the opening of the Portraits of the Wild Gallery (featuring paintings by renowned German wildlife artist Wilhelm Kuhnert), the Gloria Lupton Tennison Education Center and the Cheetos Cheetah exhibit.

Since 1995, the Zoo has opened seven new exhibits thanks to the support of individuals, corporate sponsors and foundations. These exhibits include Flamingo Bay (1995), the FUJIFILM Komodo Dragon exhibit (1995), Terminix Insect City (1996), Penguin Island (1997), Meerkat Mounds (1997), Koala Outback (1998) and Thundering Plains (1999).

The Fort Worth Zoo Association has worked diligently for decades to keep the Zoo on the forefront of animal, education and conservation programs. The Zoo will continue this momentum, and plans have been laid to keep the Zoo in the national spotlight well into the 21st century with the opening of the new Texas Wild! exhibit. Being the Zoo's landmark exhibit, the project is planned to open Fall 2000. The state-of-the-art exhibit will allow visitors to explore the Lone Star State in one day and to learn about the abundant and diverse wildlife in Texas.

As a post script: Keeping with the tradition that "everything is bigger in Texas", the Fort Worth Zoo recently introduced a 700 pound "bluebonnet". Bluebonnet, also known as Bonnie, is the Zoo's first-ever baby elephant. Born in December of 1998, the elephant calf remained nameless until the public could submit suggestions for a name. The Zoo received more than 6,500 entries from across the country in its "What's Your Name, Baby?" contest. Donna-Maria Sexton of Seagoville, Texas, was the winner, naming the baby in honor of the state flower.

Forest Park Municipal Zoo Entrance Sign, Fort Worth, Texas. This "Good Advice" at the west entrance of the Fort Worth Municipal Zoo invites everyone to enjoy the wonders of nature and to see the many interesting animals and fascinating exhibits of one of the most modern and up-to-date zoos in the Southwest. Ca. 1965

(Quentin McGown post card collection)

The Fort Worth Zoo staff is frantically trying to catch an ostrich in this picture. On occasion the animals were moved from exhibit to exhibit throughout the Zoo. Elvie Turner (lower left) was the director of the Zoo for more than 25 years.

(Courtesy of Fort Worth Zoo)

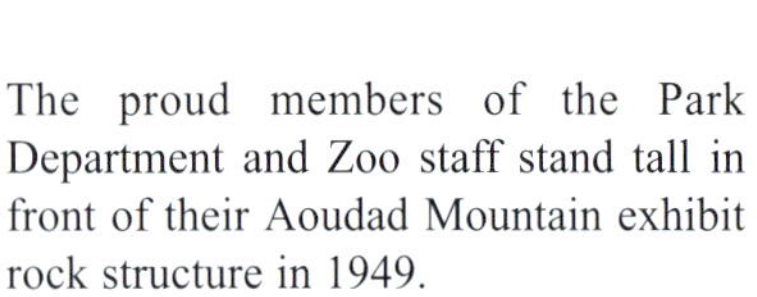

The proud members of the Park Department and Zoo staff stand tall in front of their Aoudad Mountain exhibit rock structure in 1949.

(Courtesy of Fort Worth Zoo)

Fort Worth Parks & Community Services

Fort Worth is a diverse and dynamic city which serves as the cultural hub of the western portion of the Fort Worth/Dallas Metroplex. Fort Worth Parks and Community Services Department has 195 parks to service the needs of the population of over 490,500 residents and millions of visitors.

The citizens of Fort Worth have a long history of visionary planning for the future of their parks and open spaces.

Records indicate that early park sites include Trinity Park, 1892; Haynes Triangle Park, 1893; Marine Park, 1894; Will Rogers Memorial Park, 1900; Peter Smith Park, 1903; and Maddox Park. 1905.

Public minded individuals contributed time and resources to the long term development of the city's Park system since the call to form a Park League occurred in 1908. Sara Jennings (Mrs. Thomas J.) donated land for the first park in 1873. Named for her parents, Mr. and Mrs. John Hansford Hyde, the park is located downtown on 9th Street.

In the early 1900's, as with many cities during this era, the streetcar and railroad systems were primary in determining the development of parks. Prominent landscape architect, George E. Kessler drafted a plan that created or improved twenty-three parks between 1900 and 1930 including Sycamore, Forest, Hillside, Paddock, Greenway, Sylvania, Rockwood Park and Golf Course, and Trail Drivers Park.

After Kessler's death, the firm of Hare and Hare (associates of Kessler) assumed the city's park planning. During the next era of development, from 1930 to the mid 50's, parks such as Marion Sansom Park, Meadowbrook, Lake Como, Harmon Field and Traders Oak Park were created.

Forest Park Tower Gate
(Courtesy Parks and Community Service Department)

From the mid 50's through the 1960's Fort Worth experienced dramatic post war growth and social change. The city recovered from the Depression and World War II, became a major defense and aviation center, witnessed racial strife, civil disobedience, nuclear détente and technological change. At the beginning of the era, most people on earth did not own a television, at the end of the same era, most people of the world watched America land on the moon. This growth was a significant influence on the development of future parks.

In 1964 the Parks Department and Recreation Department merged due to their mutual interest in providing services and minimizing duplication of efforts. Of the twenty seven parks acquired during this era, twenty were targeted to service neighborhoods. These included Bonnie Brae, Overton, Tandy Hills, Pecan Valley, Diamond Hill, Highland Hills and Rosedale Plaza.

From the late sixties through the mid 1980's, Fort Worth experienced a period of rapid growth as unprecedented gas and oil prices drove the economy. Seventy eight parks and recreational facilities were added to the park inventory during this time. In 1977 the City Council adopted the Parkland Dedication Policy as part of the City's Subdivision Ordinance which now serves as the primary way that the Parks and Community Services Department acquires neighborhood park sites as Fort Worth grows. Parks such as Prairie Dog, Rodeo, Little John, Worth Hills, George Markos, Riverside, Heritage, Candleridge, Sycamore Creek Golf Course, Gateway Park, General Worth Square, Oakmont, Thorny Ridge, Saunders and the Water Gardens were added during this period.

In recent years, the Department has undergone significant changes. From 1985 until 1987 growth continued as seventeen parks, mainly neighborhood and community parks were added through the Parkland Dedication policy, donations, utilizing bond funds from earlier elections or from funds from the '86 Park Capital Improvement Program Bond election. Growth in the park system diminished significantly in '87 as the oil based economy slumped. City funds were in short supply for development, maintenance and operations. Development that might have added parkland to the system effectively ceased. City leaders in government and the private sector recognized the problems of relying on a defense and resource based economy and since the late 80's have sought to diversify. This effort is now causing substantial growth in both the economy and the population of Fort Worth.

A reconfiguration of the Department resulted in the 1992 Park and Recreation Department Strategic Plan. The direction given and followed by the Strategic Plan is believed to be one of the primary reasons the Department has been selected by the National Recreation and Park Association as one of the top four managed park and recreation departments for three of the past four years and the Gold Medal Recipient in October of '96 as the best managed large park system in the country. Parks that were added to the inventory in the most recent era included parks such as Lincolnshire, Morningside Middle School Park, Lake Arlington, Cobblestone Trail, Arcadia Trail, Fairmont, Mesa Verda, Arcadia Trail North and Park Place Park.

Many parks and facilities in the current system owe their existence to the generosity of individual citizens, citizen groups and foundations. Foundations such as the Amon G. Carter Foundation, the Anne Burnett and Charles Tandy Foundation, the Sid W. Richardson Foundation, and the Communities Foundation of Texas have made significant contributions of time, land, and money to the evolution of the city and the park system. Citizen groups such as Streams and Valleys, The Fort Worth Zoological Association, The Fort Worth Botanical Society, The Fort Worth Garden Club, The Texas Garden Clubs Association, The Junior League of Fort Worth, and many neighborhood associations have also made significant contributions. Without the generosity of these groups such important facilities as the Water Gardens, Burnett Park, Heritage, Park, The Botanic Gardens, Gateway Park and the Fort Worth Zoo would not exist. Private giving has been a tradition of the citizens of the City of Fort Worth since the Sarah Jennings Donation of Hyde Park in 1873.

Swimming pool in Forest Park, *(Quentin McGown post card collection)*

(Courtesy of the Dalton Hoffman, Jr. Collection)

Forest Park
Miniature Train

(Courtesy Parks and Community Service Department)

Fort Worth Botanic Garden

Japanese Gardens
(Courtesy Fort Worth Botanic Gardens)

In 1931 construction of Rock Springs Park began, "transforming a swamp into a garden". The Rose Gardens, the first relief project in Fort Worth during the Great Depression, were dedicated on October 15, 1933. Hare and Hare of Kansas City, Missouri, was commissioned to provide a plan that the Park Commissioners, staff and dedicated residents could use to create a garden. The landscape architects were inspired by the terraced gardens of Villa Lante in Italy and the vistas of Versailles in France. The site was officially named The Fort Worth Botanic Garden in December of 1934 by the Board of Park Commissioners. The 37.5 acre park fulfilled a dream of "an outdoor library of plants" to demonstrate the thousands of plants which thrive in the South. The Fort Worth Garden Club opened the Garden Center in June of 1935 as the first established garden center in Texas (now the Rock Springs Center). The Garden library, housed in Rock Springs Center, is named in honor of Mary Daggett Lake for her dedication and achievements as the first director of the Botanic Garden Center.

Located on the southern end of the Cultural District just two miles west of downtown Fort Worth, the Botanic Garden is open every day of the year. The Garden welcomes its visitors from all over Texas, every state and many countries world-wide. Visitors number more than 600,000 annually. The Garden now encompasses many facilities including theme gardens, seasonal color plantings, expansive vistas and natural wooden areas on 110 acres. Some 40% of the acreage is in a relatively undeveloped state, which provides mature trees for the visitor's enjoyment, sites for future gardens and facilities, and a buffer from busy city thoroughfares. The Garden is owned by the City of Fort Worth and operated by the Fort Worth Park & Recreation Department and is largely supported by public funds. Organizations including the Fort Worth Garden Club , the Fort Worth Botanical Society and the Garden Club Council of Fort Worth aid the Garden with both volunteer assistance and financial support. Many significant improvements have been made possible through private fund-raising efforts.

The new entrance to the Gardens, dedicated in 1990, was designed and landscaped to catch the eye of passing motorists and entice them to discover the beauty that lies beyond the stone gates. Funds for this project were provided by the Fort Worth Botanical Society.

The Japanese Garden attracts 125,000 or more visitors each year. With 7.5 acres, it features an evergreen landscape with colorful seasonal interest, pools of koi fish, waterfalls and attractive structures.

The new garden center and a tropical conservatory were a dream realized in 1986. The 17,000 square foot center, which provides a variety of meeting rooms, office space and a gift shop, was made possible by significant contributions from Mr. and Mrs. W. A. Moncrief, Jr., the Carter Foundation, and the West Foundation as well as public support. The Dorothea Leonhardt Lecture Hall was added to the center in 1988, and provides auditorium-style seating for 241 people. Tropical plants fill the tropical conservatory. Beyond the waterfall, over 300 different varieties of exotic plants are displayed. The Beggs Garden was added along with the lecture hall and made possible by a donation from Mr. and Mrs. W. A. Moncrief, Jr., named in honor of her father, George Beggs.

Conservatory, June 1990
(Courtesy Fort Worth Botanic Gardens)

(Courtesy of the Quentin McGown Post Card Collection)

The Fragrance Garden, originally constructed in 1963, was renovated in '89. The pavestone walks, raised herb beds and half moon fountain with a ceramic facade is an inviting space. There are four pieces of sculpture placed on garden columns designed by Evaline Selolors, which feature raised patterns of foliage and wildlife. Presented first as a fragrance garden for the blind, the plants around the perimeter supply scented leaves and fragrant flowers and the Braille plant labels are provided for the visually impaired.

The Adelaide Polk Fuller Garden is a gift from the Fuller Foundation. It is located west of the center and features a classical gazebo with a slate roof and stone columns, arbors shading pathways, several fountains, a rivulet and reflection pool. Annuals and perennials provide seasonal color with a diverse collection of trees and shrubs. The Fuller family provided an endowment to guarantee the Garden's future maintenance and continued beauty.

The Leonard Courtyard is framed by the Botanic Garden Center. This extension of the Center invites visitors outdoors to experience the horticultural displays and to enjoy a tranquil atmosphere.

In 1988 a new master plan of development for the Garden was developed that will lead the Fort Worth Botanic Garden into the 21st century. The Garden Center will serve as the focal point of the complex, housing several new facilities including expanded conservatory space, a restaurant, and tram station. The BRIT, Botanical Research Institute of Texas will share a strong symbiotic relationship with the Garden, bringing the fascinating world of exotic plant materials within reach of garden patrons. A Promenade is to be a linear garden devoted to pedestrian use and to link all existing and future specialty gardens to the Center.

The future holds changes for The Botanic Gardens, but it will always remain Fort Worth's ultimate garden experience; a scenic haven, a break from the routine, or just a beautiful place to enjoy.

(Courtesy Fort Worth Botanic Gardens)

A Short History of the Fort Worth Nature Center and Refuge

As remembered by William Barney, Founder and Poet Laureate of the Fort Worth Nature Center and Refuge

Tracing the beginnings of the Fort Worth Nature Center and Refuge poses no great problem. You can put your finger on the calendar and say it began on such and such a day, when members of the Fort Worth Audubon Society acted. They decided that something must be done to assure a reasonable chance for the wildlife of our city and environs. They formed a conservation committee in January 1964 and presented a request to the Park Board. On February 12th, 1964 the Park Board designated a 360 acre location on upper Lake Worth as a "wildlife sanctuary and nature preserve," with the local Audubon Society given responsibility for "developing it."

They met the challenge, requesting information on the planning of nature centers from the National Audubon Society. Warren Pulich was employed to propose utilization and to lay out trails. Trails were cut. Moves were made toward erecting a shelter house on the island. The first naturalist, William Spalsbury, came on June 17, 1964. The presence of a nature center began to take hold in the minds of many. The enthusiasm that had fueled the growth of this project for now a quarter of century began to boil.

On October 17, 1967, Mike Ross became the naturalist. In this year, taking advantage of the expiration of leases in the area, the City of Fort Worth took one of its most inspired, far-sighted actions expanding the center to more than 3000 acres thus making it the largest of its kind in the nation. Rick Pratt became head naturalist in September, 1968. The need for a functional building became apparent, and on February 4, 1970, the Bureau of Outdoor Recreation, Interior Department, approved a grant of $40,000 matching the same amount by the city, for the construction of an Interpretive Center. In November the name of Robert E. Hardwicke, who had been active in conservation work and in legislation to protect park areas, was proposed for the new center. In January, 1971, Harold Arnold became the head naturalist. The first steps toward fencing the refuge, to prevent vandalism and dumping, were taken.

On September 17, 1971, the new Robert E. Hardwicke Interpretive Center was dedicated, a high point for all who had watched it take shape. An advisory board was formed to assist with input from various interested groups in planning for future developments. In February, 1972, the Sid Richardson Foundation granted $5000 for the development of a master plan for the refuge, with the Junior League of Fort Worth providing an additional $1500. In April, a team of four men from the National Audubon Society headed by Dr. Joseph Shoman, began their study. These men declared it a unique situation, a "prototype," no site of this size and variety could be found elsewhere in the United States. They recommended the name be changed to the Fort Worth Nature Center and Refuge, as the city justly deserved to put its name on the place. The name was changed in 1975.

Work began on one of their recommendations, for a boardwalk at the Lotus Marsh. The enthusiasm of Fort Worth citizens is shown by such actions as that of the Meadowbrook Garden Club which gave $830 toward construction of the boardwalk. The Junior League in 1973 provided $499 for the platform, and in 1974 the platform was completed thanks to a gift of $1000 by Mrs. Harry Wallenburg.

1974 saw the organization of the Friends of the Fort Worth Nature Center and Refuge. The formal organization has made possible a steady support for the staff, the development of many useful programs, the acquisition of equipment and various improvements. Even more important, it has given a growing band of supporters a sense of sharing in the growth and outreach of the Center. In 1974 the Equestrian Trail was virtually completed, all 5.1 miles. Buffalo, a cow and calf, and three deer were on hand.

(Courtesy of Fort Worth Nature Center}

The refuge has been a delight to the school children of Fort Worth. The staff, Junior League and schools arranged to provide for visits. The Fort Worth Museum of Science and History has lent its aid also. Here the work of docents must be recognized. It is impossible to guess what exposure to the wonders of the refuge can have done for youngsters.

In March, 1975, Tom Wood became an assistant naturalist; in 1977, he was made head naturalist. 1977 saw the beginning of the Prairie Dog Town and the paving of roads in the refuge. 1978 brought the closing of the North Peninsula to control vandalism and dumping. The popularity of the Nature Center became so great that it outgrew its original building. An addition, providing an auditorium, library, offices and support space was begun and ultimately dedicated in February 1981. In 1985, a new staff position, Public Education Specialist, was added to expand the educational programs. The Carter Foundation funded the pilot program, which included the purchase of a vehicle, allowing for offsite programs to schools, nursing homes, and libraries. Over 35,000 citizens have enjoyed these programs.

It would be just about impossible to list all the activities the Nature Center has provided, but let's list a few: prairie burn; first aid and rehabilitation for injured animals; hiking; wildflower identification classes and censuses; bird identification classes; night-owl sessions; star-gazing; identification of grasses; establishment of a herbarium; snake workshops; sale of books; trips to Colorado, Aransas Refuge, Big Thicket, Caddo Lake, Wichita Mountains, Davis Mountains; summer classes for children; Natural Guard cleanups; birdseed sales; photo contest; moonlight hikes; the removal of a humongous pile of throwaway tires; luncheons; bazaars, and a host of others.

In May, 1985, a windmill was erected at the newly developed outdoor educational site between the Interpretive Center and the Boardwalk. The renovation of this old homesite was completed by Women in Construction as a shelter house for programs and groups.

In June, 1987, the Nature Center received an award on Texas Wildflower Day at Denton for its work in conservation and education concerning wildflowers. In July an endowment program was initiated by the Advisory Board, looking toward the future needs of the Center. In July, 1988, Tom Wood left to take over at Ramsey Canyon, Arizona, with Wayne Clark taking interim duties (Wayne has since accepted the position of Nature Center Supervisor). In August, a new water well made sure the needs of plants and people will be met about the Center. Burrowing Owls were released at the Prairie Dog Town.

Any history should be replete with names, both of the prime movers and those who came later to lend a shoulder. This account for space reasons has focused on the Refuge itself, but a long and fervid gracias to all of them living and dead, who made this "Jewel of the Crosstimbers" a place of unending delight.

Current status of the Fort Worth Nature Center and Refuge:

The Fort Worth Nature Center and Refuge currently consists of approximately 3,500 acres making it the largest community owned nature center in the United States. It consists of prime examples of the three primary natural ecosystems of North Central Texas: the western cross timbers, the Fort Worth (or Grand) prairie and the wetlands habitats associated with the Trinity River. The current mission of the Nature Center is "to enhance the quality of life by enrolling and educating our community in the preservation and protection of natural areas while standing as an example of these same principles in North Central Texas".

Current educational programs offered by the Nature Center include: Summer Natural History Classes for grades one through eight. Canoe programs including tours and learn to canoe classes, naturalist-led interpretive hikes over the twenty-five mile trail system, Preschool Discovery Classes, grade specific school field trips, and special events including Nature Center Field Day and Snakes of Tarrant County.

The Log Cabin Village

The Log Cabin Village, a living history museum set amidst two and one-half acres of a beautiful wooded park, consists of seven 19th century log houses and a reproduction blacksmith shop. The Village depicts the life of pioneers who settled the North Central Texas area in the mid 1800's. Each authentic cabin relates the story of the pioneer family who built and owned it. In addition, different aspects of pioneer life such as spinning, weaving, and candle-making are demonstrated. Demonstrations available may vary.

Other highlights include a working gristmill; a one-room schoolhouse; and the Parker Cabin, the dogtrot home where the kidnapped Cynthia Ann Parker resided after the Parker family recaptured her from her Indian family. The impressive two-story Foster Log House, built by slaves in the 1850s, serves as the museum store and visitor center.

The City of Fort Worth Parks and Community Services Department operates the Village, which opened to the public in 1966. City staff, enrollees in the Senior Texans Employment Program, and volunteers bring Texas pioneer history to life for thousands of school children and tourists through special programs, hands-on activities, and walk-through tours.

Shaw Cabin and Grist Mill. The mill originally served as the Parker County, Texas home of Thomas J. Shaw. When the cabin was moved to Log Cabin Village, milling equipment was added and it became a working Grist Mill.*(Courtesy Log Cabin Village Parks and Community Services Department, City of Fort Worth)*

FORT WORTH WATER GARDENS

The Fort Worth Water Gardens were a gift from the Amon G. Carter Foundation to the City of Fort Worth, and are operated by the Parks and Community Services Department. They were designed by Architects Philip Johnson and John Burgee of New York, New York. Eight years in the making, from the date of conception, June 1966, to the date of completion in October 1974, the Gardens cost $7 million. They contain four and three-tenths acres. Five major water features are displayed in the Water Gardens. These attractions require water pumps with a total capacity of 440 horsepower to provide the movement of water at a rate of 19,000 gallons per minute.

At the main entrance on Houston Street is the Cascade Pool which has multi-tiered ledges with water spilling into a pool

The Wet Wall has a continuous trough, 650 feet long, built into the twenty-two foot high wall and water flows "sheet-like" into a moat at the base of the wall.

Enclosed by the Wet Wall is the Quiet Water Pool, 16 feet below ground level,. which is accessible by stairs down to the surrounding walk and Bald Cypress trees.

At the Aerated Water Pool, twelve feet below ground level, water pumps with a capacity of forty HP provide 871 gallons of water per minute through forty special spray nozzles.

The most unusual water feature is the Active Water Pool which is thirty-eight feet below ground level at its lowest point. The 710-foot concealed trough moves 10,500 gallons of water per minute, flowing constantly downward, providing a series of frolicking waterfalls from the top until ending in the Active Water Pool

The Gardens are composed of concrete and earth form. There were 17,000 cubic yards of concrete used in the seven miles of stairstep walls. Approximately 300 trees were used in establishing the Gardens. These include Coastal Live Oaks, Bald Cypress, and Bradford Pear, along with 32,000 Junipers and Indian Hawthorne which contribute to form a textured groundcover.

1981	*1982*
Worthington Hotel Opens	*First City Bank Tower is built; Bob Bolen is elcted Mayor and serves until 1991*

WILL ROGERS MEMORIAL CENTER

(Courtesy of City of Fort Worth Public Events Department)

Longhorn Cattle on the Lancaster bridge lead the way to the Will Rogers Memorial Center

(Landmark Staff Photo)

(Both photos courtesy of Fort Worth Public Events Department)

Will Rogers Memorial Center is a multi-purpose entertainment complex under forty-five acres of roof and spread over eighty-five acres in the heart of the Fort Worth Cultural District. This city-owned center generates more than $200 million to the local economy from an estimated 2.5 million visitors to a variety of events each year.

The Will Rogers Coliseum was erected along with the Auditorium and Landmark Pioneer Tower in 1936, the year of the Texas Centennial. Largest of all the buildings, the Coliseum is the first domed structure of its kind in the world.

The versatility of the 2,856 seat Auditorium has housed corporate meetings, graduations, dance recitals and many Broadway performances. The 50's and 60's hosted the likes of Jack Benny, Benny Goodman, Billy Graham, Betty Grable in *Hell's a Poppin'*, Glen Miller, The Vienna Boys Choir, The Rolling Stones and a somewhat controversial show called *Hair*. Some recent shows include Red Skelton, Barbara Mandrell, *Les Miserables, Joseph and the Amazing Technicolor Dreamcoat*, to *Jesus Christ Superstar* and a host of concerts, religious and community programs.

The Amon G. Carter, Jr. Exhibits Hall was opened in January 1984 and offers rooms for exhibit shows, banquets, meetings and performances on stage. The largest contiguous space for exhibit shows is 100,000 sq. ft. This facility hosts many consumer shows, large parties, wedding receptions and conventions.

Since the opening of the $16 million Will Rogers Equestrian Center in 1988, Will Rogers Memorial Center has become known and recognized as a world-class center with over 100,000 horses having participated in equestrian events from January 1988 to the present. The Equestrian Center includes a 215,000 sq. ft. building containing a 1, 946-seat show arena and 640-seat sale arena, an additional 197,000 sq. ft. livestock building and utilizes the 5,693-seat coliseum. This facility contains 843 permanent horse stalls.

The new $11 million, 170,000-square-foot Moncrief Building opened in January 1996 includes a 1,000 seat arena and space for up to 650 cattle or 260 horses and meeting rooms. By adding portable stalls in other buildings, the total number of available stalls can be increased to 2,200. Completion of this building makes Fort Worth the ultimate livestock show location in the nation. We now have three climate-controlled arenas in addition to the Amon G. Carter, Jr. Exhibits Hall, Will Rogers Auditorium and six Livestock Barns.

Longtime established events continue annually such as the Southwestern Exposition and Livestock Show which celebrated its Centennial in January 1996 and attracts 800,000 people in two weeks, three National Cutting Horse Association competitions, the American Quarter Horse Youth Association World Show, the American Paint Horse Association World Championship Show and the Appaloosa Horse Club World Championship Show.

The Will Rogers Auditorium was also erected for Fort Worth's 1936 Frontier Centennial celebrating Texas's 100th birthday. After more than fifty years of performances and events, the City of Fort Worth retained Hahnfeld Associates to restore this stately edifice. A goal of the architects was to respect the original design, including returning to the celebratory, patriotic, interior color scheme. As a result of the restoration, the "soul" of this theater style auditorium is rejuvenated.

Its versatility has housed corporate meetings, graduations, dance recitals and many Broadway performances.

(both photos courtesy of Fort Worth Public Events Department)

Paris Coffee Shop

The Paris Coffee Shop, established in 1926 by Vic Paris, was purchased in 1930 by Gregory K. Smith (shown in the right photo above with the cigar). Relocated in 1974 to the northwest corner of Magnolia and Hemphill, son Michael Smith now runs the Fort Worth institution where their "home-cooking and and home made pies are the best in town" according the many patrons. There are numerous vintage Fort Worth photos displayed on the walls, as the one shown below of the Pig Stand formerly located on the north side.

(Photos Courtesy of The Paris Coffee Shop)

Cattlemen's Steak House

Founded in 1946 by Jesse and Mozelle Roach, this North Side institution started as a barbecue cafe and grew to a steak house of world renown. In 1994, a group of experienced international restaurateurs purchased the assets from Jesse's widow and renamed it Cattlemen's Fort Worth Steak House, Inc.

Space Shuttle "Challenger" explodes on take-off, killing all seven crew members

George Bush elected President

Billy Bob's Texas

The building now known as Billy Bob's Texas was built in 1910 and was once a large open-air barn for housing prize cattle during the Fort Worth Stock Show. In 1936, as a centennial project, the building was enclosed and the tower added. The structure contained 1257 animal stalls, and a 1200 seat auction ring (now Billy Bob's Bull Riding Arena). The floor of Billy Bob's slopes from entry toward the showroom stage, making an ideal elevation for concert seating. This slope was originally constructed to allow easy cleaning and runoff from the cattle pens. Livestock events were held here until the stock show moved to the Will Rogers Memorial Complex. During World War I, the building was used as an airplane factory. In the 1950's, the building was home to a department store so large the stockboys wore roller-skates.

Billy Bob's Texas opened on April 1, 1981 - to national attention with it's 100,000 square foot entertainment center, forty bar stations, country music's biggest stars, and real pro bull riding. Billy Bob's can accommodate over 6000 fun lovin' folks, with something for all ages. The celebrity wall of fame displays handprints of country stars, Billy Bob's arcade features state-of-the-art video and skill games, plus over a dozen pool tables. Climb aboard the photo bull to become an instant rodeo legend.

Billy Bob's hosts the biggest stars in country music (and sometimes rock) every weekend. The list of performers is practically endless, including Garth Brooks, Alabama, George Strait, Reba McEntire, Willie Nelson, LeAnn Rimes, Clint Black, Alan Jackson, Ringo Starr, Kenny Loggins, Bob Hope, and more!

Over 23,000 bulls have bucked at Billy Bob's, with rodeo's top competitors aboard. Billy Bob's is a popular spot for movies and television shows - including Baja, Oklahoma with Willie Nelson, Over the Top starring Sylvester Stallone, George Strait in Pure Country & Necessary Roughness with Scott Bakula. Television shows and specials include: Dallas - Walker, Texas Ranger - CBS Happy New Year America - CBS This Morning - Entertainment Tonight - and Billy Bob's Country. Country Music Videos have been filmed for Collin Raye, Bryan White, Daron Norwood, BR459 and more.

With all this entertainment, it's no wonder that Billy Bob's has been named Club of the Year by the Academy of Country Music four times and by the Country Music Association three times. Billy Bob's is open daily for family fun, with live entertainment nightly.

(Courtesy Billy Bob's)

Mayfest

In 1970, the Junior League of Fort Worth and private donors funded the Halprin Plan designed by Lawrence Halprin, a landscape architect from San Francisco. The plan was developed to beautify the urban greenbelt along the eight miles of the Trinity River which runs through the heart of the city. In 1971. the Streams and Valleys Committee was created to preserve and beautify the river and parks and to implement the Halprin plan. By 1973, the greenbelt was so improved that the Trinity River Festival was held in Trinity Park to celebrate. Thus, the beginning of Mayfest.

Mayfest has four sponsors, the Junior League of Fort Worth, Inc., the City of Fort Worth Parks and Community Services Department, the Tarrant Regional Water District and Streams and Valleys, Inc. Mayfest, Inc. was created in September 1987. Its purpose is to raise funds for community non-profit programs and for continued improvement and awareness of the parks and the Trinity River through a combination of volunteerism and community resources. For the twenty-seventh year in a row, this was done by having an outdoor festival in Trinity Park along the banks of the Trinity River April 29 - May 2, 1999. Mayfest, Inc. Board of Directors, comprised of representatives from the four sponsors, oversees the operation of the corporation and advises the volunteer Festival Chairman, the Central Committee Chairmen, and their sub-committees who plan and implement the festival.

All profits from Mayfest, which to date exceed 4.5 million dollars, have been returned to the community through various projects such as the construction of miles of bike paths and rest areas and the planting of hundreds of trees along the Trinity River, and to support community programs such as Performing Arts Fort Worth, Summerbridge, Habitat for Humanity, Fort Worth Teen Court, Alliance for Children and First Call for Help. Over the course of time, the Mayfest festival has continued to grow and make changes to attract the more than 250,000 people that attend each year. The Mayfest festival includes a Children's Area, Art Market, Sports Area, Teen Area, Garden Run, Parade, Special Needs Day, Raffle, tremendous entertainment, a variety of food and beverage and various other concessions. The Children's Area features free activity booths where children can sculpt clay creatures, build wood and stick structures, create sandpaintings, search for hidden treasures in a sand pile, have their faces painted as well as enjoy special entertainment just for them.

The Art Market features fifty-four artists who are juried by a panel of art experts. These artists can demonstrate, display and sell their artwork. The Sports Area is a favorite of those who want to test their skills in sports such as fishing, ball throws, golfing, relays, obstacle courses and a variety of other sporting events. Six different stages located throughout the park display continuous and diverse entertainment. From the Fort Worth Symphony to the Party Crashers, country and western bands to children's and adult dance groups, some type of entertainment appeals to every Mayfest visitor. The Mayfest Garden Run offers the opportunity for friends, families, coworkers, even school groups to run or walk together through the beautiful Trinity Park in a race for all ages on the Saturday morning of Mayfest.

Other special events include the Mayfest Raffle-buy a ticket for a chance to win one of the many great prizes. The Mayfest Parade marches through the middle of the festival featuring bands, floats and special guests. Special Needs Day held for special needs students of the FWISD allows these children an opportunity to experience the outdoors and Mayfest during the afternoon before the park opens to the public. Food and beverage concessions abound, with everything from pizza to fajitas, funnel cakes to turkey legs, and Texas Taters awaits you at Mayfest.

(Courtesy Mayfest, Inc.)

Mayfest has served as a successful model of a private and public sector partnership for a quarter of a century. We feel that the cooperative effort and shared commitment to this festival continue to increase awareness of the parks and riverbelt, and the energy and funds we direct toward meeting our community needs will continue to enhance the quality of life in our community for years to come.

Projects and programs which have benefited from Mayfest proceeds include: Log Cabin Village Restoration; Tutoring Centers for Juvenile Probation; Legal Aid - Consumer Center; Tarrant Co. Medical Education & Research Foundation; Mental Health Assoc. of Tarrant Co. Education & Research Foundation; Music Education; Poison Education Program; North Fort Worth Historical/Architectural Survey; Management Workshops for Directors of Volunteers; Van Cliburn Competition; Eddleman-McFarland Museum and Docent Program; First Texas Council of Camp Fire, Inc.; United Cerebral Palsy of Tarrant Co.; Lena Pope Home, Special School Advocate Program; FWISD Adopt-A-School; Spruce Emergency Youth Shelter; Tarrant Council on Alcoholism and Drug Abuse; Fort Worth Teen Court; St. Joseph Hospital Family Development Foundation - Community Hospice; Gifted Students

Institute; Gill Children's Services, Inc.; Fort Worth Public Library; Citizens Crime Commission of Tarrant Co.; AIDS Outreach Center; 35 miles of paved and unpaved bike paths on the Trinity River; Trinity Park lighting, play equipment, duck pond renovation, shelter roofing; FWISD "Sister to Sister"; Easter Seal Society; Performing Arts Fort Worth; Planned Parenthood Education Bureau Volunteers in Public Schools; Camp Fire Girls; Painted Spaces, Inc.; Day Care Assoc. Group Home Parenting Guidance Center; Oral Histories of Fort Worth, Inc.; Law in a Changing Society; Summer Camp for Epileptic Children; Women's Haven, Inc.; Historic Preservation Council for Tarrant Co.; Botanic Garden Education Program; Funding Information Center; Tarrant Co. Youth Collaboration; Child Study Center; Foster Child Advocate Services; YWCA Teen Parent Support Program; Sickle Cell - Parent Support and Education; Corporate Program for Active Retirement; Fort Worth Symphony Orchestra; Women's Center of Tarrant Co.; "I Have a Dream" Foundation; First Call for Help/United Way of Tarrant Co.; First Presbyterian Church - Senior Adult Day; Historic Fort Worth, Inc.; Fort Worth Theatre; American Diabetes Assoc.; The Salvation Army; Riding Unlimited; Outreach Program at Fort Worth Nature Center; Get Involved Day; Special Needs School Children; Boys and Girls Clubs; Ronald McDonald House & Meals with Zeal.

(Photos Courtesy Mayfest, Inc.)

Oktoberfest

Oktoberfest
(Courtesy Symphony League of Fort Worth, Inc.)

Acclaimed as Fort Worth's major fall festival, the Symphony League's annual fund-raiser, Oktoberfest, has become one of the best loved festivals in the city. It all began in 1970 when Lorene Cecil, Projects Chairman, suggested the festival as a way to raise money for student concerts. She remembered the excitement of attending the colorful Oktoberfests in Munich.

Community involvement was sought, and the Oktoberfest Committee found some enthusiastic supporters — especially the late Owen Howard, General Manager of Ben E. Keith. Other community supporters included Herman Jung of Green Oaks Inn, F. Howard Walsh, Sr., Hugh Watson and Dr. Feliks Gwozdz. In later years the 200 foot German mural was painted by artist Gene Vandiver.

The first Oktoberfest was held in the Texas & Pacific Terminal, which was rented for only $1.00. Hoping at least 700 people would come to the festival, the League was overwhelmed when more than 7,000 attended.

Over 25,000 area school children are able to attend the "Adventures in Music" concerts each year because of the work and commitment of our many Oktoberfest volunteers. The Symphony League has contributed over $2,500,000 to the Fort Worth Symphony through Oktoberfest proceeds.

Many of the city's music and arts groups have participated in Oktoberfest. Highlighting the entertainment schedule is a performance by the Fort Worth Symphony Orchestra. The sounds of polka, jazz, country western, swing-time, and the activities of five stages always make a lively festival.

Working for a common goal of raising money for student concerts and general support of the Symphony, thousands of volunteers and many underwriting sponsors make this a festival of fun and fellowship in the true German tradition. This tradition will continue as Oktoberfest celebrates its 30th Anniversary festival "Longhorns to Lederhosen" in October of 1999.

TARANTULA'S HISTORIC ROUTE

In the late 1860s, as Texas left its frontier days behind, railroads determined the survival of towns and communities across the state. Without railroads, many once thriving communities withered and died. In those early days, the arrival of a railroad was reason for great rejoicing, as it assured the economic vitality of a town.

The "Cotton Belt Route," known officially as the St. Louis Southwestern Railway, was the first serious attempt at developing an extended international railroad system on the North American continent Its builders envisioned a narrow-gauge route from St. Louis to the Texas border, continuing along a three-foot gauge road to the capital of the Aztec Republic.

From its inception in the late 1870s, the route steadily spread across the Southwest spurring the development of towns and communities along its path. In the latter part of the 1880s, Cotton Belt officials, recognizing Fort Worth as an "up and coming" community, extended the line to the town. The tracks to Fort Worth were primarily for transporting lumber, which the town needed to keep pace with its "boom town" growth.

Although the Cotton Belt was not the first to extend its lines to Fort Worth, it did provide the city's first scheduled package car service; progress reports on freight shipments enroute; early second-morning delivery from St. Louis; and coordinated train and truck service. The Cotton Belt, and the economic prosperity it brought, was an integral element in the growth of Fort Worth and Grapevine - and as these cities and surrounding communities grew, so did the railroad.

Today the Tarantula Train traverses the original Cotton Belt tracks as it journeys from historic Grapevine to the Stockyards National Historic District in Fort Worth. The ride takes visitors through the cities and communities of Colleyville, Southlake, North Richland Hills (including historic Smithfield) and Haltom City.

1896 TARANTULA EXCURSION TRAIN: STEAM LOCOMOTIVE No.2248

Steam Locomotive No.2248, the primary engine for the Tarantula train, is a product of the Cooke Locomotive Works of Paterson, NJ. Built in 1896, No.2248 was considered a "heavy mountain-class" locomotive as indicated on the original Cooke drawings. As the era of steam engines waned and diesels became popular, the engine was converted to a fire control "pumper" locomotive and assigned to the Northern California mountain district to fight forest, wooden snow shed and tunnel fires.

As more modern fire control methods became available, No.2248 was remodeled and assigned to exhibition train service as a ceremonial engine for the Southern Pacific in California. When her flue time ran out in late 1959, she was retired and purchased by a private collector, Charles T. Brown of San Fernando, California. He and promoter Walt Disney had plans to build a full-size steam railroad around Griffith Park in Los Angeles. These plans never materialized, and Disney went on to open Disneyland. No.2248 went to Brown's backyard in San Fernando.

In 1974, No.2248 was purchased by the Texas State railroad for service on its fledgling Palestine-Rusk run. The engine was painted red, white and blue in honor of the United States' Bicentennial and commissioned as Engine No.200. The Palestine-Rusk excursion became very popular, and the little engine just couldn't pull the increasingly heavy loads. By 1981, No.200 had run her last mile on the Texas State line and was stored, unserviceable, at the Rusk shop.

In 1990, the Tarantula Project acquired the engine and transported it to Fort Worth. When the engine arrived, crews began extensive restoration work. The engine received new driving box brasses, driving wheels were turned, and firebox side sheet and fire tube were replaced. Both cylinders were bored and new piston rings were manufactured. The cab was lined with red oak and, along with new electrical systems, all new brass detailing was installed. Working every day, crews finished the restoration in one year. Even the engines original number, No.2248, was restored.

No. 2248 was placed into service on the Tarantula's Stockyards/Eighth Avenue Depot route in January 1992. She now pulls six cars, four passenger and two open patio coaches (circa 1920s). All coaches were beautifully refurbished in turn-of-the-century fashion, befitting the grand engine.

On August 30,1996, one hundred years after she rolled off the production line of Cooke Locomotive Works, No.2248 began daily runs from the Cotton Belt Depot in Grapevine to Stockyards Station in Fort Worth. Steam Locomotive No.2248 is the only operational steam locomotive in Texas dating prior to the turn of the century.

The "Tarantula" moniker is derived from a promotional railway map drawn by B. B. Paddock depicting Fort Worth as the center of a series of rail lines, like a spider's legs extending from its body. Thus, the name Tarantula. The map was prophetic, having first been published in 1873, three years before the arrival of any railroad into the city. By 1900, nine railroad lines radiated from Fort Worth's center, and the Tarantula dream was a reality.

(Courtesy The Tarantula Corp.)

THE OLD WEST LIVES IN THE STOCKYARDS NATIONAL HISTORIC DISTRICT

The sounds of saloon singers, lowing cattle and jingling spurs still echo on Exchange Avenue in the historic Fort Worth Stockyards. But they aren't ghosts of past inhabitants. They're real.

One hundred years after the establishment of the stopping point along the legendary Chisholm Trail, Fort Worth's Stockyards National Historic District is very much alive. In fact, the entire area is on the National Register of Historic Places.

The Stockyards grew as a satellite of old Fort Worth, 2.5 miles to its south. Fort Worth first was settled in 1849 as an outpost along the Trinity River. It became a stop for cowboys driving cattle from South Texas to Kansas along the Eastern Cattle Trail, one of the routes that fed Jesse Chisholm's trail to Abilene, Kansas.

By 1876, rail lines that extended like spider's legs from downtown Fort Worth included the Fort Worth Stockyards Belt Railway, which moved livestock from the Stockyards to the Kansas packing plants.

Within a few years, Swift and Armour, the country's two largest meat-packing companies, located packing houses in the Stockyards. The area was the second-largest stockyard in the country and the headquarters of several agricultural companies. Cattle pens extended for nearly a mile and property values were so high in the area, incorporated in 1911 as Niles City, it became known as the "Richest Little Town in the World." The area was annexed by Fort Worth in 1923.

In the years that followed, the cattle industry slowed, and although the Fort Worth Stockyards continued to function, the area deteriorated. But civic leaders with sentimental attachments to the historic area launched a major effort to restore it.

Today, the Western atmosphere and architecture have been carefully preserved. Western festivals throughout the year celebrate the city's Chisholm Trail heritage and commemorate the history of the pioneers who once settled here.

The old hog and sheep pens have been restored and now house Stockyards Station, a festival marketplace and depot for the Tarantula Steam Excursion Train. The 165,000-square-foot space has a selection of merchandise varying from art galleries and antiques to clothing, gourmet items, music, and Texas fare to please every palate. The Western theme reigns throughout the near thirty shops and restaurants in the marketplace. And a Western-style amusement park is adjacent to the Station, with fun for kids of all ages.

In shops located throughout the area, craftsmen use time-worn tools to hand-craft saddles, chaps and boots. The best Western shopping is available here, as are a number of restaurants and saloons to rest your heels.

The mission-style Cowtown Coliseum, built in 1908, was home of the world's first indoor rodeo, and hosted performances by Enrico Caruso and Elvis Presley. It's alive most weekends with professional rodeo competitions and Wild West shows.

The Stockyards Collection & Museum now occupies the Spanish-style Livestock Exchange Building, along with cattle brokers, lawyers, marketing firms, an art gallery, and the North Fort Worth Historical Society. Livestock auctions are still held weekly, although now entire herds are bought and sold by satellite in keeping with today's technology.

The Stockyards Hotel (where Bonnie and Clyde once stayed) has been restored to its original splendor, its lobby decorated in "Cattle Baron Baroque." The nearby Cowtown Corrals offer trail rides along the Trinity River. Other Stockyards' hotels include the Hotel Texas and Miss Molly's B&B.

It's all a happy reminder that the Old West - its lifestyle, culture and spirit - are thriving in the Stockyards National Historic District.

(Courtesy The Tarantula Corp.)

The Fort Worth Convention Center

The Fort Worth Convention Center opened under the name of Tarrant County Convention Center in 1968. The fourteen city-block expanse (all under one roof) is divided into three basic units: 100,000 sq.ft. exhibit hall (West Hall), 10,500 seat arena, and 3,000 seat theater. Twenty-five meeting rooms were available that would accommodate 10-200 people.

In 1983, a major expansion was completed that added an 800 space parking garage and 45,000 square feet of exhibit space (East Hall)

In 1986, the City and County developed a better of understanding and City bed tax funds were available for the first time to assist in attracting convention visitors. The facility was renamed the "Fort Worth/Tarrant County Convention Center. In addition, a priority booking policy was adopted that gave priority booking of all dates outside a two year window to the Fort Worth Convention & Visitor's Bureau. Dates within the two year window remained the responsibility of the Convention Center staff.

During the next eleven years, Tarrant County invested over $25 million in renovation of the property. The primary enhancements involved completely remodeled meeting rooms and general offices, exhibit hall divider wall replacement; enhancements to public space; arena seat replacement, ADA enhancements, two elevators and ACM abatement.

In October, 1997 the facility was purchased by the City of Fort Worth and renamed the Fort Worth Convention Center. The citizens of Fort Worth voted in favor of a bond election to enlarge the facility. City officials are currently undergoing design plans for the expansion with construction anticipated to begin in mid 2000.

(Courtesy of Fort Worth Public Events Department)

Images of Sundance Square

Sundance Square
(Courtesy Jack White Photograph Collection, The University of Texas at Arlington Libraries)

(Photos Courtesy Fort Worth Convention & Visitors Bureau)

Fort Worth - One of the Premier Aviation Cities in the United States

Douglas Harman

Douglas Harman, CDME, Ph.D., is the President and C.E.O. of the Fort Worth Convention and Visitors Bureau

Fort Worth International Airfest

Philanthropist and Fort Worth Star-Telegram publisher Amon Carter Sr. brought the first aviators to Fort Worth. In 1911, he paid $5,000 to a group of touring French aviators, who performed the city's first airshow in a field north of Seventh Street.

Not long after, the famous "Daredevil Cal" Roger stopped in Fort Worth on the first transcontinental flight across the United States. When he landed his Vin-Fiz flyer in Ryan Pasture, Amon Carter was there again, and the first to shake Rogers' hand.

World War I

The most highly publicized event associated with the Royal Flying Corps in Fort Worth was the death of Captain Vernon Castle. Castle and his wife Irene were a world-famous dance team when Vernon enlisted in the RFC. After distinguishing himself in combat over Europe, he was assigned to Fort Worth as a flight instructor at the RFC training fields.

He was killed when a student pilot flew his aircraft into the path of Castle and his student. Castle took the controls and avoided the mid-air collision, but died when the aircraft crashed at Benbrook Field. His funeral parade in Fort Worth was one of the largest in the history of the city. "The Story of Vernon and Irene Castle," a film starring Fred Astaire and Ginger Rogers, retold the story of the well-known dance team. Its premier was at the Worth Theater in Fort Worth.

Lindy Landed Here

Meacham Field, the city's first municipal airport, welcomed another aviation pioneer 70 years ago. Shortly after his triumphant return from France after successfully crossing the Atlantic in 1927, Charles Lindbergh embarked on a 95-day, 82-city tour of the United States to promote the development of commercial aviation and construction of airports.

After a short parade down North Main Street, the famous pilot greeted 15,000 school children who had gathered in Panther Park, the Fort Worth Cats' home field. Then he moved to the Hotel Texas, now the Radisson, where he stayed the night before the next day's flight to Dallas.

He also predicted that within the year, passenger and express planes in the United States would fly a daily distance equal half that around the world, that every major city would have airmail and passenger-carrying airlines, and that airplanes would travel all over the country with "a capacity of at least 12 passengers."

First flight over Fort Worth, 1911. Duration, fifteen minutes.

(Courtesy Fort Worth Star-Telegram Photograph Collection, Special Collections Division, The University of Texas at Arlington Libraries)

Carswell and the "Bomber Plant"

In 1942, Fort Worth provided the land for the "Bomber Plant" which began producing the B-24. Over the years, the U. S. Airforce Plant has built many aircraft, including the B-32, B-36, B-58, F-111, F-16, and now the F-22. Across the field is now the important Joint Reserve Base which is home to the Naval Air Station, which is important to the current military concept of training all U. S. aviation forces to work together under single command. The base was named for Major Horace S. Carswell, Jr., a Fort Worth native who died while flying a B-24 in combat in WW II, During the Cold War era, the base was home to B-52 bombers.

The Helicopter and Fort Worth

In 1951, Amon Carter Sr. brought yet another form of aviation to Fort Worth. He and other local leaders convinced Bell Helicopter to move its headquarters from Buffalo, N.Y. At the time of relocation, Bell was the leader in helicopter technology. In subsequent years, Bell established numerous production and flight records in the emerging world of helicopters. In 1963, they produced the 1,000th model 47 helicopter, the model most commonly associated with the Korean War era.

During the late '50s and '60s, Bell helicopter developed the Huey and the Bell Jet Ranger. These and other associated aircraft made Bell the dominant helicopter company in the world. In 1973, the 1,000th Jet Ranger was delivered by Bell Helicopter.

Over the years, Bell helicopters set a long list of significant records. Ross Perot Jr. and Jay Coburn, flying a Bell Long Ranger II, became the first pilots to complete an around-the-world helicopter trip. Their aircraft is now on display in the Smithsonian Institute.

Bell has produced more than 31,000 helicopters, more than any other manufacturer in the world. It currently has in production a number of different commercial and military helicopters. Bell had long been developing the technology of a convertible plane and in 1981, Bell's XV-15 tilt rotor aircraft was the first to perform at the Paris Air Show. The U.S. government eventually authorized a significant tilt rotor demonstration and a program to produce more V-22 aircraft, a contingency for U. S. Navy ships, and the Marines, and potential sales to foreign military and civilian interests.

Fort Worth Airport, late 1920's

(Courtesy Fort Worth Public Library)

Meacham Field

(Courtesy Fort Worth Star-Telegram Photograph Collection, Special Collections Division, The University of Texas at Arlington Libraries)

The Future of Aviation in Fort Worth

Fort Worth is best known for its "Cowtown" image, but it really is "Aviation City." Aviation has become the dominant industry in Fort Worth, serving in an even more influential way than cattle did in earlier years. The development of Alliance Airport by the City government and Ross Perot, Jr. has been another factor in making aviation a continuing force in Fort Worth's future.

The interest in aviation continues to blossom.

East Elevation and Passenger Loading Apron, Greater Fort Worth International Airport, Amon Carter Field, Fort Worth, Texas. Made from the balcony at the north passenger concourse, this color photograph proves the beauty and facilities of the Main Terminal Building. Several of the large Air Liners operating through this ultra-modern Airport are shown together with some of the up-to-date equipment required at all times.

(Quentin McGown post card collection)

Lockheed Martin

AIR FORCE PLANT 4 HISTORY

Air Force Plant 4, the home of Lockheed Martin Tactical Aircraft Systems, officially began operations on April 16,1942. Since then the facility's mile-long production line has rolled out more than 7,000 outstanding military aircraft and provided jobs for a total of 250,000 people.

Construction of the huge plant was completed in less than a year. Assembly of the first B-24 Liberator bomber actually began in February 1942 while parts of the facility were still under construction. Women comprised a third of the plants work force in the war years, which eventually saw production at 3,034 B-24s in Fort Worth. In the later part of the war the plant began producing another bomber, the B-32 Dominator, and rolled out 114 before the Japanese surrender.

The facility's next product was the B-36 Peacemaker, the world's first true intercontinental bomber, of which 385 were delivered in the late '40s and early '50s.

A total of 116 B-58 Hustlers, the world's first supersonic bomber, were built at Air Force Plant 4 in the late '50s and early '60s The B-58 was followed by production of the F-111, of which 562 were produced in Fort Worth. The swing-wing F-111 is still in service and played a major role in the Gulf War.

The Fort Worth plants major product today is the F-16 Fighting Falcon. Eighteen countries fly the F-16 or have aircraft on order. Production is expected to continues in Fort Worth well into the 2000s.

Lockheed Martin is developing the F-22 Air Superiority Fighter at Air Force Plant 4 and in Marlefla, Ga. The F-22 team also includes Boeing, with a one-third share. F-22 parts production and assembly are now under way.

The Fort Worth plant is also leading Lockheed Martin's efforts in the Joint Advanced Strike Technology (JAST) program to develop technologies for future tactical aircraft for the Navy, Marines and Air Force.

Amon G. Carter, Sr. with Brigadier General Gerald C. Bryant, April 18, 1941 "Groundbreaking" *(Courtesy Lockheed-Martin Tactical Aircarft Systems)*

Air Force Plant 4 has been a major force in the Texas economy throughout its existence. It has been operated under several company names in its history, including:

Consolidated Aircraft Corp., 1942-43

Consolidated Vultee Aircraft Corp., 1943-53

General Dynamics, 1953-93 (including Convair Aerospace, Fort Worth Division)

Lockheed Fort Worth Company, beginning March 1993

Lockheed Martin Tactical Aircraft Systems, beginning May 1, 1995.

B-24 LIBERATOR

More B-24 Liberator bombers were deployed during World War II than any other type of four-engined bomber. Approximately 18,000 of the Consolidated Vultee-designed bombers were constructed in addition to nearly 1,800 equivalent spares. Consolidated Vultee later became known as Convair and merged with General Dynamics. More than 3,000 B-24s and C87 cargo versions of the aircraft were assembled at General Dynamics' Fort Worth Division during World War II.

Formations of B-24s were used on the extremely long-range bombing missions in all theaters of the war, dropping an impressive total of 634,831 tons of bombs. They pounded enemy installations in Europe and Africa; dropped tons of bombs throughout the Pacific zone of war; and played the major role in the successful battle of the American and British navies against enemy sub-marines. They flew a total of 312,734 sorties. Their .50 caliber machine guns knocked down 4,189 enemy aircraft. The U.S. Navy designation for the Liberator is PB4Y-1.

Transport versions, designated Liberator Express C-87, were extensively used to carry military equipment and personnel on transoceanic and other long-range flights. Toward the end of the war a single tail version, known as the B-24K and B-24N, was designed, but only a few were built.

Maximum speed of the B-24 was over 300 mph, and maximum cruising speed was 230 mph. The Liberator operated at gross weights ranging from 56,000 to 66,000 pounds. Under emergency conditions, B-24s have taken off with a gross weight of 72,000 pounds. Heavily armed, the B-24J Liberator was equipped with four power operated turrets, each mounting twin .50 caliber machine guns. Two waist .50 caliber guns also were provided. It was powered by four Pratt & Whitney R1830 1,200 hp engines. Wingspan was 110 feet; length 67 feet two inches; height 18 feet.

The B-36s produced by Convair-Fort Worth were the world's largest bombers. At speeds of more than 435 miles per hour, the B-36 could carry a heavier load of bombs for greater distances than any other aircraft in the world. While the B-36s were never used in combat, they played a major role in the United States' policy of "peace through airpower" during the troubled decade between 1948 and 1958. The last B-36 was retired from the Air Force on February 12, 1959.

While in service, the B-36 set many records. One B-36, which could carry more than 30,000 gallons of gasoline, flew more than 10,000 miles non-stop and non-refueled, dropping a 10,000-pound bomb load midway in the flight. Another dropped a total of 84,000 pounds of dummy bombs, the heaviest load of bombs ever carried by one airplane. The B-36 also carried more defensive firepower than any other bomber: eight remote turrets containing a total of sixteen 20-millimeter cannons.

An experimental transport version of the B-36, designated XC-99, was developed for the Air Force. Flying heavy loads of high priority cargo, the XC-99 established new cargo records with almost every flight. The XC-99 could haul 400 troops of 100,000 pounds of cargo.

Another experimental version of the B-36, the NB-36H, carried an operating atomic reactor in flight to test shielding and the effects of radiation on equipment.

The RB-36, which closely resembled the B-36 bomber, was also designed to carry large cameras and other special equipment needed for long-range, high altitude reconnaissance.

Maximum gross weight of the B-36 was about 400,000 pounds, its wingspan was 230 feet, length was 162 feet, and it was nearly 47 feet high. The latest models of the B-36 were equipped with four J-47 jet engines in addition to six 3,800-horsepower, pusher-type engines.

The ten engines of the B-36 developed as much horsepower as nine locomotives, its wing tanks held enough fuel to drive a car around the world 16 times, and each B-36 electrical system required more than 30 miles of wiring.

B-36 PEACEMAKER

B-58 HUSTLER

The delta wing B-58 Hustler was the world's first mach 2 Strategic Bomber when it entered operational service in 1959. During the ten years it was flown by the U.S. Air Force, the B-58 established nineteen speed and altitude records. It was also highly accurate as a bomber because of its advanced navigation and weapons systems.

The Hustler, capable of high speed attack at altitudes up to 85,000 feet or flying at near sonic speeds at 500 feet, was flown from New York to Paris in three hours and nineteen minutes at an average speed of 1,089 miles per hour. A B-58 flew from New York to Los Angeles in 2 hours at an average of 1,214 MPH and from Tokyo to London in 8 hours and 35 minutes at an average speed of 938 MPH. These records, which were recognized with international trophies, were set by Air Force crews in standard combat-configured B-58s.

The B-58 Hustler carried a 20 mm. cannon in a tail turret with conventional and nuclear bombs and weapons beneath its large triangular wings.

It was powered by four J79-GE-5B General Electric engines delivering a total of 62,000 pounds of thrust in afterburner.

A three-man crew flew the B-58: a pilot, a navigator-bombardier, and a defensive systems operator. Only the pilot could see out the front windscreen. The two men behind him had very small windows on each side of their seats which also served as escape capsules in case of emergencies.

The B-58 was 96 feet long, had a wingspan of 56 feet, was 31 feet tall, and weighed 55,600 pounds. It was capable of flying more than 4,450 miles without refueling and could be refueled in flight.

F-16 FIGHTING FALCON

"The reason enemy piolts do not sleep well at night." The multi-role fighter for USAF, the F-16. More than 3,800 F-16's were produced worldwide to date.

(Courtesy Lockheed Martin)

A hometown built F-16 Fighting Falcon from the Air force Reserves 457th Fighter Squadron, 301st Fighter Wing at the Joint Reserve Base takes off for a local training sortie. The buildings in the background are Lockheed Martin Tactical Aircraft Systems where the F-16 was built, and are still being produced.

(U. S. Navy Photo by Marshall Lefavor)

F-22
RAPTOR

F-35
Joint Strike
Fighter

(Photos Courtesy Lockheed Martin)

Lockheed Martin Tactical Aircraft Systems was selected in October of 1998 by *Industry Week*, the leading manufacturing management magazine, to receive a 9th Annual American's Best Plant Award as one of the ten best plants in North America

(All photos this section are courtesy Lockheed Martin Tactical Aircraft Systems)

NAVAL AIR STATION JOINT RESERVE BASE FORT WORTH, TEXAS

In the time honored tradition, the crew chief and pilot exchange salutes following a Final before Flight Inspection. This F-16 is deployed to and being flown out of Aviano Air Base Italy in support of the No-Fly Zone, Operation Southern Watch over Iraq. *(official USAF photo)*

Mission statement

The mission of Naval Air Station Joint Reserve Base Fort Worth is to provide a high-quality training environment for active and Reserve components of all branches of the Armed Services; to reduce redundancy and overhead by developing joint doctrine and operating procedures that create seamless functionality amongst host and tenant commands in base support and community service programs

The beginning: Carswell Air Force Base

NAS JRB Fort Worth is located at the site of the former Carswell Air Force Base. In 1941 the installation was known as the Tarrant Field Airdrome, which served the Consolidated Vultee Aircraft Corporation. The airdrome became Fort Worth Army Air Field on January 2, 1942, following the attack on Pearl Harbor. A variety of aircraft were produced at what became "Air Force Plant 4," including the B-24, B-36, B-58, F-111 and F-16

The airfield was renamed Carswell AFB in 1948 to honor Fort Worth native Major Horace Seaver Carswell Jr. While returning from a bombing strike against a Japanese convoy, the 1939 graduate of Texas Christian University continued to fly his severely damaged B-24, enabling his crew to jump from the bomber. This unselfish act cost Carswell his life. He was posthumously awarded the Medal of Honor for this extraordinary act of heroism.

Carswell AFB was one of the first Strategic Air Command bases, hosting B-29, B-36, B-58 and B-52 bombers from the 7th Bomb Wing, which maintained a long-standing vigil during the Cold War. Carswell AFB was also one of the sites of the James Stewart classic movie *Strategic Air Command.*

Winds of change: Air Force realignment

As part of the Department of Defense's 1991 consolidation efforts, the decision was made to relocate the 7th Bomb Wing from Carswell AFB. During a 1992 Air Force-wide reorganization the famed Strategic Air Command was officially disestablished. On October 1, 1993, the Air Force Reserve 301st Fighter Wing assumed base responsibilities, establishing Carswell as an Air Reserve Base. In 1993, Congress directed the establishment of the nation's first joint reserve base under the Base Realignment and Closure authority.

"Jointness: A way of life; a model for all services"

NAS JRB Fort Worth was officially established on October 1, 1994, as the first joint-service reserve base. The 1,805-acre base is the result of the DoD's 1993 BRAC recommendation to relocate NAS Dallas and its tenant commands to the former Carswell AFB. Additional tenant commands from other closing installations were also directed to relocate to NAS JRB Fort Worth, such as U.S. Marine Corps Reserve squadrons from Memphis, Tenn., and Glenview, Ill., in July/August 1994. The 1993 BRAC proceedings also placed the Navy as the host of what has become a new joint military reserve base - a model for future consolidations.

The relocation of commands from NAS Dallas continues in stages, as renovation or new construction is completed at NAS JRB Fort Worth. Although not all units and facilities are fully in place, NAS JRB Fort Worth has already established itself as a hub for advanced joint training for pilots, aircrews and ground personnel. Since NAS JRB Fort Worth's establishment, the efforts expended to create this model base not only have increased Reserve readiness and training capabilities, but also have significantly enhanced the total capability of The U.S. military.

301st Fighter Wing
NAS Fort Worth, Joint Reserve Base Carswell Field

The 301st Fighter Wing at Naval Air Station Fort Worth Joint Reserve Base Carswell Field is the only Air Force Reserve fighter unit in the state of Texas. Its mission is to maintain a state of readiness to deploy people and their aircraft wherever needed when recalled to active duty.

People assigned to the 301st Fighter Wing repeatedly demonstrate their expertise and professionalism in Air Combat Command, Air Force Reserve Command and NATO exercises designed to emphasize "That to retain our country's combat-ready posture we must train as we plan to fight."

The 301st Fighter Wing led the way for Air Force Reserve fighter units in deploying to overseas bases for NATO exercises when it deployed to Norvenich Air Base, Germany, in August 1977. Subsequent overseas deployments by the wing include Gioia del Colle AB, Italy, in May 1979, and Cigli AB, Turkey, in October 1982. A deployment to Sivrihisar AB, Turkey, in May 1985 was an AFRES first when they operated under bare base conditions. The unit also deployed to Roosevelt Roads Naval Air Station in Puerto Rico, Nellis Air Force Base, Nevada, and Elmendorf AFT, Alaska. During Operation Desert Shield/Desert Storm, wing people were recalled to active duty and served at locations throughout the United States, Germany, England, and Southwest Asia.

In December 1993, the wing deployed twelve F-16s and approximately 350 wing people to Aviano AB, Italy, in support of the United Nations DENY Flight mission. With the wing converting from F-4 to F-16 fighter aircraft during Desert Shield/Storm, this deployment to Aviano AB was the first nonexercise operational aviation deployment since flying fighters out of Carswell in 1972. In achieving the highest rating possible from the May 1994 Operation Readiness Inspection and supporting the Deny Flight mission, the 301st was awarded the Air Force Outstanding Unit Award for the period May 1992 to May 1994.

The wing deployed ten F-16s, support equipment, and more than 300 people to Darwin, Australia, November 1994, in support of the Australian Air Force Fighter Weapons school. One year later, operation Decisive Edge called the wing to action again to Aviano AB, Italy, for forty-five days.

Brigadier General William H. Lawson, 917th Wing Commander, Barksdale AFB, Louisiana and former 301st Fighter Wing Commander, is greeted home to Fort Worth by Doc Daugherty, Executive Director, Fort Worth International Air Show. Mr. Stanley Cole, Chairman of the Greater Fort Worth Civic Leaders Association looks on. The aircraft in the background is "Diamond Lil", a B-24 flown by the Confederate Air Force. Lawson had just landed a B-52 Bomber in June 1997. The two aircraft were parked next to each other to commemorate the 50th Anniversary of the USAF. The B-24 is important to the base since this is the type of bomber that Major Horace Seaver Carswell, Jr. was flying when he was killed during World War II.

(official USAF photo by Major Clay Church)

A Barksdale AFB, 917th Wing B-52 touches down at the Joint Reserve Base in June 1997 as part of the 50th Anniversary of the U.S. Air Force as a separate service. B-52's were flown and "pulled" strategic alert for more than 35 years from the Carswell AFB.

A Barksdale AFB B-52 is parked in front of base operations at the Joint Reserve Base in June 1997 to help commemorate the 50th anniversary of the USAF. The 301st Fighter Wing former commander and then 917th Wing Commander flew the B-52 into Fort Worth. The aircraft was parked nose to nose with "Diamond Lil" a B-24 flown by the Confederate Air Force.

(USAF photo by Bob Adams)

Following on the heels of an excellent Quality Air Force Assessment, the wing again deployed people, support, equipment, and eight F-16s to Karup Air Station, Denmark, to fight MiG-29s, support ten nations defending a simulated battlefield, and keep a Russian Navy blockaded in the Baltic Sea. In May 1998, the wing deployed six Air Force Reserve aircraft in support of United Nations Southern Watch mission at Al Jarber Air Base, Kuwait.

The wing was activated as the 301st Tactical Fighter Wing in late 1944. During the last few months of World War II, the wing's P-47 pilots saw action escorting B-24 and B-29 bombers, and dive bombing and strafing on shipping and communications lines in the Far East. Prior to being deactivated in June 1949, the 301st provided air defense for Okinawa during the postwar period.

Upon reactivation in July 1972, the wing was assigned the F-105 "Thunderchief", with the Carswell-based 457th FS using a specially modified version of the F-105D called the "Thunderstick II". The 457th FS converted to the F-4D "Phantom II" in 1981 and to the F-4E in 1987. In April of 1991, the wing converted to the F-16C/D "Fighting Falcon."

Major commands/units at NAS JRS Fort Worth:

10th Air Force (Air Force Reserve)
301st Fighter Wing (Air Force Reserve)
14th Regimental Marines
Marine Aircraft Group 4l (MAG 4I)
Marine Air Control Squadron 24 (MACS 24)
Marine Fighter Attack Squadron 112 (VMFA 112)
Marine Aerial Refueller Transport Squadron 234 (VMGR 234)
Marine Aviation Logistics Squadron 41 (MALS 41)
Fighter Attack Squadron 201 (VFA-201) (Navy)
Commander, Fleet Logistics Support Wing (Navy)
Fleet Logistics Support Squadron 59 (VR 59) (Navy)
Commander, Navel Reserve Intelligence Command
Commander, Naval Reserve Security Group
9th Naval Construction Regiment
Naval Mobile Construction Battalion 22 (NMCB 22)
138th Tactical Airlift Wing of the Texas Air National Guard (TANG)
Commander, Naval Reserve Readiness Center
Commander, Naval Reserve Readiness Command, Region 11 (REDCOM 11)
Reserve Intelligence Programs Office Six (RIPO Six)

"1998 COMNAVAIRESFOR Conway Trophy Award Winner"

(Right): A 457th Fighter Squadron pilot is welcomed home by his daughters following an overseas deployment. The squadron has deployed overseas several times during the 1990's including tours in support of Operations DENY Flight, Provide Comfort, and more recently Operations Northern and Southern Watch missions over Iraq.

(official U.S. Air Force photo)

(Below): F-16 flying over Fort Worth in early 1991. The Lockheed-Martin photographer (Gary Tolbert) took the photograph for use as the unit lithograph series. This photograph has been digitally changed to update new tail or "fin flash" markings.

(Lockheed-Martin Tatical Aircraft Systems)

DALLAS/FORT WORTH INTERNATIONAL AIRPORT

The history of the Dallas/Fort Worth International Airport actually goes back as far as 1927 when Dallas first proposed a joint airport with Fort Worth. Fort Worth declined the offer and built its own municipal airport, Meacham Field. In 1940 the two cities began seeking separate federal funding for their respective airports. The Civil Aeronautics Administration (now the Federal Aviation Administration) suggested a joint regional airport, and offered $1.9 million to help build it. By 1942 the two cities still could not agree on a site, so the project was discontinued.

Fort Worth's and Dallas' individual airports continued to grow and develop until 1961 when the Civil Aeronautics Board (CAB) ordered hearings on proposals to construct a joint airport by Dallas and Fort Worth, and the FAA denied further funding of Dallas and Fort Worth's independent airports. Three years later the CAB decided that neither Dallas' Love Field nor Fort Worth's Greater Southwest International Airport was a suitable site for future needs, and ordered Dallas and Fort Worth to find a new site within 180 days, or the CAB would do it for them.

Dallas Fort Worth Airport - 1998

(Courtesy Freese & Nichols, Inc.)

In 1965 the Interim Airport Board selected a site just north of Fort Worth's Greater Southwest International Airport, about seventeen miles from the central business districts of both Dallas and Fort Worth. One year later, the first 176 acres of land were bought for the new airport. In 1968 the ground breaking ceremonies took place, and the initial phase of construction began in 1969. The dedication of the Dallas/Fort Worth Regional Airport was held on Spetember 21-23, 1973, and was attended by 200,000 people. The ceremony was highlighted by the landing of the supersonic Concord, performances by country-western star Willie Nelson and Jazz great Doc Severinson. Governor Dolph Briscoe, Senator John Tower and and Senator Lloyd Bentson also attended.

January 13, 1974 marked the official opening of DFW airport with the arrival -- on time -- of its first commercial flight, American Airlines Flight 341 from Little Rock, Arkansas. The airport opened with four terminal buildings, sixty-six boarding gates, three runways, and the most sophisticated air traffic control system in the world. The control tower held five instrument landing systems, the most ever commissioned by the FAA simultaneously with the opening of a new airport. By the end of its first year, DFW Airport had served more than 6.8 million passengers and 105,000 tons of cargo.

One year after its opening, DFW Airport was ranked as the world's fifth busiest airport. Two years later, DFW would rank as the world's third busiest airport.

By 1981 sixteen airlines operated from DFW Airport, resulting in a record 23.5 million passengers annually. By the airport's 10th birthday in 1983, it handled approximately 200 million passengers and more than 2.6 million tons of cargo and mail. The number of airlines providing service had expanded to more than forty, a dramatic increase from the twelve airlines that operated on opening day.

In 1985 the airport's name officially changed from the DFW Regional Airport to Dallas/Fort Worth International Airport.

By 1988 nearly two-thirds of all air freight in the state of Texas passed through DFW Airport. One year later, DFW became the world's second busiest passenger airport, servicing 48 million passengers annually. In 1991 the passenger traffic topped 50 million for the first time, a landmark in the airport's history.

The opening by the FAA of two new control towers in 1994 made DFW Airport the only airport in the world with three operational control towers. That same year the airport again expanded its international service to São Paulo, Brazil and Seoul, Korea. In 1995 the Founders' Plaza, the airport's observation area, was dedicated.

By 1996 an Economic Impact Study showed DFW Airport generated nearly $10.8 billion for the region annually, and created 204,000 jobs. In 1998, DFW became the first U.S. airport to offer an automated foreign currency exchange machine. Also in 1998 "Maverick" the third DVORDME (Doppler Very High Frequency Omnidirectional Radio Range with Distance Measuring Equipment) went into service. The two other DVORDME's are named "Cowboy" and "Ranger" after Metroplex sports teams.

1999 marked the 25th Anniversary of Dallas/Fort Worth Airport.

Dallas Fort Worth Airport Terminal B Skybridge including TRAM Station
(Courtesy Freese & Nichols, Inc.)

Dallas Fort Worth "Maverick" DVORDME -
Dopler Very High Frequency Omnidirectional Radio Range Distance Measuring Equipment
(Courtesy Freese & Nichols, Inc.)

Alliance Airport

In the late 1980's, the Federal Aviation Administration, recognizing the need for more airports in North Texas, approached the owners of the land that is now Alliance with the idea of locating an airport in the region. The developers envisioned more than an airport; they envisioned an entirely new type of airport and a unique business community.

In true Texas fashion, public and private entities joined to design and construct the nation's first master-planned industrial airport in a record 18 months. Its quick completion proved the value of such a public/private partnership. The team was led by the city of Fort Worth and included the neighboring communities of Denton, Haslet, Keller, and Roanoke; Tarrant, Dallas and Denton counties; the state of Texas; the FAA; and private business.

The time was right for the industrial airport. Fort Worth Alliance Airport was an immediate, unprecedented success. It surpassed traffic expectations within its first year of operation and won the praises of the FAA and the White House.

Hillwood Development Corporation focused attention on other key transportation and business components. Architects, economists, city planners, and environmental and transportation experts worked behind the scenes, exploring long-term strategies for Alliance.

Their efforts produced results. Major corporations in transportation, both air and rail, recognized Alliance's potential and opened facilities there. Other corporate users- large and small, international and regional- followed all attracted by the opportunity Alliance represents and, perhaps most of all, its vision.

Fort Worth Alliance Airport is a public airport that exclusively serves the needs of industrial, business and general aviation users, rather than commercial airlines. The airport leads the way in airport privatization. It is owned by the city of Fort Worth and is managed by privately held Alliance Air Services.

The airport operates 24 hours a day, year-round. It offers direct taxiway access to nearby business facilities at Alliance Center, giving users on all sides immediate access to the adjacent runway.

The world-class fixed base operation (FBO), in addition to providing fuel and aircraft maintenance, also features a wide range of convenient services including catering, ground transportation and business services such as fax, copying capabilities and meeting facilities. A new 32,000 square foot hangar for aircraft storage and a 20,000 square foot aviation center includes a state-of-the-art weather information and flight planning facility, a pilot lounge, a passenger lounge, and a food service area and lobby. In addition to the FBO, Alliance Airport's facilities and services include: a 9,600 x 150 foot primary runway- to be extended to 13,000 feet and an 8,200 x 150 foot parallel runway, capable of accommodating all types of commercial transport aircraft to access all global markets; a full Category III Instrument Landing System (ILS) allows airport operations to continue during inclement weather; a $4.5 million FAA-operated control tower and office building with the most technically advanced computer systems and equipment available; a U.S. Customs Service office staffed by full-time customs personnel; a unique airport overlay district providing zoning restrictions on nearby buildings and land to ensure compatible uses; and an on-site aircraft rescue and firefighting facilities

(Photos Courtesy Alliance Air Services)

Museum of Science and History

A Premier Regional Attraction

The Fort Worth Museum of Science and History has attracted an average of 1.2 million visitors each year since 1985, distinguishing it as the most popular cultural attraction in the Fort Worth/Dallas metroplex. And with 63 percent of these visitors coming from outside Tarrant County, the Museum is more than just a metroplex attraction — it is also a popular regional tourist destination.

Strong public awareness of the Museum is maintained through an active marketing program that targets areas of rapid growth in Fort Worth, Dallas and communities throughout North Texas. Press releases are mailed to more than 700 media outlets throughout the state and region and press openings introduce Omni films and major exhibitions. The Marketing Department also works closely with local corporations, schools, area convention and visitor bureaus and the tourism industry to promote the Museum to tour groups.

Reduced group admission rates make the Museum an attractive destination for school and community groups, and Museum publications help these groups plan activities to enrich their Museum experience. School groups comprise approximately a quarter of the Museum's annual attendance.

The Museum: Where Imaginations Soar - Education is at the heart of every program, exhibit and special event offered at the Fort Worth Museum of Science and History. More than 300,000 children visit the Museum each year either as part of a school group, as a Museum School® student does, or as a participant in one of the Museum's outreach programs.

Founded in 1941, the Fort Worth Museum of Science and History is dedicated to increasing the public's understanding and appreciation of science and the human experience through personal interaction with exhibits, programs and the Museum's collection. For more than fifty years, the Museum has provided a safe, inviting place where children and grown-ups - families of all kinds - can come and learn together.

Museum exhibits draw on the strength of extensive scientific and cultural collections that have been amassed over the years. Exhibit galleries include a wide range of interests, from dinosaurs discovered "in our Texas backyard" to a chuck wagon that supplied "the comforts of home" for cowboys on the Chisholm Trail.

The Fort Worth Museum of Science and History is both an important component of the educational infrastructure of this community and a key steward charged with preserving the heritage of North Texas. Through its exhibits and programs, the Museum provides life-long learning experiences emphasizing math, science and history that enrich the lives of its patrons.

Located in the heart of Fort Worth's Cultural District, the Museum encompasses eight permanent exhibit galleries, the Omni Theater, The Noble Planetarium, and Museum School. Permanent galleries include The Dino Dig®; KIDSPACE®; Hands on Science; Lone Star Dinosaurs; and People and Places. In addition, as many as three special exhibitions are offered annually.

The Museum has been recognized nationally and internationally for its innovation in educational programming and is the only Texas museum serving on the panel empowered to redirect and enhance the state's formal school curriculum.

The Ultimate Viewing Experience- Fort Worth's Omni Theater is the first and largest domed theater in Texas. It is a technical marvel incorporating the most advanced super 70-mm projection and sound systems in the world. The theater's screen is a magnificent dome, eighty feet in diameter and tilted at a 30-degree angle to the horizon. The result: a viewing system that dazzles your senses, enveloping you in sight and sound in one of the largest theaters of its kind on the globe.

Behind the dome's surface, seventy-two strategically placed speakers, driven by 18,600 watts of power, allow 6-track sound to "move" across the screen in synchronization with the action.

The patented Omnimax® projection system utilizes the largest film format in the world. Nearly ten times larger than its 35-mm counterpart, the film fills the dome with brilliant, larger-than-life images.

More than 7.5 million visitors have enjoyed Omni Theater features since its grand opening April 19, 1983.

Charlie Mary Noble and The Planetarium - The Noble Planetarium at the Fort Worth Museum of Science and History is the first planetarium in the world dedicated to a woman. As you might surmise, Miss Charlie Mary Noble was a talented educator. She taught in the Fort Worth public schools for over forty-five years, twenty-five of those as the head of the math department at Paschal High School. It was at Paschal High School that she organized the Penta Club for honor math students, which she supervised for twenty years . After retiring from the school system in 1943, Miss Noble taught mathematics, astronomy and navigation at Texas Christian University. In 1950, her fine work was recognized by an honorary Doctor of Law degree from TCU. In 1947, Miss Noble was asked by the museum to help young people become acquainted with the stars. She organized the Junior Astronomy Club.

In 1949, the Junior League gave the museum its first Star Projector. The first planetarium was an oblate spheroid, about 18 feet in diameter and constructed of plywood and cardboard. It was erected under a tent in the backyard of the museum. Miss Noble used the planetarium to teach school children and her Junior Astronomy Club. Approaching blindness and waning strength finally prevented Miss Noble's active participation in the club.

In 1955, shortly after the museum moved to its present location, the planetarium, one of the finest small planetariums in the country, was dedicated in Miss Noble's honor. Miss Charlie Mary Noble passed away in December 1959.

(Courtesy Fort Worth Museum of Science & History)

MODERN ART MUSEUM OF FORT WORTH

Chartered in 1892, as the Fort Worth Public Library and Art Gallery, the Modern Art Museum of Fort Worth is the oldest art museum in Texas. The museum focuses on modern and contemporary art, including paintings, sculpture, works on paper and international contemporary photography. The Modern exhibits works from its extensive 3,000-piece collection, in addition to special traveling exhibitions. Contemporary sculpture is on view outdoors on the grounds of the museum. With an extensive permanent collection and a vibrant exhibitions program, the Modern makes a key contribution to Fort Worth's celebrated cirde of museums.

The Modern offers a variety of educational programs including lectures, guided tours, adult and children's classes and workshops, summer art camp and occasional family activity days.

In 1995, the Modern opened a downtown annex featuring additional gallery space for exhibitions and a larger branch of the museum's unique gift shop. The Modern at Sundance Square is located on the ground floor of the historic Sanger Building, on the northwest corner of Houston and Fourth Streets in downtown Fort Worth. Built in 1929 to house Sanger's department store, the Sanger Building is listed on the National Register of Historic Places. The renovation of the Modern Art Museum's annex was designed by Fort Worth architect Ames Fender, grandson of Wyatt Hedrick, the original architect of the Sanger Building. The Modern at Sundance Square serves as an additional venue for the museum's permanent collection and small-scale traveling exhibitions and is within walking distance of all the downtown hotels.

Exterior view of the Modern Art Museum of Fort Worth.
(Courtesy Modern Art Museum of Fort Worth)

A new facility for the Modern Art Museum of Fort Worth, designed by Japanese architect Tadao Ando, will open in Fort Worth's Cultural District in 2002. The purchase was made possible by a generous grant from The Burnett Foundation of Fort Worth. The Modern's new home will feature a significantly greater amount of exhibition space, a restaurant, a state-of-the-art auditorium and additional classrooms and studios.

New Modern Art Museum of Fort Worth, 1998. View of Main entrance on Darnell Street. Tadao Ando Architect & Associates.
(Courtesy Modern Art Museum of Fort Worth)

Amon Carter Museum

The Amon Carter Museum is a treasure not only for the Fort Worth community, but also for art lovers throughout the world. An extraordinary collection, special exhibitions, education programs, community events, and publications make the Museum a major center for the gathering, interpretation, and enjoyment of American art.

Fort Worth publisher and philanthropist Amon G. Carter, Sr. (1879-1955), founded the Museum to house his collection of paintings and sculpture by Frederic Remington and Charles M. Russell. His unwavering commitment to excellence is still very much alive in the Museum today.

Since its opening in 1961, the Museum has broadened the scope of its collection by adding outstanding works of 19th and 20th-century American art. The Amon Carter Museum houses a collection of over 300,000 objects, including paintings, sculpture, and prints, as well as one of the foremost collections of American photographs. The Museum's collections, exhibitions, public programs, and publications support the study and appreciation of American art. The Museum boasts one of the most active art museum publishing programs in the country. Since 1962, the Amon Carter Museum has published over 100 books, both independently and in conjunction with major publishers.

The Carter is open Tuesday through Saturday, 10 a.m. to 5 p.m.; Sunday noon to 5 p.m. Closed Mondays and major holidays. Admission is free; free parking is available. Handicap parking spaces are located on Lancaster Avenue. Galleries are barrier-free.

The Amon Carter Museum closed temporarily for extensive remodeling on August 1, 1999. The original 1961 shellstone building will remain intact. The entire area to the rear will be removed and replaced with a larger, multi-level structure in rich brown granite. The building expansion will more than triple the size of the galleries. Until reopening, scheduled for Fall of 2001, visitors are welcome at The Carter Downtown, located near Bass Hall.

(Courtesy Amon Carter Museum)

The Cattle Raisers Museum

Preserving the Heritage of Ranch Life

From cattle barons to cowboys; from Special Texas Rangers to rustlers. From boots to branding irons. You'll find it all at the Cattle Raisers Museum—-where the real West begins.

This entertaining, interactive museum tells the story of the cattle and ranching industry in Texas and the Southwest. Talking mannequins, authentic artifacts, and an exciting theater presentation all make the legends and lore come alive.

The museum is filled with fascinating tales of ranch living. Meet Special Texas Rangers who have been catching cattle rustlers for more than 100 years. Be transported to the most famous ranches in history for a look into the lives of men like Charles Goodnight and Captain Richard King. Encounter cowboys who drove cattle hundreds of miles to market. And learn more about ranch hands, past and present.

At the Cattle Raisers Museum, you'll see the world's largest documented collection of branding irons —- including brands used by Stephen F. Austin, baseball great Nolan Ryan, and the "running W" from the King Ranch; see a pair of boots owned by renowned Western artist Charles Russell; more than fifty pairs of famous maker spurs; saddles just like the ones used on the dusty Chisholm Trail; and a wide variety of photographs and personal items depicting life in the West.

For a genuine glimpse into the West, the Cattle Raisers Museum is not to be missed. The Museum is open Monday through Saturday from 10 am until 5pm and on Sunday from 1pm until 5pm. School and visitor tours are available by advance reservation.

In 1979, with a rich history behind them and a vision of continued progress ahead. Texas and Southwestern Cattle Raisers Association members formed the Texas and Southwestern Cattle Raisers Foundation. Intent on preserving and protecting the heritage of the livestock industry of the Southwest, their specific goals included educating students and the general public as to the cattlemen's independent nature, pride in the free enterprise system, devotion to private land ownership, and commitment to environmental stewardship.

From the outset, the Foundation was envisioned as having three interrelated and constituent parts: (1) the W.T. Waggoner Memorial Library, a specialized research collection that now contains more than 1,000 volumes as well as periodicals, reference and manuscript material plus 25,000 historic photographs devoted to the cattle and ranching industries; (2) educational support that fosters tomorrow's agricultural industry leaders with academic scholarships and other awards of merit including livestock judging and beef education honors; and (3) the Cattleraisers Museum.

(Courtesy The Cattle Raisers Museum Photo by Geno Loro, Jr.)

The Cattleraisers Museum opened in 1980. Over the years, the museum has expanded to more than 8,000 square feet of exhibits including dioramas, interactive computers, talking mannequins, and the Amon G. Carter Theater which together tell the all-important story of the cattle industry. The number of visitors grew as well. From fewer than 500 the first year, it now attracts more than 15,000 school children, tourists, and area residents annually. The Texas and Southwestern Cattle Raisers Foundation is continuing to build a greater public awareness of and appreciation for ranching heritage.

(Courtesy The Cattle Raisers Museum)

(Courtesy The Cattle Raisers Museum Photo by Steve Edmonds)

Kimbell Art Museum

Kay Kimbell was a successful entrepreneur in grain, retail, real estate, and petroleum. He and his wife, Velma Fuller Kimbell, along with Mr. Kimbell's sister and her husband, Dr. and Mrs. Coleman Carter created the Kimbell Art Foundation. This was in the 1930's shortly after Mr. and Mrs. Kimbell purchased their first paintings. The Kimbell's continued to collect artworks, and when Mr. Kimbell died in 1964, he bequeathed his art collection and entire personal fortune to establish and maintain a public art museum of the first rank in Fort Worth. Shortly thereafter Mrs. Kimbell contributed her share of their property to facilitate the full implementation of her husband's wishes.

By 1966, the Kimbell Art Foundation board of directors had appointed Dr. Richard F. Brown as the Museum's first director and adopted the policy to "form collections of the highest aesthetic quality, derived from any and all periods in man's history, and in any medium or style." They envisioned a small assembly of objects that exemplified that highest quality aspirations of past generations, enshrined under natural light in modestly scaled galleries of fine materials that would "charm" as well as enrich the visitor.

The Kimbell Art Museum's holdings range in period from antiquity to the 20th century, including masterpieces from Fra Angelico and Caravaggio to Cezanne and Matisse. The Museum is one of the only institutions in the Southwest with a substantial collection of Asian arts, and has also assembled small but select groups of Mesoamerican and African pieces as well as Mediterranean antiquities.

Since its opening in 1972, the Kimbell Art Museum has won acclaim for its classic modern building designed by the great American architect Louis I. Kahn (1901-1974). Kahn's innovative use of natural light and subtle articulation of space and materials enhance the experience of the art. The building's gracious proportions, fine craftsmanship, and beautiful landscaping lend a further sense of serenity and restraint. The Kimbell Art Museum is widely regarded as one of the most outstanding modern public art-gallery facilities in the world.

The Kimbell Art Museum provides metropolitan Fort Worth and Dallas an ongoing program of interpretative exhibits and publications. Displays initiated and organized by the Museum include The Blood of Kings: A New Interpretation of Maya Art and Monet and the Mediterranean as well as important retrospectives dedicated to Elisabeth Louise Vigee Le Brun, Jusepe de Ribera, Nicolas Poussin, Giambattista Tiepolo, and Georges de La Tour. The Museum has also hosted major traveling exhibitions, such as Impressionist Masterpieces from the Barnes Collection: Cezanne to Matisse.

The Museum offers a full schedule of public programs to promote appreciation of the collection and special exhibitions, including symposia featuring guest speakers, regular lectures and gallery talks by the professional staff and regional artists, and storytelling for children. Workshops on the arts - especially designed to share the resources of the Museum with all levels of the community - are held regularly for children, high-school students, adults, senior citizens, and the hearing-impaired and are based on the principle that increased understanding is the key to an expanded enjoyment of art.

(Courtesy Kimbell Art Museum)

FORT WORTH SYMPHONY ORCHESTRA

John Giordano, Music Director and Conductor; Ron Spigelman, Associate Conductor; Enrique Arturo Diemecke, Principal Guest Conductor

The Fort Worth Symphony Orchestra Association grew from a community effort behind the dream of Brooks Morris, the Orchestra's founder and first conductor. The Orchestra debuted on December 11, 1925 before an audience of more than 4,000. Morris served as conductor from 1925 to 1943. During this time the Orchestra's season increased to six concerts per year.

During the past seventy-three years, the Fort Worth Symphony Orchestra has grown to become one of the most successful orchestras of its size in the U.S., with an annual budget of $7.9 million. The Fort Worth Chamber Orchestra, an ensemble of thirty-eight musicians, as well as the Fort Worth Symphony Orchestra, are under the artistic leadership of Music Director John Giordano.

While the Fort Worth Chamber Orchestra is recognized in the U. S. and overseas for touring, the Fort Worth Symphony Orchestra remains an integral part of the local community. This season the FWSO will present nine sets of Classical concerts and seven sets of Pops concerts. In addition, the Symphony is the principal Orchestra for the Fort Worth Opera, the Fort Worth/ Dallas Ballet and the Southwestern Baptist Theological Seminary Oratorio Chorus. In 1991, the Association inaugurated its Concerts in the Garden Summer Music Festival; a series of outdoor performances at Fort Worth's Botanic Garden. The sixteen concert series entertained over 42,000 individuals in 1997. Along with this series, the FWSO also participates in many local events which reach thousands of first-time listeners, including free performances at Mayfest, Riverfest and Oktoberfest each year. Education is also a priority. Starting with our first Young Persons concert in 1926, our youth activities include interactive children's concerts and participation in Imagination Celebration, a national children's arts festival. During the season, the Orchestras perform 190 concerts for more than 285,000 people.

The Symphony serves as the host orchestra for the Van Cliburn International Piano Competition which receives worldwide attention via radio and television broadcasts of the Competition's finals. In 1994 the Symphony hosted the first preliminary round of the Tokyo International Conducting Competition ever to be held in the United States. The symphony has received tremendous acclaim by performing with Van Cliburn in 1990, Luciano Pavarotti in 1992 and recording with Peter Nero.

The Fort Worth Symphony Orchestra Association and all Orchestra activities are governed by a volunteer Board of Directors and thirty-five member Executive Committee. Additional volunteer leadership comes from a 500-member Symphony League. Admnistrative support is provided by a staff of eighteen full-time employees, led by Executive Director Ann Koonsman. In Koonsman's nineteen year tenure, the Symphony has balanced the operating budgets consistently and has established an Endowment of $4.5 million.

(Courtesy Fort Worth Symphony)

Fort Worth Symphony League

The Symphony League was organized as a volunteer support group for the Fort Worth Symphony Orchestra in 1957. That same year the Orchestra reorganized and became a permanent organization. The early years were formative for the League as members became active volunteers for the Orchestra in many capacities.

With the Orchestra's growth additional office staff help was needed, and a Symphony League Office Staff Committee was formed to provide volunteers. The league helped conduct the Season Ticket Renewal Campaign, held in the front window of the former Monnig's downtown store. Joint efforts of the League and Orchestra placed emphasis on music education for our youth. The League sponsored children's concerts performed by the Orchestra. In later years the League has prepared students for the concerts through their Docent Program. The program has expanded over the years, involving many League and Orchestra members. They present a music education program to school children. A school contest, "I Came, I Saw, I Heard," is held after the children have attended the concert. Participants are awarded prizes. This docent program has now become one of the most sought-after volunteer educational music programs in Fort Worth.

To achieve the type of educational programs desired by the League, fund-raising had to become an integral part of the League's activities. Kleenex sales, coloring books, garage sales, cooking schools, and Pops concerts were some of the fund-raising events. The annual Helen Corbitt Cooking School held at Neiman Marcus Hedges Restaurant raised $25,000 for the League. The last cooking class was held in 1976. The need for an even bigger fund-raiser was apparent and 1969 became a crucial financial turning point for the League. The first Oktoberfest was held at the old T&P Station with major financial help from the Ben E. Keith Company. Over 7,000 people attended and $6,700 was raised. For the next two years Oktoberfest was held at the Will Rogers Roundup Inn which it quickly outgrew. Oktoberfest was moved to the Convention Center where it has been held ever since. Oktoberfest has raised over two million dollars for the Fort Worth Symphony Orchestra. Other notable fund-raisers besides Oktoberfest were "Symphony of Trees" and the Oktoberfest Preview Party and Art Sale. Presently the League's fund-raising events also include the Southern Living Cooking School and Note Card Sales.

In 1980 the League began sponsoring the Brooks Morris Concert. Other projects and activities were the Coffee/Lecture Series with the Chamber Orchestra started in 1986, Pre-Concert lectures for the Masterpiece and Virtuoso Series, Ballinger/Padgham Memorial Scholarship Fund providing funds to support young musicians, Symphony League Singers, Volunteers for the Van Cliburn Competition, Starpath Committee to assist in Guest Artist transportation needs, Docent Education Program, the "Prelude" that is the League's newsletter, welcome flowers for the guest artist dressing room, and the annual Staff Appreciation Luncheon. Most of these projects are still in effect today.

Hospitality has long been synonymous with the Symphony League. The League has served refreshments to the orchestra after the concerts, as well as lunch during the rehearsals. In previous years an "Orchestra Appreciation Dinner" was held each season. Refreshments are served by the League for Orchestra auditions. The league has hosted many parties on various occasions through the years. These parties have included Pre and Post-Concert receptions following the Masterpiece and Pops Concerts, Season Ticket Renewal Party at Ridglea Bank, Dixieland Jamboree Membership Party at the Botanical Garden Conservatory featuring Don Thomas's Dixieland Band, and a Thirtieth Anniversary Soiree at Ridglea Country Club that featured Doug Pummill's music. Special lyrics were created and performed by the Symphony League Singers touting the League's accomplishments and good times throughout those thirty years. Other parties have included a President's Tea honoring past presidents, New Member Welcome Parties, parties in beautiful Fort Worth homes spotlighting Symphony Orchestra Members, the Oktoberfest 25th Silver Anniversary Party held at the original site of the first Oktoberfest, and the annual Spring Installation Luncheons honoring the League officers.

The Symphony League is associated with the American Symphony Orchestra League (ASOL) and Texas Association of Symphony Orchestras (TASO formerly Texas Women's Association Symphony Orchestras). Delegates are sent to these annual conventions. The League continues to bring honor to our membership by winning awards and honors at the special competitions held at TASO and ASOL.

Thousands of volunteer hours, over two million dollars to the Symphony Orchestra and lasting friendships make up the Symphony League's past. This rich heritage is the foundation for the success of the Symphony League.

The Fort Worth Opera

The story of the oldest continuing opera company in the state of Texas is one filled with vision, dedication hard work, and community spirit. The Fort Worth Opera seed was planted in May 1946, when local music leaders, frustrated with having to drive to Dallas to see a touring production of The Metropolitan Opera, decided to bring opera to Fort Worth permanently. Seven months, thousands of dollars, and 400 volunteers later, the curtain at Will Rogers Memorial Auditorium rose on November 25, 1946, to a sold-out performance of La Traviata.

From 1959 to 1981, Maestro Rudolf Kruger transformed the small opera company into one of the country's most highly regarded regional opera entities, bringing up-and-coming stars to the Fort Worth operatic stage. Many great artists of today, including Placido Domingo and Beverly Sills, made their American debuts with Fort Worth Opera. Over the years, Fort Worth Opera has enjoyed other special moments including Lily Pons' final operatic performance in Lucia di Lammermoor.

Today, Fort Worth Opera continues to provide countless memorable performances under the direction of General Director William Walker. The tradition of excellence is increasingly evident as Fort Worth Opera welcomes to its stage bright stars, including Frances Ginsberg, Mikhall Svetlov Knitikov, Robyune Redmon, Louis Otey, Jane Thorugren, Allan Glassman, and Frank Hernandez, among others.

One of the fourteen oldest opera companies in the entire nation, Fort Worth Opera has also served as a catalyst in the creation of the Fort Worth Symphony Orchestra, Fort Worth Dallas Ballet, and Casa Mañana In all, Fort Worth Opera has presented more than 180 productions. But longevity, although impressive, tells only part of the story. Fort Worth Opera combines vocal, choral, and orchestral music with drama, dance, costumes, sets, and lighting to create the glorious synthesis of sight and sound that can only be found in opera, and can only be experienced at the Nancy Lee and Perry R. Bass Performance Hall. Here, the true grandeur of opera is unleashed, and the magnificence of Fort Worth Opera is realized.

The Fort Worth Opera has made a tremendous impact on the North Texas performing arts community since its first production in 1946. The formation of an opera orchestra helped to influence the post-war revival of the Fort Worth Symphony Orchestra. Casa Mañana's Summer Musicals were begun in 1955 under the direction of Melvin Dacus, the business manager of the Fort Worth Opera The need for a corps de ballet for opera productions also served to encourage Fort Worth's interest in a professional ballet company.

Under the direction of Rudolf Kruger, Fort Worth Opera also made important contributions to opera in America. Many great singers appeared in important leading roles on the Fort Worth Opera Stage. The roster includes John Alexander, Luigi Alva, Martina Arroyo, Enrico di Guiseppe, Placido Domingo, Cornell McNeil, Alberta Masiello, Samuel Ramey, Beverly Sills, Diana Soviero, Giorgio Tozzi, Norman Treigle and William Walker. This tradition continues as the great singers of tomorrow join Fort Worth Opera today.

In addition to six main-stage performances of the traditional repertoire, Fort Worth Opera's Children's Opera Tour brings the exciting and colorful world of opera to over 30,000 school children each year. For many elementary and middle-school students, it is their first experience with classical music and drama. Fort Worth Opera's other educational and community outreach programs bring an operatic experience to an annual audience of 19,000 in every age, ethnic and social group.

Fort Worth Opera employs over 500 performers and production personnel each year, as well as contracting local performing arts groups, including the Fort Worth Symphony Orchestra, the Fort Worth Dallas Ballet and the Texas Boys Choir. Approximately 85% of Fort Worth Opera's budget is returned to Tarrant county each year.

As the oldest continuing opera company in Texas, Fort Worth Opera looks back on fifty-three rewarding and eventful years, and looks ahead to our most important commitment - the future. In 1992, former Metropolitan Opera baritone, William Walker, joined Fort Worth Opera as General Director. A Fort Worth native and graduate of Texas Christian University, Mr. Walker endorses Fort Worth Opera's commitment to America's developing artists and to present productions of the highest quality. Under his leadership, Fort Worth Opera has shown remarkable growth in audience participation, financial, and community support.

Photo is the Fort Worth Opera production of the Flying Dutchman
(Courtesy Fort Worth Opera)

VAN CLIBURN FOUNDATION HISTORY

Van Cliburn's sensational victory at the first Tchaikovsky International Competition in Moscow in 1958 made international history and marked a new era in cultural relations between East and West. Celebrating this remarkable achievement, a group of music teachers and citizens of Fort Worth, created the Van Cliburn International Piano Competition. Since the first medals were awarded in 1962, the laureates of this quadrennial competition have repeatedly demonstrated the tremendous impetus a major competition can lend to an international career. Medalists receive the unparalleled prize of two years of concert management and hundreds of concerts around the world, thus fulfilling the Foundation's purpose of bringing the highest quality of music to audiences everywhere.

Widely recognized today as one of the most important musical events, the Competition has become a festival showcasing the pianists in solo recital, in chamber music with the world's most prominent string quartets, and in concert with orchestras under illustrious conductors. Covered by the media from around the globe, the Competition is also recorded by major recording companies and broadcast on radio. Van Cliburn International Piano Competition documentaries are seen on five continents.

In addition to its dedication to nurturing a new generation of musicians, the Foundation has cultivated a broad audience in North Texas through its Cliburn Concerts. This annual series presents renowned international artists as well as a variety of rising young stars, many of whom have emerged from major international competitions. The Foundation is actively involved in educational endeavors and participates in outreach programs, sponsors lecture demonstrations, and performs in underprivileged communities.

The Van Cliburn Foundation has established the International Association as a membership program for people around the world who share a love of classical music and support the efforts of the Foundation.

(From left to right): Van Cliburn, Jon Nakamatsu
Tenth Van Cliburn International Piano Competition
(Photo by Ron Jenkins for the Van Cliburn Foundation)

Fort Worth Dallas Ballet

The evolution of Fort Worth Dallas Ballet has had many significant milestones. Formed in 1961 and incorporated as a non-profit organization in 1964, the Company has presented a broad range of dance experience to the Fort Worth Community. Over the years, Fort Worth Dallas Ballet has enjoyed continued artistic growth, first as a civic company, then as a civic regional ballet and finally as a professional chamber company in 1985. Fort Worth Dallas Ballet has developed a national reputation as a classical ballet company of the highest caliber, performing regularly throughout Texas and touring nationally and internationally. Lavish full-length and mixed repertory programs have graced the stages of Chicago, New York, Washington DC, San Antonio, Dallas, Taiwan, and Japan, in addition to full production seasons locally. For the 1998-99 season, the Company produced eight full programs (five in Fort Worth and three in Dallas) as the resident professional ballet for two cities with nearly five million citizens.

The pillars of the current organization are firmly rooted in an idea begun in Fort Worth over thirty years ago with the formation of the Fort Worth Ballet Association. As the century nears its close, Fort Worth and the Ballet's founders can celebrate the success of the organization that now is Fort Worth Dallas Ballet. The Company entered a joint venture in 1993, signed by representatives of both cities, approving the formation of Fort Worth Dallas Ballet. The idea of a joint ballet company between Dallas and Fort Worth had been discussed for years as both cities recognized the difficulty in funding two major ballet companies. Following the demise of the Dallas Ballet in 1988, its major financial and cultural supporters desired a high-quality, professional ballet company that would perform on a regional scale. Looking to Fort Worth, they found a major professional resident company seeking broader audiences and larger earned and contributed income to continue its steady progress of prosperity and performance.

In June, 1998, Benjamin Houk was named artistic director for the Company. Mr. Houk had been artistic director for Nashville Ballet for two years and was previously a principal dancer with Pacific Northwest Ballet. He brings considerable experience as a director, performer, choreographer, teacher, and lecturer to his role. In his first season, Mr. Houk has expanded the repertoire to include a number of notable 20th century choreographers. He has also created an all-new production of The Nutcracker, his first full-length ballet for the Company. In addition, the Company has found a new home for its Fort Worth performances in the beautiful new Nancy Lee and Perry R. Bass Performance Hall in downtown Fort Worth.

Fort Worth Dallas Ballet will continue to perform in and garner financial support and audiences from Dallas and Fort Worth and the entire North Texas region. In a continual quest for artistic excellence, audiences can look forward to an ongoing process of expansion, development and achievement that is associated with the premiere classical ballet company of North Texas - Fort Worth Dallas Ballet.

Gretchen Patchell and Michael Clark from the Fort Worth Dallas Ballet Company premier of *Rodeo,* November 13, 1998.

(Courtesy Fort Worth Dallas Ballet)

THE TEXAS BOYS CHOIR:
A Brief History

The Texas Boys Choir celebrated its 50th anniversary in 1996. The Texas Boys Choir's superb showmanship and disciplined ensemble have earned worldwide critical acclaim for hundreds of performances in major concert halls of the United States, Europe, Japan, Mexico and Australia.

Exceptional young singers are selected from throughout the state of Texas and the United States to be in the touring choir of The Texas Boys Choir. Headquartered in Fort Worth, the boys attend a fully accredited private school for grades four through twelve. Their facility includes an elegant concert hall, rehearsal areas and classrooms. The Choir has over thirty recordings to its credit and has appeared on major national and international television networks.

The Choir's mission is to provide to any boy who qualifies, regardless of socioeconomic or ethnic background, a structured environment for the development of a world-class professional choir of boys.

Auditions are held on an individual basis throughout the year. Boys, beginning from age eight, may receive instruction in musical fundamentals. After preparatory classes boys may enter into the graded choir program and eventually audition to enter the top touring choir.

The Texas Boys Choir is a non-profit independent arts organization. It is through the generosity of our corporate friends and individuals that this organization is able to continue.

(Courtesy Texas Boys Choir)

Theater Groups

Fort Worth is home to several theater groups. Here are only a few:

Allied Theater Group
(formerly Stage West / Shakespeare In The Park)

Stage West and Shakespeare in the Park are pleased to present their first combined season under the name Allied Theater Group. The two companies announced in June of 1999 that they intended to join and create a new company in October. The new group will continue to present indoors at Stage West, located on University Drive and outdoors at Shakespeare in the Park located in Trinity Park. There will be two outdoor productions in the park and seven indoor productions at Stage West, creating a year-round theater festival for North Texas. Shakespeare's plays will provide the heart of a continuing commitment to plays with high literary value in a season that will balance contemporary and classical material. By combing and expanding current educational programming of both organizations, Allied Theatre Group also expects to offer more comprehensive services to area schools.

Circle Theatre

In a 125 seat black box theater, with seating on three sides, Regional Theatre produces professional, innovative plays in an intimate setting. The specialty is premiers of first run plays. There is also an ongoing art gallery in the lobby of the theater to support the visual arts as well as the performing arts. The facility is available for meetings and other groups looking for a performance venue. The year-round theater began the 19th season in October with the premier of "The Woman In Black", an English Gothic Horror Story that has been hugely successful in England.

Fort Worth Theatre

Fort Worth Theatre is in their 45th season of producing mostly comedies, drama, and some musicals. Anything from family to adult theater is presented, with primarily contemporary shows. The Theatre has a Main Stage season, Hispanic Series, and a Labor of Love series that benefits AIDS charities of Tarrant County. They also have an educational outreach series, headed by Lynda Rodriguez, Master of Education. This series primarily benefits at-risk students from minority neighborhoods. The theater does cutting edge studio productions, which are smaller in scale and have shorter runs (they are usually more risqué material). The current location is at Orchestra Hall, which is also the home of the Fort Worth Youth Orchestra.

William Edrington Scott Theatre

Named for a member of one of Tarrant County's pioneer families, this building was designed by Donald Oenschlager and constructed to serve as headquarters for Fort Worth's performing groups and to include a small theatre. The Scott opened in 1966, with the Community Theatre, the Texas Boys Choir, the Opera, Symphony and Ballet associations as performers. The Scott Theatre is a building, not a producing organization. Fort Worth Theatre was the major tenant from 1966 to 1996. The Theatre seats 481 and recently underwent a renovation with upgrades to lighting and sound system, seats, and carpet. Scott Theatre is also the civic venue for The Junior League, The Junior Women's Club Spring Show, Texas Wesleyan Theatre Department and Kids Who Care.

Nancy Lee and Perry R. Bass Performance Hall

(Courtesy of Performing Arts Fort Worth)

The following pages will speak for themselves . . the Hall will speak to your senses and your soul.

David M. Schwarz / Architectural Services, Inc. created the interior design of Bass Hall. Dr. Christopher Jaffe of Jaffe Holden Scarbrough Acoustics provided the acoustic design. Scott and Stuart Gentling coordinated the artwork and the Heralding Angels are by sculptor Marton Varo.
(Courtesy of Performing Arts Forth Worth, Inc., Hedrich Blessing Ltd.)

(Hedrich Blessing, Ltd.)

May 1, 1998 Dedication Ceremony

(Courtesy of Performing Arts Fort Worth, Inc.)

May 8, 1998 First Performance - Carol Burnett; Frederica von Stade and Van Cliburn with the Fort Worth Symphony Orchestra, Fort Worth Dallas Ballet, Fort Worth Opera and Texas Boys Choir. The Grand Opening Festival featured over a month of celebration with the participation of the above as well as Fort Worth native Betty Buckley, and the World Premiere of Red White & Tuna with Joe Sears and Jaston Williams.

The Hall's Children's Education Program brings children of the elementary grades to Bass Hall. Each grade will be given the opportunity to visit and experience first-hand the performing arts. Sue Buratto, Education Director for Performing Arts says, "The Board of Directors of the Performing Arts of Fort Worth wanted the Hall to be a classroom for the children." Working with the Fort Worth Independent School District, as well as private Fort Worth schools and area Catholic schools, the programs are designed to progressively adapt to each grade level. In 1998 over 60,000 children were involved in the program.

(Courtesy of Performing Arts Fort Worth, Inc., Hedrich Blessing Ltd.)

HONORING THE PAST, IMAGINING THE FUTURE

By Fernando Costa, Planning Director, City of Fort Worth

The theme of Fort Worth's sesquicentennial celebration "Honor the Past, Imagine the Future" underscores the importance of preserving our heritage as we seek to build a city in which our children and grandchildren will want to live. Throughout our rich and colorful history, Fort Worth has always welcomed growth and progress, but our city has also succeeded in retaining a remarkable sense of community identity. Despite the many changes that Fort Worth has experienced over the years, we still see ourselves — and others still see us — as the city where the West begins, as the Texas-most city, as Cowtown. Regardless of our city's size and sophistication, we still have the friendly, down-home quality of a small town. Most of us tend to like Fort Worth essentially as it is; we do not want it to become more like Dallas, or like Houston, or like any other place. Yes, we can justifiably take pride in knowing who we are as a community, but what kind of city will Fort Worth become within a generation or two? What lessons can we draw from our history to help us in making sound decisions about our future?

Our city government's mission statement begins with the simple sentence, "Fort Worth, Texas, is a city focusing on its future." Indeed, our civic leaders have been focusing on our future at pivotal points throughout the city's history. In 1876, for example, our leaders took the initiative of bringing the first railroad to Fort Worth, thereby linking us with major cities around the country and establishing the foundation for our industrial development. In 1909, our leaders laid the groundwork for our award-winning park system by adopting a long-range plan for the acquisition and development of open space along the Trinity River and its tributaries. Our leaders created Lake Worth in 1914 and Eagle Mountain Lake in 1931 to meet the city's long-range needs for water supply, flood control, and recreation. In 1923, our leaders created the Fort Worth City Plan Board — the forerunner of today's City Plan Commission — to prepare and help implement a long-range comprehensive plan for the city's growth and development. More recently, the opening of DFW International Airport in 1973 and Alliance Airport in 1989 have positioned our city for long-term economic growth. In these and many other instances, our leaders have understood the importance of formulating a long-term vision for our city's future and then making practical decisions to realize that vision.

Replicas of the flagpole and the flag that once flew over old Fort Worth were dedicated June 5, 1999 on the lawn of the Tarrant County Courthouse

(Landmark Staff Photo)

The need for visionary leadership has never been greater than it is today. According to the North Central Texas Council of Governments, Fort Worth's population has recently grown to approximately 504,000, surpassing the half-million mark for the first time in our history. If our current birth, death, and migration rates were to continue into the future, then our population could possibly exceed 600,000 within the next twenty years. Our employment base is projected to grow at an even faster pace. On the basis of current trends, we can reasonably expect the number of jobs in Fort Worth to increase from approximately 375,000 today to more than 500,000 by 2020. All of this growth will create extraordinary opportunities for revitalization and new development, and our city certainly has plenty of land to accommodate that development. We have approximately 302 square miles of land within our city limits and nearly half of that land - some forty-six percent - is undeveloped. Furthermore, we have an additional 348 square miles of predominantly undeveloped land in our extraterritorial jurisdiction, the area beyond the city limits into which we can expand our boundaries.

In view of this potential growth, what patterns of development should we promote? How would those development patterns affect the volumes of traffic along our streets and highways, our access to public transportation, and the quality of the air that we breathe? How would they affect the capacity of our schools, parks, and other public facilities? How would they affect our access to jobs and the quality of life in our neighborhoods? The City Council seeks to answer these and many other important questions about Fort Worth's future through the city's comprehensive plan. The comprehensive plan serves as a general guide for making decisions about the city's growth and development. It sets forth a broad vision for the kind of city that we want to create, and it presents a summary of the policies, programs, and projects by which we might realize that vision. The comprehensive plan thus helps the City Council and others to make logical decisions about how we allocate financial resources for capital improvements, how we provide incentives for development, and how we regulate the use of land.

In the process of updating the comprehensive plan, citizens and community leaders have identified various critical issues that will influence the growth and development of Fort Worth. Realizing that a healthy city must have a healthy core, the City Council has assigned priority to the revitalization of our central-city neighborhoods and commercial districts. The economic and cultural renaissance that Downtown Fort Worth has experienced during the past decade or so, and the broad benefits of that reinvestment to the city as a whole, have plainly demonstrated the value of central-city redevelopment. Accordingly, our civic leaders have recently undertaken several important projects to capitalize upon that momentum. The Lancaster corridor redevelopment project, for example, seeks to use the redesign of Lancaster Avenue as a catalyst to revitalize the south end of Downtown and to connect Downtown more effectively with the Southside Medical District and the Cultural District. Toward that end, the Lancaster project brings together various initiatives that affect the south end of Downtown. These initiatives include the relocation of Interstate 30, the removal of the overhead freeway from Lancaster Avenue, the redesign of Lancaster Avenue itself, and the reconstruction of railroad underpasses along Main Street and Jennings Avenue. They also include the expansion of our convention center, the development of a commuter rail system that would link Downtown Fort Worth to Downtown Dallas, and the development of a light-rail trolley system that would connect Downtown to other commercial districts in the central city. Through this project, Lancaster Avenue could become a great street with a mixture of residential, retail, and office uses, and the south end of Downtown could recapture the vitality that it enjoyed during the height of the railroad era. Additional central-city redevelopment projects include improvements to the North Main Street corridor from the Tarrant County Courthouse to the Stockyards, the development of a Mexican marketplace or mercado along North Main, improvements to the Berry Street corridor from University Drive to Evans Avenue, and the development of an African-American cultural district in the historic Near Southeast neighborhood.

Of course, many other critical issues will also influence our city's growth and development. Our community realizes, for instance, that the quality of our public schools will significantly affect our ability to attract families and businesses to Fort Worth. We also recognize the importance of conserving our natural resources. The quality of development along the Trinity River and around our major lakes, and the public's access to these scenic and recreational resources, will certainly affect the attractiveness of our city. On a regional scale, traffic congestion and air pollution will inevitably focus more public attention upon transportation options, including pedestrian activity and the use of mass transit. The design of the proposed Southwest Parkway, and the use of land along the parkway corridor, will appreciably change the landscape in the southwest quadrant of our city. Our effectiveness in addressing these and other critical issues will determine, to a considerable extent, the kind of city that Fort Worth will become in the years ahead.

The pioneers who established a frontier outpost on the Trinity River could not have imagined the great city that Fort Worth would eventually become. Throughout our 150-year history, we have been blessed with far-sighted leaders who have combined broad vision with decisive action to create a remarkably livable city. Of course, none of us can safely predict the kinds of changes that lie beyond the horizon. Technological, economic, and societal changes will surely create opportunities and challenges that we can scarcely imagine today. Nonetheless, by studying our history and understanding the long-term trends that are affecting our city, we can proceed with confidence to make Fort Worth an even better place for future generations.

Early view of the Tarrant County Courthouse shows the Horse Fountain that served horse, rider and pedestrian

(Courtesy of the Dalton Hoffman, Jr. Collection)

The Women's Humane Association dedicated the original horse fountain in 1892. In 1999, for the sesquicentennial celebration, a reconstructed horse fountain was rededicated after a longer than fifteen year effort.

(Landmark Staff Photo)

And the herd returns . . .

Leading the Fort Worth Longhorn Herd down North Main, Trail Boss, Dennis Merrell is followed by the lead steer, Ned, a red and white spotted steer. Ned and his buddy to the right, Chocolate Chip, black with white splotches, are both veterans of the 1995 Great American Cattle Drive from Fort Worth to Miles City, Montana. Merrell and his fellow drovers led the herd from the downtown area to the Stockyards. The same destination awaited the herd on July 5th, 1999 and will become their home. There will be daily drives from there to the Trinity River for grazing and once again, the breed known as Texas Gold will become a part of Fort Worth's living heritage.

(Courtesy of the Fort Worth Star-Telegram, Photo, Carolyn Bauman)

APPENDIX

Information about our contributors:

MUSEUMS:

Amon Carter Museum
3501 Camp Bowie Blvd.
Fort Worth, Texas 76107
Open Tuesday – Saturday, 10 a.m. to 5 p.m.
Sunday noon to 5 p.m.
Admission is free
(817) 738-1933

Cattle Raisers Museum
1301 West 7th Street
Fort Worth, Texas 76102
Open Monday - Saturday, 10 a.m. to 5 p.m.
Sunday 1 p.m. - 5 p.m.

Modern Art Museum of Fort Worth
1309 Montgomery Street
Saturday, 11 a.m. - 5 p.m.
Fort Worth, Texas 76107
Open Tuesday - Friday, 10 a.m. - 5 p.m.
Sunday, noon - 5 p.m.
(817) 738-9215
Admission free

The Modern at Sundance Square
410 Houston Street
Friday - Saturday, 11 a.m. - 10 p.m.
Fort Worth, Texas 7
Open Monday - Thursday, 11 a.m. - 6 p.m.
Sunday 1 p.m. - 5 p.m.
Admission free

Museum of Science & History
1501 Montgomery Street
Fort Worth, Texas 76107
(817) 732-1631
Museum Exhibit hours

	Sept - Feb	March -Aug
Mon- Wed	9 - 5	9 - 9
Th- Sat	9 - 9	9 - 9
Sun	noon - 9	noon - 9

Admission:
Exhibits: Adults $5 Seniors $4
Children (3-12) $3
Children under 3 free with adult
Omni: Adults $6
Seniors and children under 12 $4
Noble Planetarium: $3

The Kimbell Art Museum
3333 Camp Bowie Blvd.
Fort Worth, Texas 76107
Open Tues. - Thur., 10 a. m. - 5 p.m.
Friday 12 - 8 p.m.; Saturday, 10 - 5 p.m.
Sunday, 12 - 5 p.m.
(817) 332-8451

Stockyards Museum
131 E. Exchange Avenue, #110
Fort Worth, Texas 76106
Open Monday - Saturday, 10 a.m. - 5 p.m.
(817) 625-5083

LIBRARIES:

The Fort Worth Public Library
300 Taylor Street
Fort Worth, Texas 76102
(817) 871-7700

University of Texas at Arlington Libraries
Arlington, Texas
Fort Worth Star Telegram Photo Collection
Jack White Photography Collection
W.D. Smith, Inc. Com. Photo Collection

Southwestern Baptist Theological Seminary
Special Collections Librarian

Texas Wesleyan University Library,
Special Collections
Robert R. Bragan Fort Worth Cats Collection

Tarrant County College (formerly TCJC)
North East Campus Library, Special Collections

Texas Christian University

THE CITY OF FORT WORTH:
Parks & Recreation Department:

Botanic Gardens
3220 Botanic Garden Blvd.
Fort Worth, Texas 76107
(817) 871-7686
Open daily from 8 a.m. to 11 p.m.
Admission free
Call for information regarding
Conservatory, Japanese Garden

Parks and Community Services Department:

Fort Worth Nature Center & Refuge
9601 Fossil Ridge Road
Fort Worth, Texas 76135
(817) 237-1111

Log Cabin Village
2100 Log Cabin Village Road
Fort Worth, Texas 76109
Open Tuesday - Friday, 9 a.m. - 5 p.m.
Saturday, 10 a.m. - 5 p.m.
Sunday 1 p.m. - 5 p.m.
(817) 926-5881
Admission: Adults $2, Senior$1.50, Children age 4 - 17 $1.50. Offer History Program and Pioneer School to groups

Fort Worth Water Gardens:
located in downtown Fort Worth south of Fort Worth Convention Center
Open daily 7 a.m. - 11:30 p.m.
no admission

Public Events Department:
Will Rogers Memorial Center
1 Amon Carter Square
Fort Worth, Texas 76107
(817) 871-8150

Fort Worth Convention & Visitors Bureau
Douglas Harman, President & CEO
415 Throckmorton
Ft. Worth, Texas 76102
(817) 336-8791

Planning and Growth Management Department
Fernando Costa, Director
1000 Throckmorton
Ft Worth, Texas 76102

FORT WORTH INDEPENDENT SCHOOL DISTRICT:

H.Y.P.E.
(Hispanic Youth Promoting Excellence),
Jo Linda Jara Martinez, Coordinator

Archives, Billy W. Sills

Athletic Department, Jack Billingsley

Fort Worth Police Department
Officer Curtis Chesser
& Captain Bryan Sudan, Director,
Police Department Training Division

Naval Air Station -
Joint Reserve Base at Fort Worth
Major Clay Church

United States Postal Service, Fort Worth
Olde Tyme Postique
Jeanette Hodges

ORGANIZATIONS:

Fort Worth Zoo
1989 Colonial Parkway
Fort Worth, Texas 76110
(817) 871-7050
Open daily 10 a.m. - 5 p.m.
weekend hours extended seasonally
Admission fee, Adults $7;
children (3-12) $4.50
children under 3 free; Seniors (65+) $3

North Fort Worth Historical Society
Sarah Biles
131 E. Exchange Avenue, #110
Fort Worth, Texas 76106

Fort Worth Metropolitan Black
Chamber of Commerce
3607 E. Rosedale
Fort Worth, Texas 76105
(817) 531-8510

Tarrant County Black Historical and
Genealogical Society
Mr. Frank Moss, President
(817) 871-8805

Fort Worth Hispanic
Chamber of Commerce
1327 North Main
Fort Worth, Texas 76106

Texas and Southwest Cattle Raisers Association

National Oceanographic Atmospheric
Association

The Woman's Club

The Fort Worth Club

Nancy Lee and Perry R. Bass Performance Hall
(817) 212-4200 (administration)
1-888-597-7827 (ticket office)
(817) 212-4325 (information hotline)
Performing Arts of Fort Worth Inc.
330 E. 4th Street
Fort Worth, Texas 76102
(817) 212-4300
Bass Performance Hall Photographs:
(those credited to Hedrich Blessing, Ltd.)
information: Hedrick Blessing, Ltd.
11 W. Illinois
Chicago, IL 60610
(312) 321-1151

Fort Worth Dallas Ballet
6845 Green Oaks Road
Fort Worth, Texas 76116
(817) 763-0207

Fort Worth Opera
3505 W. Lancaster Avenue
Fort Worth, Texas 76017
(817) 731-0200

Fort Worth Symphony Orchestra
Fort Worth Chamber Orchestra
330 East Fourth Street, Suite 200
Fort Worth, Texas 76102
(817) 665-6500

Texas Boys Choir
2925 Riverglen Drive
Fort Worth, Texas 76109
(817) 924-1482

The Fort Worth Star Telegram

Casa Mañana Musicals, Inc.
3101 W. Lancaster
Fort Worth, Texas 76107
(817) 332-2272

The Van Cliburn Foundation
2525 Ridgmar Blvd., Suite 307
Fort Worth, Texas 76116
(817) 738-6536

Thistle Hill
1509 Pennsylvania Ave
Ft Worth, TEXAS 76104
(817) 336-1212
Open Monday - Friday, 11a.m. - 2 p.m.
Sunday 1 p.m - 3 p.m.
Admission $4 Adults, $2 Seniors and
children, ages 7-12

Allied Theatre Group
Stage West / Shakespeare in the Park
(817) 784-9378

Fort Worth Theatre
Orchestra Hall Trail Lake Drive
Fort Worth, Texas 76109
(817) 921-5300

Circle Theatre
230 W. Fourth Street
Fort Worth, Texas 76102
(817) 877-3040

William Edringon Scott Theatre
Public Events Facilities
3505 W. Lancaster
Fort Worth, Texas 76107
(817) 738-1938

Mayfest, Inc.
1110 Penn Street
Fort Worth, Texas 76102
(817) 332-1055
Mayfest is held each spring in Trinity Park
Call for information

First Presbyterian Church
Saint Patrick Cathedral
First Baptist Church
Midtown Church of Christ
First United Methodist Church
Travis Ave Baptist Church
Congregation Beth-El Archives
Congregation Ahavath Shalom
Mount Gilead Baptist, Joy Thomas
Oakwood Cemetery Association
Shannon Rose Hill Cemetery
Harris Methodist Fort Worth
All Saints Health System
Cook's Children's Medical Center
University of North Texas Health Science
Center at Fort Worth
JPS Health Systems
Acme Brick, Britt Stokes
Alliance Air Services
Dallas Fort Worth International Airport

Oktoberfest
330 E. 4th Street, Suite 200
Fort Worth's Convention Center
Fort Worth, Texas 76102
Oktoberfest is held each fall in
Fort Worth Convention Center
Call for information
(817) 332-2560

Tarantula Steam Train of the Fort Worth
& Western Railroad
for information and reservations call
(817) 625-RAIL (7245)

Jacqueline Price of Freese and Nichols, Inc.

Karen Hagar of Lockheed-Martin Tactical Aircraft Systems

Mark Leaf of The Pinkerton Agency

Louann and Bob Rubel of Old Glory Gallery

T. Joy Webster, Director of Facilities,
W. T. Waggoner Building

Carter & Burgess

Pam Minick of Billy Bob's Texas
2520 Rodeo Plaza
Billy Bob's is open daily for family fun,
Fort Worth Stockyards
with live entertainment nightly
(817) 624-7117

Britt Sharp, Manager
Cattleman's Fort Worth Steak House
2458 N. Main Street
Fort Worth, Texas 76106

Michael Smith of Paris Coffee Shop
704 W Magnolia
Fort Worth, Texas 76104
Open 6 a.m. - 2:30 p.m. Mon - Fr
6 - 11 Sat

Mark Angle of Lee Angle Photography
Congresswoman Kay Granger
Speaker Jim Wright
Judy Alter, Texas Christian University Press
Delbert Bailey
Mrs. Leon (Fay) Brachman
Duane Gage
Dalton Hoffman, Jr.
Quentin McGown, Texas Wesleyan University
Jim Noah, Retired Battalion Chief
Fort Worth Fire Department
Bill Morgan
Dr. Ben Procter, Texas Christian University
Dick Ramsey
Richard Selcer
Betty Porter Walther
Hollace Ava Weiner
Joyce M. Williams
Dave Naugle

BEACH AND BATH HOUSE, LAKE WORTH, FORT WORTH.

REAR OF MESS TENTS, CAMP BOWIE, FORT WORTH, TEXAS.

BIBLIOGRAPHY

Fuller, Larry Paul, editor. *The American Institute of Architects Guide to Dallas Architecture with Regional Highlights*. McGraw-Hill Construction Information Group, 1999.

Freese, Simon W., P. E. and Sizemore, Deborah Lightfoot, *A Century in the Works: Freese and Nichols consulting engineers, 1894-1994.* Texas A & M University Press, 1993.

Farman, Irvin, *The Fort Worth Club, A Centennial Story,* The Fort Worth Club, 1985

Selcer, Richard F., *The Fort that Became a City: an Illustrated Reconstruction of Fort Worth, Texas 1849-1853* / drawings by William B. Potter: text by Richard F. Selcer, Texas Christian University Press, 1995.

Selcer, Richard F., *Hell's Half Acre: The Life and Legend of a Red Light District, (Chisholm Trail Series No. 9),* Texas Christian University Press, 1991

Sanders, Leonard, *How Fort Worth Became the Texasmost City* / text by Leonard Sanders with captions by Ronnie C. Tyler, Amon Carter Museum, 1973

Urdang, Laurence, editor, *The Timetables of American History,* Simon & Schuster, Inc., 1981

Register, Phil R., *The White Man and the Negro Magazine,* Vol 2, No. 10, December 1933

Tell Their Stories, Women in Fort Worth History, Joyce Williams, References:

Garrett, Julia Kathryn, *Fort Worth a Frontier Triumph,* Texas Christian University Press, Fort Worth, 1996.

Knight, Oliver, *Outpost on the Trinity,* University of Oklahoma Press. Norman. 1953.

Pate, J'Nell, *Livestock Legacy: The Fort Worth Stockyards 1887-1987,* Texas A & M University Press, College Station, 1988.

Pate, J'Nell, *North of the River: A Brief History of North Fort Worth,* Texas Christian University Press, Fort Worth, 1994.

Pirtle, Caleb III, *Fort Worth the Civilised West,* Continental Heritage Press for the Fort Worth Chamber of Commerce, 1980.

Selcer, Richard F, *The Fort that Became a City,* Texas Christian University Press, Fort Worth, 1995.

Selcer, Richard F., *Hell's Half Acre,*. Texas Christian University Press, Fort Worth, 1991.

Oral History interviews and research files. Fort Worth Museum of Science and History.

The photographs featured in the Appendix and Bibliography are courtesy of (in order, as featured):Children with elephant, Fort Worth Zoo. Frog sculpture, Landmark Staff. Chishom Trail Mural, Sundance Square, Fort Worth Convention and Visitors Bureau. Junior Woman's Club Building, Woman's Club. Family posing on porch of house, Fort Worth Public Library. Lake Worth, Quentin McGown Postcard Collection - Camp Bowie, Quentin McGown Postcard Collection. Trinity River Scene, Fort Worth Parks and Community Services Department.

Thanks, Dad, for your guidance, counsel, love, patience, and most of all, ongoing support.

Bob

INDEX

— A —

— B —

— C —

— D —

— E —

— F —

— G —

— H —

— I —

— J —

— K —

— L —

— M —

— N —

— O —

— P —

— Q —

— R —

— S —

Above photo of Bass Hall is courtesy Performing Arts Fort Worth, Inc., Hedrich Blessing, Ltd.

The back endsheet photograph was taken from approximately the same southeast angle as the front endsheet photo, seventy-two years later. Photograph, Robert LaPrelle, Lee Angle Photography, Inc. 1999. Compare to front endsheet photograph.